THE DUST DIARIES

Owen Sheers was born in Fiji and brought up in Abergavenny, South Wales. He is the author of the acclaimed poetry collection *The Blue Book*. *The Dust Diaries* is his first prose book.

'No ordinary biography. The writing is beautiful and so emotionally charged that Sheers addresses his uncle directly, as if speaking to him at his graveside, or after a day sifting through his letters in an Oxford archive.' *Daily Mail*

'In style *The Dust Diaries* is beautifully elegiac, at times reaching a mystical intensity, but it is never sentimental or pretentious. Sheers writes with warm admiration for his extraordinary ancestor and simultaneously captures the strange experience of being a biographer, who must try to breathe life into the facts to the extent that he almost begins to think like his subject . . . This is an important debut by a young writer who is sure to go far.' *Literary Review*

'At the start of the story are a love affair and an illegitimate daughter left behind in Britain. Sheers's quest to uncover their secret is one of the most compelling strands in an audacious piece of literature that, emotionally but not emotively, tackles the roots of the Zimbabwean land crisis today.' *Independent*

'Like many good stories, this one begins with the discovery of a book . . . The result is a poetic, moving and vivid narrative that spans the twentieth century, eloqently using history and travel with a fiction-alised account of his ancestor's life.' *Mail on Sunday*

'A poetic, moving and brilliantly imagined semi-fictional account of the strong-minded missionary making his home on the veld. He suc-ceeds in making the reader equally fascinated in what could have remained a private obsession and in the process turns up a great deal that is relevant to Zimbabwe's political situation today.' *Observer*

by the same author

poetry

THE BLUE BOOK

The Dust Diaries

OWEN SHEERS

faber and faber

First published in 2004
by Faber and Faber Limited
3 Queen Square London WC1N 3AU
This paperback edition published in 2005

Typeset by Faber and Faber Limited
Printed in England by Mackays of Chatham plc,
Chatham, Kent

A CIP record for this book
is available from the British Library

ISBN 0–571–21026–0

2 4 6 8 10 9 7 5 3 1

To Arthur
and in memory of
Leonard Mamvura

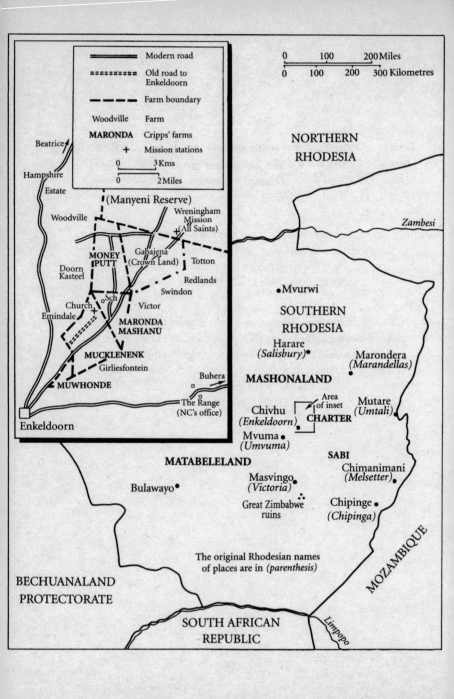

Dust . . . 2. a dead person's remains (*honoured dust*). 3. confusion or turmoil (*raised quite a dust*). 4. *archaic* or *poet.* the mortal human body (*we are all dust*). 5. the ground; the earth (*kissed the dust*).
The Oxford English Dictionary

History is as light as individual human life, unbearably light, light as a feather, as dust swirling into the air, as whatever will no longer exist tomorrow.
Milan Kundera, *The Unbearable Lightness of Being*

This *decaying sense,* when wee would express the thing itself, (I mean *fancy* it selfe,) wee call *Imagination,* as I said before: But when we would express the *decay,* and signifie that the Sense is fading, old, and past, it is called Memory. So that *Imagination* and *Memory* are but one thing . . .
Hobbes, *Leviathan*

Arthur Cripps with Leonard Mamvura, *c.* 1942

Prologue

Mpandi was one of the Shona names given to my great, great uncle, Arthur Shearly Cripps, Independent Missionary to Southern Rhodesia. The name was translated for me in Mashonaland, where he lived, as 'the man who walks like thunder' or 'the man who shakes the earth with his walking'. He was given many names during his life, but this is the one I have thought of most often as I followed in his footsteps, literal and metaphorical, over the past three years. Because for me he has always been walking, always on the move. Always a few steps ahead of me as I tried to track him down, as I tried to understand him. What follows is an account of this search: the story of my contact with him and of how the unfolding of one man's life can resonate down the years in the lives of others. This account of my search is true. It happened, just as Arthur's life happened, but the story of his life that I have written is not true in the same way. This story is written as a fiction, the fiction I formed in my mind so as to better understand Arthur's life. It is, however, a fiction based on the facts, stories, myths and tales I gathered while looking for Arthur Cripps. Some of the people who feature in this story are imaginary, but most are not. Of those who really existed, some of their actions I have invented, many, again, I have not. It is the story of Arthur Cripps' life reflected through my imagination. It may not always be true to historical fact, but I hope it is true to the essence of Arthur's story and to the essence of the man I discovered buried in the nave of a ruined church far out in the Zimbabwean veld.

PART ONE

Maronda Mashanu, Mashonaland, Southern Rhodesia

---◇---

It is dawn in the African bush. Light is expanding from the horizon, growing over the veld of rock, grass and dust. The first birds are calling in the winter trees. Arthur Cripps, Independent Missionary to Mashonaland is lying awake in the rondavel he built next to the church he named Maronda Mashanu, the Saint of the Five Wounds. He is lying awake and he is dying. It is his last day on earth. He is eighty-three years old.

He listens to his breath and counts backwards.

Ten years since he lost his sight.

Thirty-seven years since he went to war.

Thirty-eight years since he built the church.

Fifty-one years since he came to Africa.

Fifty-five years since he fell in love.

Beira Bay, Portuguese Mozambique

◇

The irregular coughs of the man sleeping in the bunk beneath him had been chiselling into his sleep all night, but it was the slap of the sea against the ship's hull that finally woke Arthur. There was something different about it, a change in its register and rhythm. Keeping his eyes shut, he tried to work out what it was. And then he realised: they were still, the ship was no longer moving. They must have finally been allowed into harbour. They had arrived.

He felt a dip of excitement in his stomach at the thought of being on land again. The journey from England had been more laborious than he'd thought it would be; at least, the sea voyage had. He had enjoyed the earlier train trip through Europe. In Rome he'd even got a chance to visit the room where Keats died and the Protestant cemetery, where he'd seen the poet's grave. Standing above the simple headstone near the grand Pyramid of Cestius he'd looked down at the engraving of a broken lyre and the strangely ambiguous epitaph: *Here lies one whose name was writ in water.* The poet's friend Charles Brown had interpreted this as Keats' abandonment of any hope of posthumous fame, but standing there looking at it with the perspective of eighty years' hindsight Arthur liked to think it was not this simple. His name is writ *in* not *on* water. Part of nature, not fleeting but eternal, twisted into the currents of history. He had often talked about visiting the grave, but once there it had felt strangely unreal. But then maybe that was because he had never expected to be visiting it alone.

From Rome he had travelled to Naples, where he boarded the *Hertzog*, and that is when the harder part of the journey began: the unforgiving hours of boredom looking out at an indifferent sea, the forced formalities of the captain's table and the joking sarcasm of some of the pioneer crowd. Most of his fellow travellers were tolerable, and there was a particular group with whom he had become good friends. He had a postcard in the pocket of his jacket hung at the end of his bed with these people's signatures on it, a memento of their shared trip. But there was another group of men, 'entrepreneurs' they called themselves, who thought it fun to gently mock him and his vocation, often late at night, out on the deck when everyone was enjoying the cooler air. Their breaths heavy with port and cigar smoke, they would interrogate him about his work in Africa – was he ready to battle with witchcraft? Did he know they still ate missionaries in the Belgian Congo? How would he resist the charms of the native girls, out there alone in the bush? Inevitably the jokes would wane and they would soon be talking among themselves about their own schemes for fortune on the dark continent, but they had often irritated Arthur to such an extent that he longed to take one of them on in a boxing ring.

Zanzibar had come as a welcome break from life on board ship. They had made a double stop there and Arthur had taken the opportunity to catch up with his college friend Frank Weston, who was a missionary on the island. The voyage down from Aden had not been easy. Just two days after leaving port the *Hertzog* ran into the south-west monsoon, a curtain of storms and high winds that lasted for three days. They were so fierce that when they finally abated and he emerged from his cabin he saw that the two black funnels rising above the centre of the deck had been turned a dull grey/white, coated with a layer of brine from the waves that had broken into and over the ship. The hull bore marks of the storm too. Immediately below the railings of the lower decks he could see it was streaked with long pale splashes of dried vomit, fanning out down to the waterline. Like the other passengers he had not had a good time of it, feeling the sea beat itself against the outer wall of his small cabin through long, sleepless nights, so it was a relief when the clustered white buildings of Zanzibar's capital, Stonetown, came into view.

The strong smell of cloves and spices carried on a warm trade wind had heralded the presence of the island hours before anyone on board could see her shores. The captain told them this would be so. But there had been another smell too, equally strong, coming in gusts, that puzzled Arthur. He enquired of it to a passing crew member. The boy (he looked no older than sixteen) told him simply, 'Oh, that's shark, sir. They salt 'em in vats on the shore before selling them to the niggers on the mainland.' Shark and spices. Not for the first time on that voyage, Arthur felt he was inhabiting someone else's life, a Rider Haggard-type fiction, and not his own at all.

As the *Hertzog* steamed nearer through a flat, hot morning with heatwaves tricking the eye, the buildings of Stonetown became clearer. A broad white palace with pillars and grand steps dominated the immediate ground behind the port and its frilling of palm trees. Part of its façade was covered in a crude scaffolding and half-naked workmen clambered over its stone like animated hieroglyphs. Arthur realised it must be Beit el Ajaib, the House of Wonders that Frank had written to him about, and on closer inspection he saw he was right. There, behind the scaffolding, the white walls gave to a shattered dark hole, the last remaining damage of the British shells that had thudded into the palace back in 1896 in what turned out to be the world's shortest war. Just forty minutes long, Frank had said. To the south of the House of Wonders the massive bastioned walls of the old fort rose from a packed confusion of smaller, square coral-rag buildings, their wooden carved doors of red, green and blue the only colours in the white and dull fawn of the new and old stucco plasterwork. Behind these, the towers of minarets and the domes of mosques were the only buildings tall enough to be seen. Arthur had expected to be able to see the spire of the Anglican Cathedral that Frank had also written to him about, but however much he scanned the outline of the town, he couldn't find it. There were just the delicate minarets, wavering in the haze against an African sky so blue he felt the colour as a sensation in his chest.

As the *Hertzog* came into port both the town's buildings and the noise of the place came into focus. A crowd of hundreds of people were shouting from the quayside, woven baskets of fish and fruit carried on their heads. After the flat emptiness of the sea and then the cramped conditions of his cabin Arthur had been disorientated by the crush of them about him as he disembarked from a launch onto the harbourside. The dull familiarity of the ship fell away and suddenly everything was strange again: men with bloodshot eyes appearing close to his face asking questions in broken English that sounded more like demands; the musty stench of goats wandering among the crowd; children tugging at his jacket, softly chanting 'Meester, meester'; the smells and colours of the fish, nuts and fruit they carried in their baskets.

Frank was there waiting for him. Arthur spotted him through the crowd, jogging towards him, his arms outstretched as far as the crush of people would allow and his voice a welcome foothold of familiarity, 'Arthur! Who'd have thought it? God bless you for coming, God bless you!' Arthur held out his own hand but his friend dodged it and embraced him instead.

Frank was soon guiding him out of the port area and into the narrow alleys and passageways behind the main coastal road. It had been three years since they had seen each other, and he saw Frank had changed. His pale complexion was now tanned a dark brown, and the broad face of his youth was leaner, narrower in appearance. He wore a light safari suit with a clerical shirt and collar and the same wire-rimmed spectacles he had worn in England. He looked older. There were flecks of grey in his neatly-parted dark hair and Arthur thought again of the white brine on the black funnels, the signature of the storm. But he was still the Frank he had known at college: energetic, nervy, excited, with hands that explored the air around him as he talked, and a face that managed to express both a frown and a smile as he listened to you.

This morning he was as excitable as ever, anxious to show Arthur his world on the island and what he had done there. He walked ahead, one arm out in front finding a way through the flow of people pressing against them, talking to Arthur over his shoulder, asking questions about home, their old tutors, their mutual friends.

'And what of old Gore?' he asked, breathing heavily in the heat and looking back at Arthur.

'No, unfortunately I didn't manage to see him,' he replied, 'but I wrote to him and he answered. I have his blessing it would seem.'

'Of course you have, of course you have,' said Frank. 'Why on earth shouldn't you?'

Arthur tried to continue the conversation as best he could, but he was distracted, still coming to terms with his new surroundings. Smells came to him like colours, distinct and pure, while his eyes tried to keep up with the onrush of new sights after the boredom of the ship at sea. Thin, leathered old men crouched in groups, dicing or smoking on tall hookahs, children played at the edges of the passageways, throwing marbles at tins, and women passed by quietly, obscured in purdah, their heads averted as if they would rather be invisible or a part of the walls they kept so close to. All of this seemed to wash over Frank like the air he breathed, but for Arthur everything struck him for the first time, as if his senses had been recharged. He had hardly ever left England before, except for a couple of trips to the continent, and now, just weeks after sailing from Southampton, he was walking through the morning life of a world completely alien to him, and yet so established in itself, comfortable with its own weight of history (and this is what, on looking back from his bunk in the *Hertzog*, he realised had shocked him the most), a world so Arabic. Frank had told him in his letters about Zanzibar's Sultans and Arthur himself had read of the Arabic influence on the island, but somehow he hadn't expected this to be so pervasive, so ingrained in the lifeblood of the place. And yet it was, and its existence there, in Africa, in the reality of this unreal life he was leading, focused his newly sharpened senses on his own situation. As he followed Frank through the narrow streets, a thin showing of blue sky between the close buildings, he felt the pressure of history at his back and he felt small in its presence.

Later that day, after Frank had settled Arthur in his own quarters at Kiungani, he took him to see the Anglican Cathedral which had eluded him from the deck of the ship. It was an impressive building, solid and imposing among the shacks and crumbling stucco of the surrounding houses. 'The first Anglican cathedral built in East Africa,' Frank had said proudly, as they approached its broad plastered walls and tall spire that tapered into the clear sky above a blank patch of ground.

'This is where the island's slave market stood.' Frank gestured to the bare dusty earth around the Cathedral. As they walked towards the Cathedral's entrance, he continued over his shoulder, 'Together with the trade in ivory, it was this market that ran the island.'

Frank was still explaining the history of the site when they entered the Cathedral's nave through a heavy carved door, stepping into the relief of the building's cool darkness from the rising heat of the day outside. Impatient to show him the peculiar features of the building, Frank didn't wait for Arthur's eyes to adjust to the dim light, and immediately began his well-rehearsed tour. In the nave, the huge font made from Italian marble shipped in from the Apuan Alps, and next to this, twelve pillars, all upside down, mistakenly erected that way by the local workmen while the Bishop was off on safari. In the body of the cathedral he drew Arthur's attention to the elegant Moorish windows, and a dark crucifix made from the wood of the tree under which Livingstone's servants had buried his heart. At the altar a single round piece of white marble was inlaid where the whipping post of the slave market had stood. Around this, to represent the blood that had fallen there, were slabs of grey marble veined with red as if that blood had just been shed and was still unfurling in the stone's frozen water.

Behind the altar itself was the grave of the Cathedral's founder, Bishop Steere, buried there in 1882, two years after the building was completed. Behind this again was the entrance-way down into the old slave chambers, into which Frank crouched with a lit candle. Arthur followed, bending down low to avoid the stone of the door frame above him.

The chambers were low-ceilinged dungeons of disturbingly small proportions. Frank continued his tour, his soft voice falling like ash in the bare rooms. This, he explained, was where fifty men or seventy-five women and children were chained and kept for three days. One deep channel for faeces and urine ran through the centre of each chamber, and one narrow slit at the level of the street outside provided a dusty ventilation. There was nothing else. It was a culling ground. The weak did not survive, and the strong emerged back into the light barely human.

After their visit to the Cathedral Frank had left Arthur to his own devices and he'd taken a walk through the town again. This time, walking through the streets alone, he found the strangeness of the place he'd felt that morning had begun to settle into a rhythm of its own. A rhythm he could identify and feel a part of. He talked to some of the traders in the tiny, cool shops that punctuated the narrow streets, and even bought himself a new khaki safari suit from one of them. It was a little short at the sleeves, but he was pleased with his rare purchase. Then he had lain down for a few hours in the cool of his lodgings, listening to the town outside, the distant roll of the port's noise and the nearer quick talk of women and children, in both Arabic and Swahili. Eventually he slept, shedding his body of its sea weariness, until he was woken in the early evening by the muezzin's call to prayer, skittering across the sky from one of the minarets that rose above the town's bustle of people, plaster and dust.

That evening he and Frank took a pony and trap out to the British Governor's house for dinner. His sleep, seeing Frank again, the impressive Cathedral, feeling the foreignness of the town ebb about him, all of these had left Arthur with a sense of contentment that he hadn't felt for years, either in England or on his journey south. Lying with his eyes closed in his bed on the *Hertzog* outside Beira Bay, feeling the gentle rock and swell of the ship, he remembers now how that short trip out to the Governor's house had seemed so perfect, as if just momentarily he and his surroundings were in harmony. The sun blinked, low and orange, between the coconut palms at the side of the road and dazzled in the sea beyond them. Through the trees he'd been able to make out the dhows coming home from the evening catch, each with its single sail, a white wing of wind. Beyond these the reef turned on itself like a seam in the sea, while on the beach he'd caught a glimpse of a boy and a girl playing under a stranded dhow's dropped rigging. Even the swirls of dust thrown up by the pony's hooves had appeared to turn and wheel as part of a greater synthesis with which he was in tune. For the first time since departing from England he had felt he was no longer leaving, but going somewhere instead.

But that was before the dinner. The dinner which had, for some reason, so unsettled him, and sent him off kilter as easily as the pieces of driftwood he'd seen that afternoon caught up against the harbour wall, turned and swayed on the wilful motion of the waves.

The British Governor's residence was a large coral limestone house on the coast a few miles north of Stonetown. Again, Frank fulfilled the role of guide as they rode out there, explaining that the building had once belonged to Princess Salome of the Omani.

'Quite a woman apparently, marvellous gardener. You'll see when we arrive, extraordinarily beautiful,' he said, shaking his head in admiration as he spoke.

Walking through the Princess's gardens, with the scent of jasmine and honeysuckle in the air and the evening light of a sinking sun, Arthur saw what Frank meant. The house and the grounds were both of a remarkable, exotic beauty. A long, open veranda ran the length of the ground floor, with only a few potted plants and one large round table occupying its generous space. At the centre of the back wall a pair of dark wooden carved doors stood open, giving a view into a large room with a window open onto the sea. White drapes beat over the window, blown pregnant by the wind off the water. The first floor was also open on the front of the house: a long covered balcony on which Arthur could make out an African in a white robe walking the length of it, lighting the candles that stood in tall holders around its edge. He could also see that a wooden table occupied the centre of this balcony and that a group of Europeans stood at its furthest end, holding drinks and talking. One of them, wearing the white uniform of the Colonial Service, saw them approaching and came to the balcony railings. 'Father Weston! Good evening! Do come up and join us. If you hurry, you'll catch the sun!'

The company at that dinner comprised Arthur, Frank, the British Governor, his almost silent wife, Mr Beardsley, a merchant from Essex, Charlotte, his timid and much younger female companion, and a man who introduced himself to Arthur as 'S. Tristam Pruen, Fellow of the Royal Geographical Society'. As they watched the sun sink into the sea a servant brought a tray of pink gins and a bottle of quinine. Arthur declined the gin, but still took his five grains of quinine. The medicine was bitter on his tongue and he wondered briefly if he wouldn't rather suffer malaria than this taste lingering in his mouth every evening.

They ate at the large dark wood table, its surface softened by the touch of hands over time, and were served crab, red snapper and rice by wordless, effortless Africans dressed in the same simple white robes as the candle-lighter. Of the guests, Mr Beardsley, the merchant, was by far the loudest. When he laughed Arthur watched the tips of his ginger moustache tremble and he thought he saw the girl by his side visibly wince at his volume. She looked worried, her strained smiles failing to convince Arthur of anything other than her anxiety. The merchant, however, seemed oblivious and was having far too interesting a time quizzing S. Tristam Pruen to notice his companion's apparent distress.

S. Tristam Pruen (he never said what the S. stood for) was a writer of some repute among the European community in Africa, though the party only had his word to go on for this. A few years earlier he had published *The Arab and the African*, which he described to the assembled company as 'a handbook of my own experience written down to help and introduce others to the dangers and excitements of this dark continent'.

On hearing this Mr Beardsley, who had arrived only a few weeks before, began to ask Pruen for his advice on various matters concerning adjustment to tropical life. Which did he consider the best cash crops to grow on the mainland of British East Africa? What was the most effective method of sisal production? How to prevent white ants getting in his food cupboard? The best way to approach a native village? Arthur watched him as he stabbed at a forkful of crabmeat while asking 'And what about the rats, eh? Bloody things, oh, sorry fathers, yes, the things keep getting at my meat wherever I seem to hang it. Size of dogs they are!'

'Yes, that took me a while to work out myself,' Mr Pruen replied, 'and in the end it was my cook who solved the problem. We simply hung the meat in the centre of the pantry from a rope with a knot in it, and a square sheet of tin skewered through resting on this knot. The rat will climb down the rope as far as this tin, but then find its desires frustrated, slipping off the sheet clear of the meat.'

'Damned clever, very clever, sir. Why didn't we think of that, eh, Charlotte?' Mr Beardsley turned to the girl at his side who forced out a weak smile. Arthur thought she was going to cry. The Governor, recognising that Mr Beardsley was in danger of monopolising the conversation, interjected before he could ask another question.

'I understand you're quite a hunter too, Mr Pruen, is that right?'

Mr Pruen looked up at the Governor over his food, smiled, and sat back, placing his cutlery on his plate.

'Well,' he started with a heavy sigh, 'during my time in equatorial East Africa I have come to know the ways of the bush, and so yes, I have had my fair number of run-ins and tangles with the wildlife which lives there. I do therefore also have some knowledge on how best to bag them. Or escape them, depending on the appropriate action at the time,' he added with a snort.

The writer continued, his gift for verbosity leading him into a series of anecdotes about his African hunting experience. Arthur noticed how these stories all followed a similar pattern. Mr Pruen would amaze the table with the plumage of the sun-birds or plantain-eaters or the peculiar habits of the gazelle, leopard or crocodile, speaking with the authority (and, Arthur admitted, often the love) of the naturalist. Then he would explain in exacting detail the best method to capture, shoot, trap or skin the creature in question. It was a surprisingly candid display, he thought, of man's ability to worship and destroy. To love and to kill.

He looked around the table. Mr Beardsley was enraptured by the hunting stories, while the Governor nodded politely, obviously having heard such facts and myths before. His wife, in contrast, a stout woman in her forties, ate throughout Mr Pruen's speeches, silent as she had been the whole evening, her eyes downcast at her plate, while the young Charlotte looked straight ahead of her into the garden, where the midges hovered around the candle flames and the fireflies ignited themselves in short bursts of electric green. Frank, meanwhile, sat quiet and small at his side, the way he used to sit at college when in the presence of authority, real or imagined, as if he could by will alone remain unnoticed. It was getting late, but the heat had still not drained from the day, and as he drifted towards his own thoughts against the distant stream of Pruen's stories Arthur felt a long tear of sweat gather behind his knee and run the length of his calf into the heel of his boot.

'But I mustn't talk about this kind of thing all night. Not when we have new blood at the table . . . How about you, Father Cripps? I'd be interested to hear what brought you to Africa.'

Arthur was only aware he had been addressed when the faces of the others at the table followed Pruen's gaze. He felt himself redden at being caught out not listening, but the Governor, who was experienced in this kind of social situation, stepped in to help,

'Yes, Father, I'd be interested to hear what brought you here as well, if you don't mind. From what Father Weston has told me you had quite a literary career in the offing back home, and a Trinity living too, I believe?'

Arthur turned to the Governor, at once grateful for his help, but also reluctant to be drawn on his motivations for missionary work, especially in the company of people he had only just met.

'Well, there were many reasons really,' he replied, 'and actually Frank was one of them. I mean, Father Weston and I are old college friends, and he used to write to me about what he was up to here . . .' He talked on, sketching out his education under Bishop Gore at Oxford, how he had met James Adderley, a travelling preacher he'd accompanied on treks through the Essex countryside, how he hoped, in coming to Africa, to lessen the blow of two cultures meeting. He said nothing, though, about why he had chosen Southern Rhodesia. Nothing about the book he had read a couple of years before, sitting in his armchair under a veil of light from his standard lamp, the winds of an Essex night beating in waves at his window. The book was *Trooper Peter Halket of Mashonaland*, written by Olive Schreiner in a white heat of anger after the '96 Mashona uprising. It told the story of trooper Peter Halket, who is ordered to shoot an African prisoner, but who helps the prisoner escape instead, and so is executed himself. But he said nothing about this book or how its story lit his imagination. And he said nothing about the book's frontispiece either, a photograph that had burnt its image onto his mind. A tree, a mimosa tree as he would come to learn, around which a group of white Rhodesian pioneers rested, all men, lying on the grass propped up on their elbows, leaning on their long rifles, smiling into the camera. And hanging from the tree three more men, all black. Three Africans on long ropes, naked, slow-turning, hanging from the branches of that mimosa tree, their heads dropped, chins to their chests, the bad fruit of a day's work. He said nothing about any of this; somehow he knew it would not have been welcome information at the table. And he said nothing about Ada either.

He stopped talking. A change had come over the company when he said 'Christianity', the word travelling down the table like a cold wind. He smiled briefly at the Governor, then looked down at the scratched and dented surface of the table. Clearing his throat in preparation, it was Pruen who first spoke again,

'Yes, well, at least Mohammedanism will not be a stumbling block for you, Father,' he said. 'Not that I consider it to be a really serious one anywhere on mainland Africa. Apart from here and maybe in Dar I've never seen a native perform any Mohammedanistic religious duty beyond turning a sheep or a goat towards Mecca before cutting its throat.'

He laughed, and Beardsley and the Governor joined him. Arthur thought of the elegant minarets and the women in purdah.

Pruen carried on. 'And I know what you mean about the meeting of two cultures. I've spent much of my own time in Africa trying to right the wrongs of such a meeting. Just last month I was at a freed slave station, arranging apprenticeships for the boys there. But you'll not have that problem in Rhodesia either; the natives there have, I understand, managed to escape the plague of slavery.'

Arthur looked up at him. 'I was thinking more of the meeting between our own society and the African,' he said, 'rather than the Arab and the African.'

'Oh, come now, Father, I think you have nothing to worry about on that count,' Pruen said, looking a little surprised. 'The natives of Mashonaland have not suffered from their meeting with the white man, I assure you. No, your concerns in a place like that should not be with worries of native suffering, but with the natural obstacles you will come across in bringing the gospel to the heathen. Indifference, slow minds and witchcraft, that's what you should prepare yourself for, Father. But the Mashona are a humble people too, full of humility, and once converted can be quite perfect Christians, I believe. Good material to work with, I'd have thought.'

Before Arthur could reply the Governor addressed Pruen himself, taking in the attention of the whole table at the same time, speaking as he did, a little too loudly. Arthur suspected a case of tropical deafness.

'I don't believe I've told you the history of this house, have I, Mr Pruen? Or indeed any of you. Except Father Weston' – he smiled at Frank – 'and of course my dear wife, who has heard it all before.' The Governor turned to his wife. She did not look up from her plate on which she was pressing her fork onto the last grains of rice that had, until now, eluded her. He turned back to the assembled company and as the servants cleared the plates and served coffee, he began his story of the house and its previous owner, Princess Salome.

Settling back into his chair, the Governor told them how the Princess had been betrayed by her brother, the Sultan Mahjid, when in 1870 he gave the house they were now sitting in to the British to use as their consulate. The Princess, an emotional and passionate woman, was distraught. She had put the energy of a mother into the gardens that surrounded them, and she wept bitterly when she had been guided out of the house with her servants under the watchful guard of her brother's men. She was moved to a third-storey apartment in town, where she pined for her house with its spacious rooms and balconies through which the coastal wind wandered freely. Her apartment was cramped in comparison, and without character. From its high window she watched her island change at the hands of commerce: the influx of Europeans, the bustle and activity of slave market days, the tall ships that sailed into harbour to take their spices across the oceans to the tables of Russia, Europe, the Americas. It was not, however, the view of her pulsing capital that came to fascinate her, but the view of another window, opposite her own. This window looked into the rooms of a young German merchant from Hamburg and, lit at night by oil lamps, it provided an insight into another life too tempting for the Princess to resist.

She had watched the young man move in and unpack his belongings: a few books, his new solar sun hat, a sepia photograph of his mother placed on his desk. Then over the following months she had watched him grow into the island, and it into him. She traced the sun's effect on his pale skin, from the red blushes on the back of his freckled neck to a darker brown that showed in contrast to the milky whiteness of his torso when he took off his shirt. She watched him acquire friends and observed their Western dinner parties, bright with laughter and the sound of glasses in the night. He bought a gramophone and she listened with him when he played his scratched records of Bach and Wagner. She watched him when he was alone and despondent, dreaming of home, and she watched him when he was cheerful and excited, dressing for a party. And in this way she fell in love with him.

When they finally met (ironically, introduced to each other at a British consulate party, so that just for one night she had both her house and the man she loved together in her life), the attraction was instant. She wore her traditional dress with long amber beads looping around her neck down to her exposed waist. But what the young man had noticed was not the finery of her jewellery or the scent of her perfume but the smoothness of her skin and the darkness of her eyes. They spoke to each other in broken English, each understanding more than they said, and that night, for the first time, she appeared in the window she had watched for so long, finally a part of its small, bright life.

Shortly after news of their affair reached the Princess's brother, the couple left the island, and Princess Salome sailed with the merchant back to his home in Hamburg. It was the first time she had left the island other than to travel to Dar es Salaam, and as the ship steamed away from its shores she tried to locate her beloved house and gardens. But all she could see was palms, dipping onto the sands, and dhows, circling inside the reef.

In Germany they married; the Princess converted to Christianity and they set up home in Hamburg. Life was strange for her. Some people wouldn't talk to her, and in the winter the bitterness of the cold made her cry. But she loved her husband and the two children she gave him, a girl and a boy. Then, three years after their arrival, her world fell apart when he slipped on some ice avoiding a salesman's cart and fell under a tram. He was dead before the screech of its brakes had died on the November air.

'She did return once, back in '85 I think, before my time.' The Governor looked away, moved for a moment by his own story. 'She wanted her children to see her island, and of course this place. She got quite a welcome, but didn't stay. Apparently by then she spoke Arabic with a German accent, but I'm not sure if I believe that.'

The table was quiet and even Mr Pruen just nodded sagely rather than offering comment on the Princess's story. Arthur looked out past the other guests into the unmanned dark. The Governor's tale had saddened him, and not just out of feeling for the Princess whose house they now sat in. It was a more personal sadness than that; a sadness of empathy as well as sympathy.

It was Mr Beardsley who broke the silence, nudging his young companion and jokingly admonishing her, 'You see, Charlotte, that'll teach you to go running off to strange lands with merchant men!' He followed the remark with a hearty laugh that sent his head back and his mouth open so Arthur could see the rotten state of his lower teeth.

Charlotte did not share his amusement, and the gentle nudge in her ribs finally upset the tears that had been brimming inside her all night. Her face dismantled under the weight of them, and gave way completely with a bursting sob as she pushed her chair away from the table and ran through the huge double doors into the central vestibule. They heard her small feet on the wooden floorboards receding behind them, then the slam of another heavy door.

The merchant looked sheepishly around at them all. 'Gosh, I do apologise. It's been a long day, and the heat you know . . . I'll just . . .' He made to get out of his chair.

'No, don't bother yourself, I'll go and see to her.'

It was the Governor's wife, speaking for the first time that night. With a sigh which seemed to say that she'd seen it all before, she rose from the table, ample in a bottle-green evening dress, and walked slowly and purposefully through the carved double doors. While she was gone the servants served port. Again, Arthur declined but he did allow himself a smoke of his pipe as he sat back and listened to the others talk about matters of commerce, the railways and the war in the south. The cicadas sang their static song in the darkness beyond the balcony and he wondered if he would ever get used to their sound, or indeed any of Africa.

Eventually the Governor's wife returned, but just to excuse herself and say goodnight. She was about to leave when Mr Beardsley cleared his throat,

'Er, Charlotte. Is the old girl all right?'

She looked at him as a mother might at a tiresome child.

'Oh, yes, fine. Silly girl was wearing a corset. In this heat,' she added, shaking her head, and then as she turned to leave, 'Nearly cut in two with heat rash, no wonder she looked so miserable.'

The merchant managed a weak smile. 'Oh good, jolly good,' he said quietly, avoiding the eyes of the others and swilling the last dash of port in his glass.

The dinner party ended not long after the Governor's wife retired. Mr Beardsley and Mr Pruen were both staying at the consulate, so a car was ordered for Frank and Arthur to return to Stonetown. Beardsley made his excuses and also left them, apparently now back in buoyant mood.

As they waited on the balcony for their car to arrive Mr Pruen also retired to his room, but returned again just as they were taking their leave of the Governor. He had a brown leather-bound book in his hand, which he held before him as he approached Arthur.

'It was very interesting to meet you, Father Cripps. I wish you well on your mission.' He took Arthur's hand and shook it, then placed the book in it. 'A copy of my book. I always try to travel with a few. I'd like you to have it. Never know, may come in useful.'

He let go of his hand and Arthur thanked him as the headlights of their car swept and trembled up the rough track towards the house. The four of them made their way down the exterior steps into the garden, and at the bottom of the steps they all shook hands once more. With a crunch of tyres over stone the car pulled up outside the garden wall and Frank and Arthur walked down the path, through the jasmine and honeysuckle, the cicadas loud in their ears as the footsteps of the two men behind them receded up the stone steps back into the house. As he got into the car Arthur noticed how its headlights lit the beach at the end of the track, spotlighting the waves, bowing again and again in their beams like actors at the end of a play.

After his prayers that night Arthur had looked through the pages of Mr Pruen's book, lying on his bed with a flickering kerosene lamp beside him. There were sketches of animals, traps, how to build a bush dwelling, descriptions of sicknesses and their bush cures, and a daunting appendix listing the supplies considered necessary for 'one person travelling in Central Africa for one year'. He skimmed over the lists, noting Pruen's advice after some of the items. From 'Personal Supplies':

One tent, 8ft. or 9ft. square, with fly, and extra ceiling inside of dark green baize
One canvas camp bedstead, with unjointed poles
One Willesden canvas bag, open at one end only for bedstead
One very easy folding chair
One ribbed hair mattress
Two small pillows
Four pillow cases
Two pair of sheets
Six blankets
Mosquito net, arranged on cane ribs, in shape like the hood of a perambulator, but 2ft.3in. wide, and half instead of one-quarter circle. It should have a linen fringe all around and tuck in.
One dressing case, well fitted
One India-rubber camp bath, whalebone ribs
One ebonite flask
One bull's-eye lantern
Four dozen boxes of matches
One luminous match box-case
Six 'Charity' or 'Art' blankets (two for servants, two for headmen, two for sick porters)
Two policeman's capes, for messengers in rainy season (N.B. Tents, blankets, etc., must be *lent*; on no account given as presents, or they will be bartered for food or drink at the first opportunity).

From 'The Outfitter':

Clothes pegs, half gross. (Very necessary articles, usually forgotten)
Alarum – No wild animal will enter a tent at night where an alarum is ticking. A luminous face (which shines well after exposure to the brilliant African sunshine) is useful.
Two tweed suits, unlined
Two canvas suits for marching and hunting
Two flannel suits
Flannel shirts with good collar-bands but *no collars*

Three travelling caps
Two helmets (both good and cheap in Zanzibar)
Brown-leather, broad-toed, thick-soled boots
Strong, thick-soled slippers
Comfortable, easy slippers
Two pairs thin cork soles
One pair of lasts for boots
Spare laces
Linen towels
Turkish towels
Six pyjama suits

He put the book down, wondering why anyone would need six pyjama suits and leaving the lists that followed for 'Cooking Appliances', 'Scientific Instruments', 'The Luncheon Basket', 'Groceries' and 'Packing Cases' unread.

Turning off the lamp, he pulled the side of his mosquito net down and tucked it under his mattress. A short gust of air blew in from the open window above his bed, indenting the net and briefly cooling his skin. It was still hot and he was sweating despite his decision to abandon his one pyjama suit and sleep naked. He lay there for a moment, listening to the night outside: the turning of the sea's pages, the hush and fizz of the waves on the shore, the sudden screeching and confusion of two cats fighting, then silence. Just his breath in the sparse room. Turning onto his side, he thought of his small packing case in the corner, and of how his belongings compared to Mr Pruen's recommended supplies. Two suits now (counting his purchase this afternoon), some notebooks, pencils and one pen, his Bible and Book of Common Prayer, a photograph of his mother (also called Charlotte – he had thought of her when introduced to the girl tonight), an old hat, some shirts, underwear, a pair of boots and not much else. He rolled onto his back again, closed his eyes and waited for sleep to take him. The whine of a mosquito caught inside his net swung loud then quiet then loud in his ear, and he wondered, once again, if he was prepared for what lay ahead. Or, as he thought of the Princess's story, for what he had left behind.

That had all been just over a week ago, but already Zanzibar seemed far away to him, already that visit was organising itself into memories and so much of what he had thought and seen there had been lost or altered. But at least now he would know if he was prepared, because the journey was over, and he was here. Snatches of conversation in the corridor outside his door confirmed that the *Hertzog* had been allowed into harbour and they would be disembarking soon. He considered going up on deck to take a look, but he was tired and he knew he would be needing his sleep over the next few days, so turning onto his side, he pulled the thin pillow over his exposed ear and tried to get another hour's rest, or at least back to the half-waking thoughts of a poem that had been drifting in his mind before he had woken. It was a poem he had been working on throughout the voyage, a version of the Orpheus and Eurydice myth, and there on the inside of his eyelids he could still see the imprint of the lines he had formed in his semi-conscious state. They were just about tangible and he tried to call them back once more, but like the ridges on a sand dune, they disintegrated under his touch, slipping away, edging back from language towards images again. Orpheus at the lip of the cave, turning and condemning himself with every degree of his turn. And there behind him, Eurydice, his lover, willing him not to, and at the same time drinking in every molecule of his being before she is tugged back to her darkness. Yes, he had the image, but not the words. They had gone, silting somewhere in his sleep. He hoped they would surface again, somehow they had felt right.

Turning onto his back again, he opened his eyes. Above him the same dimly lit patch of ceiling that he had woken up to for the past month came into focus, its cheap paint blistered with damp. From Naples, through the Suez Canal, Aden, Zanzibar, and now Beira Bay, Portuguese Mozambique. In all these places he had woken up to this sight. All his dreams ended here, in this damp patch of ceiling inches above his head. But he had chosen this, to travel steerage rather than in the more spacious cabins of 2nd or 1st class. And he wouldn't have had it any other way, despite both his brother William's protestations and the concerns of the church committee, both of whom were dismayed by his choice. Once on board, though, he'd soon realised that he was still relatively well off, at least compared to the native passengers, who were restricted to the open deck accommodation.

He had taken a look at their quarters on the second day out of Aden, and was disgusted at what he found. The men (they were all men) were Somalis picked up to work on the Rhodesian railways. They were crouched beneath an ageing green canvas stretched above them as an improvised roof. The rain, spray and sea wind all blew through holes in the material, giving the cramped collection of dark arms, legs and heads a persistent skin of moisture, slick on their bodies. The area was completely inadequate, the space having been reduced to make room for extra cargo, and he went straight to the German captain of the ship and complained, demanding he take some action to improve the conditions for these men. To his credit the captain listened and agreed with him that something ought to be done, though Arthur was aware of an irritation in his manner running beneath the smooth surface of his words. When he returned in a couple of days the canvas had been replaced, and a number of the men had been moved to other quarters further along the starboard side of the ship. But the situation still frustrated him. The divide in comfort was a gross insult and Arthur made sure to take half his food there every day for the rest of the voyage. And he made sure the captain knew that he did.

The man beneath him was still having a restless time of it, not just coughing now, but turning on the axis of his sleep as well. With each shift of his weight the flimsy bunks rocked and creaked, and the loose screws holding the bed to the wall of the cabin slid in their worn holes. The man, whose name was Joseph O'Connor, was younger than Arthur, more of a boy than a man. He was thin and pale, sent on this voyage by his father to follow in the wake of Rhodes and his pocketfuls of diamonds. From what Arthur could make of it his father had booked this voyage for his son because he wanted a new world for him. London, he had told him, was no place to start a life now, not when there was so much of Africa to make your own, to build your dreams in. He himself had travelled from Ireland as a boy to follow his dreams in England, and now his son would follow his to Africa. And that was what the boy seemed to be travelling on: dreams, borrowed dreams, not even his own. But then who was he to dismiss Joseph's borrowed dreams? Wasn't he, after all, travelling on dreams himself? Towards them and away from them, pushed and pulled, by borrowed and broken dreams alike.

He knew his decision to leave England had caused pain. He thought of his mother's distress, her worries for his safety and his promise to her to stay in Africa for just two years. But then he thought of his brother too, William, how he had glanced at his pocket watch as the train pulled out of the station, as if even then he wasn't leaving quickly enough. He knew his brother loved him as much as his mother, but he showed it in a very different way. And he would, there is no doubt, be feeling some relief now his troublesome younger sibling was so far away, now that things could finally be allowed to settle. Except of course, lying there looking at his damp patch of ceiling, Arthur knew they would never settle entirely; not in him or, he found himself hoping, in her. What had he done, leaving like that? Maybe he should have taken the risk and, like Orpheus, not gone on, but should have turned back instead. And if he had done, then maybe she would, after all, have still been there, waiting for him to turn. Waiting for him to come back to her, for the touch of his hands on her face, the sound of his voice in her ear and the taste of his breath on her skin.

Joseph O'Connor's dreams obviously weren't going to let Arthur return to his, so, swinging his legs off the edge of the bunk, he let himself down onto the floor of the cramped two-berth cabin. He reached for the khaki suit he had bought in Zanzibar, hanging on the end of his bed. Though a little on the small side, wearing it made him feel suitably adventurous. He pulled on the trousers and put the jacket on over his cotton shirt, before slipping his bare feet into his boots. Turning to the cabin door, he reached for its handle. As he did, he glanced back at the sleeping form of Joseph, who looked even younger now, frowning like a confused child over the top of the twisted sheets that had wound themselves around him. Arthur looked at him and could not help but feel a pang of concern about what lay in store for this boy in Africa. Joseph rolled over again, away from him, and Arthur turned away too, opening the cabin door, stepping through it and walking up the narrow corridor, acknowledging as he went that the concern he felt was not just for Joseph. It was for himself as well.

He heard the noise as he climbed the steep stairwells towards the top deck of the ship. Muffled at first, it became clearer the nearer he got. It was the noise of men, not at work, but at argument. The cadences of two languages were confronting each other above him, and while he could not make out what those languages were, he could tell from their pitches and rhythms they were infused with high emotions. Aggression, fear and panic. Coming up onto the first level beneath the deck he pushed through a heavy door, and the two tongues suddenly became more forceful, like the heat from an opened oven. He broke into a jog and took the steps up onto the deck two at a time.

As he emerged into the morning air the brightness of the light took him by surprise, and his eyes were momentarily confused, shot with white stars and a prism light reflecting in his pupils. He put his hand out to steady himself on a rail, vaguely aware of the activity far below him on the dock to his right, and, shading his face with the other hand, waited for his eyes to clear. As they did the source of the argument came into focus. The Somalis from the native accommodation stood as a crowd further up the starboard side of the ship. All of them seemed to be there, about fifty in total. They were tightly bunched, and moving, swaying together, a muscle of men. As Arthur watched they suddenly contracted as one, recoiling from something he couldn't see beyond them. They were all agitated, but the raised voices came from the front of the group, the part he couldn't see despite his height. The Somalis were a tall people.

As he walked towards the group he could hear the language opposing the Somali: harsh, Hispanic, but not Spanish. He glanced to his right. There was the dock, and there was Africa. Black bodies worked everywhere, carrying, pushing, lifting. A few Europeans stood among them. Not carrying, not pushing, not lifting. They pointed. They shouted. And they all wore khaki like he did.

It was the first shot that snapped his attention back to the deck. It cracked and echoed through the air, leaving a sense of sound displaced. He didn't think it was a shot until he heard the second, then the third. He began to run towards the group. But then came the fourth and the fifth in quick succession, each ear-jarring crack chasing the tail of the other. The Somalis had broken on the first, and were now fanning, spreading, melting towards him as he ran towards them. They hit him like a wave, a riptide of feet rolling him, pulling him under. He saw the flash of a blade swipe through the corner of his eye, more feet, more legs and arms, then a body falling, its black chest unfurling a sheet of blood to the floor. More shots. Six, seven, eight. He was clear of the feet and legs now, but he remained lying on the deck, his arms over his head, the same words repeating again and again in his mind. Why don't they stop? Why don't they stop? And then they did.

Suddenly, as suddenly as it had begun, it all stopped, and for a few seconds silence came ebbing back into the vacuum. But it was not long until more noise arrived, the sound of aftermath rising to the occasion. More shouts, the German of the crew, an undertone of groaning, the sea's slap and clap against the hull, his own breath, short and close in his ear, the winch and pulley of a crane that had worked throughout. One woman's scream, long on the morning.

The whole incident had passed in seconds, and already it was over, it had happened. But Arthur's mind had not caught up, and as he lay there on the deck, his eyes closed, he was still trying to register it, to adjust himself to the sudden disturbance, the violent brevity of it. The whole, sight, sound and smell of it. He opened his eyes. From where he lay he could see the legs of the remaining Somalis, thick together like a copse of closely planted saplings. Looking up their bodies he saw they were being rounded up, collected, gathered by men in uniform. Policemen. Two held drawn swords, one held a revolver, clumsy and smoking in his hand. Then there, closer to him, were the bodies. Two, no, three of them. The man closest to him lay on his back, his head thrown back, exposing his neck, his pointed Adam's apple jutting from his throat. His mouth was open, and leaked blood from the commissure of his lips which trailed down his tilted face to his open eyes, where it collected in an eyelid. A red tear, ready to drop.

He was still staring at the dead man when he felt the pressure of hands on his body. He was being picked to his feet. Hands under his arms, pulling him up. A face swam into view, one of the young German crew, speaking in faltering English.

'You are hurt, *Vater*?'

No, he was not hurt. His body was fine. He gently pulled his arms away from theirs and waved a hand in front of his face, making it clear they should leave him. Behind them other members of the crew were clearing the bodies. He watched, still stunned, as the man with the blood in his eyes was hauled over a broad shoulder, and carried off the ship, like one of the thousands of sacks being carried back and forth on the dock below him. He felt the bitter taste of bile rise in his throat, the swelling of nausea in his stomach and, thinking he was going to vomit, he turned again to the ship's railings, resting his hands on them, his head bowed, breathing deeply. The urge to be sick passed and he raised his head once more to look down on the dock, which was teeming again with work. In fact, it looked like it had never stopped. It was all energy. Energy and sweat. The essential ingredients for empire building, for the building of new countries, new lives. New dreams. But energy and sweat would never be enough on their own. As he had just witnessed, there was always blood too.

One of the Europeans standing on the harbour side, a stocky man in khaki, had spotted him looking out over the dock. Arthur saw him now, squinting up at him, one hand shielding his eyes beneath his solar hat, the other raised above his face, waving. He seemed to be smiling, but it was hard to tell. Arthur raised his own arm in reply, and waved back, not sure in himself if he was waving a greeting to this man or waving goodbye.

◇

Bishop William Gaul had been waiting in Beira Bay since the previous day, and on the dockside since dawn. He was, he knew, by nature an impatient man, but this delay, he felt, would have tried the patience of even the most saintly of constitutions. The Boer War grinding on in the south didn't help, cutting off all supply routes from Cape Town, making Beira Bay the main point of entry for anything and anyone from Europe (and from where he was standing it seemed as if Europe was sending most of herself to Africa). The port was impossibly busy. The ship he had been told was carrying Cripps had stayed stubbornly anchored far out all yesterday evening, and was still there earlier this morning. Now, at last, it had been allowed in. But he was still waiting, and the sun was rising, and the heat of the day was finding itself, flat and harsh on his skin. So he stood there, at the back of the docks, stock still among the hundreds of moving bodies and voices, looking up at the high sides of the ship. Anyone standing close enough would have heard him muttering frequently under his breath, damning the Boers for their stubborn persistence in this war, and even occasionally the British too, for theirs.

Like the other Europeans on the quayside the Bishop wore khaki. Both his drill apron and his clerical coat were of this colour. He was small, only five feet tall in his boots, but stocky with it. His face was clean-shaven, and his skin a sun-burnt brown, taut across his cheekbones despite his age. He was fifty-five. The only discernible lines on his face were about his eyes, deep crow's feet, developed by years of squinting through the sun's glare. His cheeks were lean, and beneath his helmet, which was tipped back from his forehead, was the suggestion of closely cropped grey hair, receding above the temples. His eyes were blue, and made all the brighter in contrast to the bloodshot whites about them.

Bishop Gaul had been stationed in Rhodesia for seven years now as

Bishop of Mashonaland, and on meeting people had taken to introducing himself as 'the smallest bishop with the largest diocese in Christendom'. His listeners often found it hard to distinguish with which of these feats he was most proud, but he liked it as a line. He liked people to know where he stood, of the scale of things here. And he liked to be the first to mention his height, denying anyone else the chance of an early jibe or comment.

The Bishop had lasted a long time, much longer than most. A total of nineteen years of service, starting off in the south, far south, in the diamond town of Kimberley, then migrating north, into Mashonaland and the sudden violence of the native uprising of 1896. A widower, he'd arrived in Southern Rhodesia seven years ago a hollow man, a husk blown north on little more than the wind of his wife's death and his own song lines of grief. He'd come to replace Bishop Knight Bruce, looking for more of the pioneering work he'd done in Kimberley, where he had risen to the challenge of that town to become both rector and archdeacon. It was a hard town, hard as the diamonds at its core, where the prospectors spent the days flogging their bodies in the mines and the nights dreaming of the future happiness their riches would bring them. They mined the earth for the elusive diamonds, while he mined their souls for an equally elusive faith. It seemed like an agreement, a contract, and over time he'd gained a respect in the town, and not just when he was needed, to marry, bury, christen. He also won the respect of the miners for who he was – a man doing his job just like them. And diamonds and God, he'd come to decide, had a lot in common. They both held promises for men, and were received either by those who worked hard, who went looking, or more often than not, by those who just stumbled upon them. No logic. Gems, hidden in the dirt. Soul prospecting.

He'd had some success with this prospecting in Kimberley. Not much, but enough to keep his belief lit, enough for him to feel he was touching the edge of something, here on this wild continent. But that was a long time ago, and more recently he'd begun to feel his energy dwindle, his eye wander more towards what was to come, rather than where he was now. Towards the end, and where that might be. Natural, maybe, for a man of his age, away from home for so long. Not that he was sure where home was any more. When he was married it had been anywhere with her, his wife. Now, however, it was often bush camps, ramshackle churches, one-horse towns. Would he return to

England? Perhaps. Or would he end in Africa? He'd often thought about this, ending it in an African way, not an English. Waking one night in his camp to the sound of the old elephants, swinging their huge weight through the bush on their way to their mausoleums of bone. How he'd walk out of his tent and watch their ink-dark shapes pass before him, and how he'd follow in their giant footsteps, walking with them to the secret place where he would take one last look at the veld stars before lying down with them. To end. To disintegrate and subside into the country which had for so long been calling out for his body, which had for so long craved this union. Dust to dust, bone to stone, his blood seeping into the soil.

As he stood there, waiting, the bishop absent-mindedly flexed his right hand, and rubbed it with his left where it still ached and blushed across the knuckles. A punch. An upper cut, yesterday, clean between the man's arms, cracking on his chin. A hard chin, he thought now, as he opened and closed his hand and felt the soreness of the bone under the skin. He hadn't wanted to hit the man, but as was so often the case in this country, it happened almost naturally, violence evolving like a strange flower out of the barest of provocations. Like yesterday. A hot, cramped train shunting along, stopping for long moments of time under the midday heat. Flies in the carriage, the boring veld outside. And inside, a furnace, where he sat, sharing his hard seat with a bunch of railway workers, Irish navvies, work-dirtied hands and week-old stubble darkening their faces. The close space was filled with their smell, stale and new sweat pungent on their clothes. They were eating and drinking, swigging beer from the large brown bottles favoured by the working men. He didn't mind this, the drinking. That was something else that happened here, and he understood why it did. But their language, he minded. It was coarse and blasphemous. The Bishop liked language, he liked words, and to hear them defiled was for him like watching someone take a sledgehammer to a beautiful gold watch. Sitting there, his eyes glancing off the dull yellow and browns of the view, it got to him, the insult on his ear. So he asked them to stop. Once politely, then, when they did not, a second time more forcefully, hoping his clerical dress might at least induce a sense of propriety in them. It did not, and the loudest of them let him know this. A fat man, his shirt open to his navel, revealing whorls of matted hair across his chest and overblown stomach. He leaned over to the Bishop and spoke close to his face.

'If yooze weren't a fecking sky-pilot I'd knock you down for that. We'll talk haws we want, won'we, lads?'

The smell of the beer, sweet on his tongue, his friends' drunken agreement. The Bishop felt his anger rise and the adrenalin rush in his body, making his hands sweat and his balls tingle. He stood up, to the inevitable response.

'Jeezez Christ, e's a bloody dwarf!'

'Are yooze still sitting there, Father?'

'Feck me if it isn't a pigmy we've got here!'

The man stood up opposite him, again to the laughter of his mates. He looked down on the Bishop, enjoying the height difference. The Bishop, however, held his stare while he removed his collar and drill apron, throwing them on the seat behind him. His heart beat fast, pumping his anger around his body, but his mind was calm. Still.

'There lies Bishop William Gaul of Mashonaland. Here stands' – more laughter – 'Billy Gaul.'

The veld rubbing by outside, the sun, brash through the open window.

'Now you can knock me down.'

An awkward pause, in which the man put down his beer bottle on the bench behind him, then turned slowly to the others, who were all looking at him, quiet with expectation. He met their gaze, then a smile opened across his tobacco-stained teeth. He laughed, and they responded. That laughter pulled at the Bishop's nerves, tugged them tight, and it was as the man was turning back to him, still smiling, as he was raising his hands, clenched, that he hit him. Clean on the chin. And he went down. With the weight of a shot horse, he went down, and with him went the Bishop's heart, sinking at the sight of this man folding to his knees.

He looked up from his knuckles to the ship again. Apparently violence had risen its head there this morning too. From what he could gather from the rumours and reports doing the rounds of the port, the German crew had told a group of Somalis brought from Aden they would be used as slaves, not workers on the railways. It was the young Portuguese policeman who came to collect them this morning who bore the consequences of this information. Badly beaten by all accounts. Which of course had brought his colleagues with their swords and pistols. He'd heard the shots. He sighed. Thick-skinned as he was, the indifference with which life was treated here still got to him.

In the past ten years the Universities Mission to Central Africa had already lost fifty-seven men from the two hundred missionaries sent to them. Blackwater fever, diarrhoea, animals, uprisings. The country could find a hundred ways to kill a man, and the Bishop was all too aware that they were taking its soul with their graves. The new missionaries knew it too and were now even told to write their will before making the journey. And choose their epitaph. From what he could gather though, Cripps was a harder man than most. A boxing and cross-country blue. Quite a runner apparently. Still, you can never tell, he'd seen good men go under before. And apparently Cripps was also a poet.

An increase in activity on board and around the ship's gangway caught his drifting attention. The first passengers were disembarking. A bustling stream of hats, leather trunks, dresses and parasols. Women and children first. The Bishop scanned the people behind the women, the men, for Cripps, wondering as he did what kind of epitaph a poet chooses for his grave. He thought he knew who he was looking for as he was sure he'd seen him earlier, shortly after he'd heard the shots on board. A tall figure silhouetted against the morning glare, resting his hands on the railings of the deck. He'd waved, and the figure had waved back. Disorientedly, slowly. His arm delicate against the sky.

Half an hour passed before the Bishop finally caught a glimpse of Cripps coming down the steep gangway. Yes, it was the same man. Head and shoulders above his fellow passengers. He was walking beside a younger, pale-faced man and looking about him, his long, thin frame making him resemble a curious heron. As he neared, the Bishop took stock. An awkwardness about him. Sun-blushed skin, the tops of his ears blistered and burnt by the voyage. His safari suit far too small. Thin wrists. Not those of a boxer really. Striking eyes, not a stare as such, but certainly a deeper gaze than most. The Bishop took this all in, his own practised eyes skimming over Cripps once more before passing judgement. He gave him five years at the most. Five years before the fever, the sickness, the home-lust, the whole truck and trial of this country buckled him. He was close now, and the Bishop walked towards him, revealing himself from the crowd, his sore right hand outstretched.

'Father Cripps, I presume? Welcome to Mozambique. Bishop Gaul. The smallest Bishop with the largest diocese in Christendom.'

'I beg your pardon?'

'The smallest Bishop with . . .'

Cripps' eyes were on him; in his, studying him from below a frown. The Bishop petered out. '. . . the largest . . . oh, never mind.' Then, indicating the one small suitcase he carried, 'Is this all your luggage?'

'Yes.'

'Well, let's get you out of here. This way.'

Indicating to an African boy to take Cripps' suitcase from him, the Bishop turned and began to make his way through the moving crowd to where his car and driver were waiting, thinking as he went that he'd never trusted poets anyway, but also, that he may have been wrong about Cripps lasting only five years. His handshake had been that of a physical man, and his body, though slim, seemed taut with muscle. And those eyes too, they promised more.

That evening Arthur took a walk along the beach that laced the shore to the north of the harbour. The sand was pale in the dusky light, and the remaining threads of a sunset lay across the horizon. He was relieved to be walking on the beach, out of the quarters where he and the Bishop were billeted for the night at the Universities Mission to Central Africa. They were comfortable, very comfortable compared to his weeks at sea, but he found the place somewhat oppressive. The talk after dinner had been mainly about the war in the south, or of other matters of which he knew little. Unlike the other men there he had not spent his recent years on the African continent and he found the discussion alien and awkward. The Bishop, too, he was finding difficult. He was hard to connect with and Arthur felt he had failed to win his trust, though he couldn't think why. '*A peppery fellow, who I hope to be great friends with in the future*' is how he had described him to his mother when he'd retired to his room after dinner to write to her. And he did hope they would grow to be friends. There was the potential, he was sure, somewhere beneath their awkwardness, for a genuine connection.

Though he knew his mother would want to know every detail of his first impressions, he'd played down the incident on board the ship that morning. He could not, however, disregard it completely in the letter, and had slipped in a few lines about it in the closing paragraph, hoping it wouldn't register too strongly there. He told her what he knew of the events leading up to what he had witnessed, then brushed over the actual confrontation as a '*bit of a set-to on board*'. The platitudes of the phrase jarred in him as he remembered the man with blood in his eyes, and they were, he feared, betrayed anyway by the sentence he wrote immediately afterwards. '*I fear,*' he told his mother '*that it may be an all too characteristic introduction to this dark continent.*' Perhaps he would try and write the letter again. She knew him well and he knew her. That line would ring back through the letter like a plague bell at dawn, transfiguring every other phrase it met until she would see nothing but danger and death in his writing. And maybe she would be right. The shooting did after all hang heavy on his mind, especially since the Bishop had told him the pathetic chain of events leading up to what he saw.

The evening was on the cusp of night, but he wanted to remain outside, on the beach. Ahead of him, further up the shore, he had spotted a cluster of men dragging something from the sea. It was hard to tell in the half-light, but they looked like fishermen, and he assumed the weight they were pulling in was a net of fish. But as he got nearer he saw he was wrong. The shooting had lingered not just in his mind alone, but also in that of the sea itself, and now it was remembering, recalling a body onto the shore and delivering it into the hands of these fishermen, who were tugging its dead weight up the sand away from the blink and shovel of her waves. As he neared them he could make out the corpse they carried. There were four of them, one at each limb, and the body was a man, ingested and swollen with sea water. It was one of the Somalis from the *Hertzog*. The whites of his open eyes were the brightest part of the scene.

As Arthur got nearer still he watched as the men struggled with the body's wet skin. The left arm suddenly slipped free from its bearer's grip, and the body tilted, slipped again in their grasp, then fell onto the sand, face down. The men turned it onto its back, tenderly, and one of them went to the head, passing his hand across the dead man's face, wiping his eyes shut. Another folded his arms across his chest, dusted now in a fine coating of sand. Then they simply stood and looked down at their strange catch. Arthur looked too, from outside their tight circle. Nobody spoke. Everyone was looking at the same thing. A rose of proud flesh, pink and lurid, blossoming above the man's left nipple. The exit wound of a bullet shot from behind and at close range. Shot as the man was running away.

The darkness was almost complete when one of the fishermen eventually left to fetch a policeman. Shortly afterwards Arthur left too, and made his way back to his billet on the edge of town, which now shone from its lit windows in the night, transformed by darkness from a scramble of tin shacks and people into a yellow constellation, grounded. He walked up the beach, towards these lights, and towards sleep, trying to expunge the image of that opening flower of flesh from his mind. His journey was not over yet. Tomorrow it would continue, and he would need his sleep for it, he told himself. For tomorrow, when he and the Bishop would ride the train out of Mozambique to Umtali, and then on into central Mashonaland. For tomorrow, when he would travel deeper into the strange country that was to be his home for the next two years.

Maronda Mashanu, Mashonaland, Southern Rhodesia

———◇———

He is awake. How long has he been awake? Certainly for longer than he has known. He can't be sure. It is more and more often this way, his dreams spilling over into wakefulness, his night bleeding into his day. Though what do those words mean to him now? So much less than they used to, that's for sure; no more than variances of light through the darkness of his blindness. Certainly his left eye is always night. Or rather, as he still has to remind himself in the first minutes of waking, the empty socket where his left eye *was* is always night. Because they took it out. Sometimes he forgets this. They took it out.

> Light seeking light, doth light of light beguile

Yes. And this is why he stays in the dreams, or rather, why the dreams stay with him, floating on in the night that swills in his eyes, even when awake.

But he is awake now, he's sure of that. He can hear the grasshoppers and cicadas in the tall grass a few feet from his rondavel. So it must almost be morning. What else does he know? That he is lying on his back in his rondavel. That he is eighty-three years old. That above him there must be a star of early light shining through the hole in the thatched roof where the wooden poles intersect at the top. That over the next hour the same morning light will begin to wash grey over the little kopje that overlooks the mission. That it will ripen into a deep red before diluting in the full heat of the day into a winter light, harsh and hard-edged. A heat light. That he is dying.

He can hear something else as well as the cicadas. It's the earth. Spadefuls of earth falling. No, it is footsteps. *Footfalls echo in the memory.* The distant bare footsteps of a woman walking outside. She is walking up from the river and now he can hear the slap and wash of the water in the bucket she carries on her head. Why so early? Maybe she has been dreaming herself awake as well.

Over these past years, as his sight has failed him, so his hearing, or at least his use of hearing, has improved and with it his imagination.

He has found a new chamber of his mind – a chamber for the imagination of sound. For years he fed his stories, poems and daydreams with the visual. With the light seeking light. And he still has his archive of images, but now he is learning the language of sound again. Because this is where he lives now: in a sound world. It is how the world meets him, with its tongue, palate and breath first. He concentrates on the sound of this woman's footsteps and slowly, carefully, forms the image of her walking feet in his mind. Yes, he can see them now: pale soles coated with the red dust, her toenails hardened to claws in the heat and dry air. A scar on the left heel where she fell from a tree as a child.

There is little else to listen to. Something scratches at the base of the wall outside his hut, probably a chicken, but it is hard to tell. Maybe it is a bold rat. No, he prefers to think it is a chicken. The only other sound this early is his own breath. Long, shallow and dry. It sounds alien to him, not like his breath, not the breath he knows. Like so much of his body now it is unfamiliar to him. He has listened to his own breath for years – for hours across the veld, then at night, as he lay to sleep under the sky. Just his own breath and his own thoughts. But this is not his breath. This is the breath of an old man, a man with beaten lungs. This is the breath of a man who is dying. But he will not believe he is dying. Not yet, because there are things he has to do. Even with this unfamiliar body and this empty eye socket, there are things he has to do.

> Old men ought to be explorers
> Here or there does not matter
> We must be still and still be moving.

Tomorrow he would travel deeper into the strange country that was to be his home . . .

Tomorrow. How careless he had been with that word then, how casual. *Tomorrow and tomorrow and tomorrow.* Not like now, when each tomorrow reaches him like a gift from the gods, precious and rare. His daily reprieve. But still he won't believe it, that he is going, leaving all this. And he feels again the shot of fear that pushes him past what he knows in his heart and on through panic to denial. The fear in him. He is eighty-three years old, he should have no fear. He has his God, he should have no fear. But he does. With every thought of the tomorrows gone, and the tomorrows that will never be, he has fear. Primal, heart-beating, sweat-inducing fear. Is this how he thought it would be when he was a younger man? Probably not. The young expect the old to approach death with grace, with acceptance, expectant and resigned. Well, it hasn't been like that, not for him. The life lust, however old, does not ebb. Yes, his eyes have failed, his legs, arms and bowels long past his control, and he is an old man, thin with long-living. But inside he is young, and burning for every breath, sight and sound he can experience. And, if he is honest with himself, still burning for her too. Still. For her and her daughter.

But he won't think of her, not now, not after the weight of time that has passed: *wait without thought*. So he turns his blind eyes to the low, narrow doorway of the rondavel instead and senses the light of the day growing there, petals of it unfurling onto the smooth floor of caked cattle dung, and he thinks again of the half-waking dream of his arrival in Africa fifty years before. But he knows it is not a dream. It all happened, this, his life, and now it is passing before his eyes. Not flashing as it is meant to, but passing, deliberately, in sharp focus. So, what sort of a man was he then? How old, to start? Thirty? Thirty-one? Yes, just thirty-one and not long out of college. Seven years at the most. An innocent. And yet not an innocent. But certainly adrift, washed up on the shores of Africa, the 'Dark Continent' which he had read about, heard about, spoken about so often. A continent of dreams and nightmares depending on who you spoke to. Of opportunities and destinies. But that, Beira Bay, had been just the edge of her, the outskirts of her, where her temperament was washed cool by the ocean. It was where he would start but not where he was destined to be. Where he was heading, into Southern Rhodesia, there was no calming influence of the sea. It was a landlocked country of heat and veld and thorn trees, a ridge of mountains bulking out its eastern flank, the torrent of the Zambesi running along its northern border. A country only years young, and still healing from its forming, the blood of the '96 *chimurenga* still seeping into her soil. An ancient country with a history that was no history, living in the minds and memories of the people, not on paper. An unknown history. Above all, then, in 1901, it was a country stunned by the influx of white men rifling her pockets for gold and diamonds, digging in her earth, sifting in her river-veins and herding her people like cattle into reservations. But then, waiting for the train to take him through Portuguese Mozambique to Umtali, he knew almost nothing of this.

He had read about Africa: in Olive Schreiner's book, in Livingstone's diaries, and even in the novels of Rider Haggard, and he had looked at her on maps. Frequently on the voyage down he had unfolded his *Philips' Authentic Imperial Map of Southern and Northern Rhodesia with British East Africa* and studied the names he found there, strange on his ear. *Bulawayo, Matobo, Lomagundi.* The rivers of *Bubye, Nyadazidza* and *Buma.* And then the more familiar names of the settlements and townships: *Daisyfield, Hartley* and the impressively large and bold *Salisbury.* But still, as he realised now, he knew nothing of Africa. For him then, a thirty-one-year-old Anglican missionary standing on the shores of Beira, it was a vast country which he had filled in his absence from it with ideas and expectations. A physical landscape on which he hoped to practise the ideals that Bishop Gore had inspired him with in Oxford. The African native had no preconceptions of Christianity, no awareness of its history of divisions and institutions. He would be approaching them as untainted individuals. He wanted to immerse his religion, his beliefs and his life in the soil of the country. To discover its rhythms and tides and to fit them to his understanding of the gospel. Above all though, he wanted to prove himself worthy. He remembers some lines from a poem he wrote around that time, 'The Death of St Francis':

> I seemed in one great stab of eager pain
> To feel his heart beating within my heart . . .
> It seemed he lent his Sacred Heart to me:
> One moment did I know his wish, his work,
> As if mine own they were, and knew with them
> The worm-like weakness of my wasted life,
> My service worthless to win back his world . . .
>
> I knew in blissful anguish what it means
> To be a part of Christ, and feel as mine
> The dark distress of my brother limbs,
> To feel it bodily and simply true,
> To feel as mine the starving of his poor . . .

'To feel as mine the starving of his poor . . .' That is what he had wanted as he waited for the train to take him into Rhodesia. To feel. To feel

God, not on the tables of the English rich, but in the hunger of the starving poor, who, being close to the earth, were already so much closer to Him.

Is that how he felt, or how he thinks he felt? It is hard to tell now, fifty years later, how much of his life he really remembers and how much he has recast in memory. Even that train journey, his first voyage into Africa, into her heart, comes to him down the years as a montage of images, reflections, snatches of conversation. He and the Bishop had sat alone in the carriage, he is sure of that. Near the front of the train, so he felt every jolt and kinetic tug of its halting movement. There never seemed to be any reason for the stopping and starting. Other than the heat, which he does remember, and which maybe affected the train as it would a human or an animal: slowing it down, getting under its skin. The heat. He remembers he found it hard to think under its flat, oppressive pressure. A clear sky and a white sun shining at them through the window, burning on the right side of his face.

The country had passed them erratically. He remembers squinting out at it, through the glare, watching it pass, sometimes at a crawl, then shooting off behind them in a sudden burst of energy like a badly scrolled roll of film. Then it would slow to a crawl again, and then stop altogether, paused in the frame of the window. He thought it was a harsh land, he remembers that. Malarial lowlands, then stony veld covered in tall blond grass and low bushes. The odd swampy area above which huge clouds of flies hovered and twitched. He remembers watching those clouds and thinking of Keats' gnats, *bourne aloft or sinking as the light wind lives or dies*. But there had been beauty too, and all the more beautiful to his unaccustomed eye. Shoals of gazelles and impalas, shying away from the train, bounding over the long grass, performing sudden voltes. Or an eagle, circling a solitary tour of the sky. Or the hills, purple in the distance.

The unadulterated country made him aware of the mechanisation of the train, the clumsy weight of its engineering and metal. He remembers one image clearly. Looking back as it took a long bend in its stride, seeing the other carriages curving away behind them, the sun flashing on and off in their windows. He had thought, as he looked at the train sweeping through the veld, of Bishop Knight Bruce who had trekked this way just a few years earlier. It had taken him and his three English nurses three months to reach Umtali then. Bishop

Gaul and he would do the same journey in a day. Bishop Knight Bruce had fallen ill as soon as he arrived, as if it had been the journey that was his mission, not the destination. He was shipped home to England where he died not long after his arrival, blackwater fever spreading like a stain of ink through his kidneys. He was forty-four years old.

What else did he remember? Talking with the Bishop, asking him where were the native settlements. And the Bishop telling him they had been cleared to make way for the railway. What else had the Bishop said that day? Words of advice, opinions. He had talked a lot, but he could only remember two moments now. In the first the Bishop is looking out at the passing veld, and he keeps looking out as he speaks.

'You ask a native where they live,' he says, 'and they won't say Southern Rhodesia. Doesn't mean a thing to them.' Then he'd stopped, rubbed his nose and said in a quieter voice, 'Mind you they haven't heard of Africa either.'

In the second he is more animated. He's talking about the mission work he can expect.

'You'll get the hang of it pretty quickly. It's education most of them want, give them that and they'll be happy. They can be pretty unforgiving Christians though, some of them. If the white God doesn't bring the rains, the crops or the children they want, they'll soon abandon him for their own again. They're practical like that.'

He'd paused, cleared his throat, then carried on.

'Anyway, it's not them you should worry about, so much as the Europeans. They're the ones whose souls need saving.' He'd leant forward, looked him in the eye. 'They can be a pretty rough lot. Think you can manage?'

He can't remember what he'd said in reply, just the sensations he'd felt, then, fifty years ago. The hardness of the bench he sat on. The train stopping, jerking him forward, juddering then going still. Looking out of the window as its engine thrummed through the carriage. The sun burning in the sky and the tall blond grass, stretching away over the veld, unmoving in the windless air.

But he doesn't want to remember anymore. And he doesn't want to listen to his breath, weak and dry in his throat. So he thinks of Noel Brettell instead, the young teacher who will visit him today. Because there is, after all, something else that he knows, another foothold for his mind. That it is Thursday. The names of the days may not have much sense out where he is in the middle of the rural lands, especially to a blind man, but he needs to know them. He needs to know it is Thursday: the day Noel will visit him, bringing with him his books and his clear voice, that still bears the accent of a Black Country childhood. It's an interesting lilt, and one he enjoys listening to. It was not often he had listened to poetry and heard the word 'bronze' rhyme with 'sons'. Today Noel would read Keats and Tennyson. Last week it was Eliot, whose writing he'd found intriguing. *The Waste Land, Four Quartets* and others. To hear poems he had not heard before, even if Noel told him they had actually been written thirty years earlier, fascinated him.

> The winter evening settles down
> With smell of steaks in passageways.
> Six o' clock.
> The burnt-out ends of smoky days.

He sighs, bringing his broken breath back to his hearing. That is how he feels. Burnt out. Burnt out under an African sun. And his eyes too (*look those were pearls that were his eyes*), those burnt out as well, by the sun during the day and by the quick-burning candles at night. He turns his thoughts back to Noel Brettell, who will ride to him this afternoon down the long dust trail from Wreningham to read him poetry. (*Here I am, an old man in a dry month,/ Being read to by a boy, waiting for rain.*) He remembers their first meeting well, when Noel approached him in Enkeldoorn. He had stayed over after his weekly service at the hospital. It was early morning and he and his boy, Thomas, were preparing to leave once more for Maronda Mashanu, when Brettell approached them. This was over three years ago, but his eyes were already almost useless, the darkness seeping in from the edges, the patches knitting together across his cornea. So the first he knew of Brettell was his voice, that accent from so far away, a Black Country childhood, tempered by an adult life in Africa.

'Good morning, Father Cripps.'

He hadn't recognised the voice and was startled by the sudden interruption. He looked in the direction of its speaker and after a pause replied, 'Good morning', then turned back to his preparations for leaving. But the voice persisted,

'Forgive me, let me introduce myself. My name is Brettell, Noel Brettell.'

He sensed a hand rising to greet him, and then Thomas's was at his own, lifting it to meet Noel Brettell's. An awkward pause, which he filled with nothing but his silence in return. Brettell squeezed his hand, calluses on his palm, working hands, a firm grip, then let go.

'I'm the teacher at Wreningham school.'

He didn't know what to say. He looked into the mist that was his vision and then addressed the form he saw there, 'Good,' he said. 'Good. I am glad the school is still doing well.'

As if sensing that the conversation would not continue much further, the young man came straight to his point. 'I've read some of your poetry, Father, and I admire it. To tell the truth I was very impressed. I write a little myself, although I can't pretend to be as accomplished as you.'

Brettell was aware he sounded sycophantic, and from what he knew of Father Cripps, this wouldn't go down well. Praise was only more likely to send him back into the bush even faster than usual. He was nervous, but continued, speaking into Arthur's silence and his still face, which looked back at him with unfocused eyes and an expression that conveyed both inquiry and a gentle alarm.

'I was wondering if you might let me discuss poetry with you next time we are both in town. Maybe I could read to you. I have quite a good collection.'

He stopped, then added, 'I know your eyes are not so good as they used to be.'

Arthur waited to see if this Brettell had anything more to say, but the only sounds to reach him were those of the town waking. He was thrown. These days he spoke to few of the Europeans, and then it was only with people he had known for most of his life. He had given up meeting new people, thinking he had met everyone he wanted to meet and had lost too many of them to want to build new friendships. As a consequence he was aware he had become awkward and irritable in the presence of strangers, that he had lost any ability he once had for small talk or for the speech of new acquaintances. His first reaction was to refuse the young man, to not disturb his way of things, but this was checked by a genuine sense of gratitude, as if this man's words had punctured a tiny hole somewhere in his chest, through which a pressure had been allowed to ease. Eventually he answered.

'Yes, I would like that. But not here, come to my place. Next Thursday.' And then he added, in an awkward attempt at hospitality, dredging the formality from some distant memory, 'I shall give you some tea.'

Noel watched the old missionary leave town, walking the dust track back to Maronda Mashanu, his tall frame, even with the arc of age in his back, stepping out beside the slight figure of Thomas. In one hand he held an African walking stick, ornately carved, and in the other the shoulder of his young helper who also carried his old leather satchel, spilling over with books and letters. Together they shuffled their way out of town, walking the unforgiving twelve-mile road that wound its way back to their peculiar church in the veld.

The following Thursday Noel borrowed a bicycle from a farmer and cycled down the winding track from the school at Wreningham, past the two huge gum trees that stood on the hill and down through the dropping lilac of the jacaranda trees towards Maronda Mashanu. Coming over the lip of the final dip before the clearing where the mission stood, he saw Arthur waiting for him. He was sitting outside his rondavel, beside his beloved, oddly deformed church, its five thatched, high-domed roofs looking like huge termite mounds growing from the granite of the misshapen walls. He was sitting alone, staring straight ahead, though it was hard to tell if his eyes were open or not, as he wore a pair of oversized round medical sunglasses. Beside him a table had been fashioned from some wooden planks and upturned oil drums. As he got closer he saw it was laid. With tea, biscuits and peanut-butter sandwiches. Along with the goat-cropped grass surrounding the church resembling a lawn the whole scene gave, for a moment, the impression of a proper tea party. And Noel could indeed have thought himself transported back to England, having tea with this eccentric priest, were it not for the eagles circling above the church and the screams of the baboons swinging in the branches at the edge of the clearing.

That day Noel had read Keats to him. And he would again today. Not that he needed the poetry read for him to remember it. He knew it off by heart. Keats, with his sensorium tuned to vibrancy. How could he ever forget those lines? No, he didn't need it read to him, but it was not just for his reading that he still asked Noel to come to him every

Thursday. And not just for his voice. He valued Noel for his mind too, for the contact it gave him with an intellect that was of the same making as his. An English education, a love of literature, and a life in Africa. A mind requires contact with another, he reasoned, if it is to have confidence in its own existence.

There was also the secondary physical experience Noel's visits gave him: an appreciation of the veld by proxy. He liked to think of him cycling or riding over to his rondavel, down the narrow dusty paths, of the wind he would feel, at his back or at his side, cutting one cheek cold while the other heated in the sun. Of what he saw as he rode: the long horizon, the burnt colours of the trees, the granite rocks topped with orange lichen, sculpted and shaped by millennia of wind and rain. It was what he had not seen for himself for years, and what he mourned in the quiet hours of dusk and dawn. His lost landscape, just the other side of the thin wall he lay against and yet further from him than any distance on earth, being as it was, two blind eyes away.

The scratching at the hut wall has stopped, and there is no other sound to replace it other than the ongoing trill of the cicadas. The veld was waking, but the people of Maronda Mashona were not. The woman with the water must have been on her own, a lone early riser. Maybe the sun wasn't even up, in which case it would be a long time until Noel arrived. He shifted himself on the straw mattress that made his bed, sensing sleep ebbing back to him and his mind beginning to loosen as it did so, like a boat slow-slipping from its mooring. He felt uncomfortable with this free-wandering of his mind. He was a man who had always valued control, both physical and mental, but his body had disobeyed him for quite some time now. Hurting. He had come to terms with this, but his mind, however, he would not let slip from under his restraint so easily. That at least was his wish. In reality he was helpless, as he lay there, feeling his head lighten, his linear thought waver, and the dreams and memories gather at the edges of his sleep.

A fleeting idea brought him some relief. If he *was* dying, then maybe this is how the soul prepares, emptying itself of memories so it can leave the body how it entered it – unburdened. But there were some memories he did not want to return to. He had kept himself at a distance from them for over twenty years now, and that is how he wanted it to stay. He refused to even think of them as memories anymore. They were just thoughts, thoughts from another life, a life before this, before him as he is now, lying here, sick and old. Thoughts and memories, the difference was important. Memory was a place re-visited. And he could not re-visit. He had held on to those memories for long enough, until he could no longer endure the pull of them. The unbearable sadness of them, opening like a universe in his ribs.

So, just thoughts then, and old ones too, worn out with examina-tion long ago. Thoughts that had happened, and had gone. Not just been but gone. He could not return there again.

Harare, Zimbabwe

———◇———

Last night I danced on your grave. There must have been more than two hundred of us crammed into the ruins of your church: old men and women, children, mothers with babies swaddled on their backs, young men in Nike and Puma tracksuits, young women wearing coloured headscarves. And all of us dancing . . .

But this isn't where we begin. This is the end of our story, and I should begin at the beginning. Before all this, when I didn't know you at all. Before I had ever set foot in Zimbabwe. Three years ago. That is when we begin. The summer of 1997. The end of a hot day, when I entered my father's study, the whisky-and-water light of an evening sun burning up the room, lighting up the bookshelves along the back wall and playing over a scattering of photographs propped there. The photographs are of my family in the past, together and apart. We look out from them, our future selves just beneath the skin, waiting to happen; the scars, the growing, the gaining and losing.

There is one of my mother as a young woman when she met my father. In monochrome, she smiles out of the shot, looking like a young Liz Taylor, dark hair, white dress, Welsh eyes. My father's head is in her lap, held in the bottom left corner of the frame. He is looking up at her as she looks away. He looks young and completely happy.

I am escaping inside from the day outside and from the same family as in these photographs. We are all home, back in the old Welsh longhouse that has been home to me for as long as I can remember. Even when we didn't live here it was home. We are all together, my parents, my grandparents, my two brothers and myself. We have been eating outside, and now the plates and leftovers litter the plastic table with the sun-shade at its centre, the odd bluebottle dog-fighting over them while my family rest back into the long light of the evening. Except for me. I have come inside to release the pressure of other people for a while. And, of course, to come and find you.

Your name was mentioned that afternoon, just in passing, by my grandmother. We were talking about writing, and about poetry in particular. She said that her uncle Arthur had written poetry, her uncle Arthur the missionary to Africa. I had never heard of you before and I asked who you were. My father said he had a book about you somewhere. That someone had written a book about you. And then the conversation turned, passed on, and you weren't mentioned again. The swallows cut between the telephone wires above us, the horses flicked their tails in time to the touch of flies on their flanks, and somewhere in the distance a tractor turned waves of cut hay in a field. But already I was interested in you. A missionary in Africa. A poet. And a relation, tenuous, the shared blood thinned by marriage and time, but still a relation. It was enough to ignite an interest, and enough to send me inside the cool of our thick-walled longhouse to look for you, leaving my immediate relations outside in the sun while I looked for a distant one inside instead.

And this is where I first saw you, in my father's study on the cover of a book I took down off the shelf that late summer's afternoon. It was jammed between a collection of yellow and yellowing *National Geographics* and an old Penguin Classic. The title on the spine had been faded to ghost-writing by years of low evening suns through the facing window, so I pulled it out to take a closer look, turning it over in my hand. And there you were, in a sepia photograph washed orange, standing outside a thatched hut, your battered hat in your hand, your tall body sloping to the left as you posed awkwardly for the camera, and your broken boots gaping at your feet like two panting puppy dogs. You're wearing a dog collar, bright in the sun like a hoop of hot steel about your neck. Your face is handsome, a strong face, but somehow mistrusting of the camera, which your eyes look past, way past, out of the photograph altogether.

I open it and smell the musty, damp smell of old books. The smell I think of as that of the sixties, associating it as I do with my parents' ageing student books. It is these that occupy many of the shelves in this room, a mix of classic literature and sociology, their jackets faded like the spine of the book I am holding. Both sets of books are often faithfully inscribed on the title page, sometimes with love notes written beneath: on a paperback of Shakespeare's Sonnets, *June 1964. To my darling Eryl. Yours always, David.* Yours always. Love between the covers. I flip this book open, but there is no written inscription inside. Just a gold address sticker, with the name and address of my great aunt

46

on it. Elizabeth Roberts. My grandmother's sister, and, I realise standing there, your niece.

I close the book again and take another look at you. You do not look like an ancestor of mine. You are tall for one thing, and I am not. You look English. I am Welsh. At least, I look Welsh, and feel Welsh. And then there is that dog collar. Where do I stand in relation to that? I have often intellectualised God out of existence. I have claimed, in arguments, that man has outgrown the need to rest his troubles on the shoulders of a deity. I have spoken against organised religion. I have written academic essays about the inbuilt ideological obsolescence of Milton's *Paradise Lost*, how the very system of belief the poet tries to explain deconstructs itself in exposition. I am secular and of my time. I am twenty-two years old. I know nothing and I am confused about my intentions in the world. Only the night before I stood in the top field and looked out over the hedge at the sunset cloaking the hills red and considered a letter on my desk from the army: an invitation from the Worcestershire and Sherwood Foresters to visit their barracks.

The title of the book is written above your head: *God's Irregular: Arthur Shearly Cripps, A Rhodesian Epic.* Then below, beneath your feet, the name of the author, Douglas V. Steere. Steere. This, then, is the man who had written about you: the man who first organised your life, made chapters out of it, gave it headings. Who made you history. And over the next few days it is Steere who introduces us, who is our go-between as I read about your life in his words.

When I finish the book I know about you. I know the shape of your life, I know the facts. Your birthday, your deathday. I know you were one of the young men at Oxford who listened to Bishop Gore as he outlined the blueprint of a new kind of faith, a socially responsible Christianity. How his ideas lit you and how you became his word made flesh, campaigning against employers who paid their workers sub-union wages, against sweated conditions in industries employing female labour. I know the day you left England and the promise you made to your mother to return. I know you were in the Great War at Lake Victoria, that you took on the colonial administration over land reform. I know the day they took out your eye and when you wrote what to whom.

Already I am making connections. You wrote and I write. You were a runner, not just a competitive one, but an instinctive one. You ran for the running, for the essence and escape of it. I think I know how that feels. I have always run too: through the lanes, up the hills of the Black Mountains. For the primitive feel of its simple exhaustion.

But there are pieces missing. Triggers and gaps in the story, and you are strangely absent. This is you the history, not you the man, and for some reason I am left wanting more. Steere has done his job though, he has brought us together. His prose is dry and functional, but without it I would not have pursued you down the years; I would not have tried to get under your skin. I would never have met Leonard, Jeremy, Betty Finn, Ray Brown, Canon Holderness. I would not have camped in the Red Cave. I would not have danced on your grave last night. And, of course, there would have been no you and me. There would just have been you. Then me. Two people separated by a hundred years of forgotten memories, by a hundred years of dust, settling between us with every year past, covering your tracks and obscuring mine.

Mashonaland, Southern Rhodesia

◇

Arthur has been running across the veld for over four hours. His feet are bleeding in his boots and his lungs feel the colour of the ground beneath him: red, coarse and grained. Drained of fluid, they hang within his ribs like drying tobacco leaves, rubbing against the bone. With each breath a loose covering of dust seems to rise in him, silting in his throat and burning in his chest. He finished the last steel-tasting drops of water from his billy-can ten miles ago. His mouth is parched and his tongue sticks to the skin behind his teeth. He can feel his lips drying out, cracking like waking pupae. His breath clicks in his windpipe.

The veld at his feet is as dry as him, deprived of water these last few months when it should have been raining. And not just any rain, but the downpours of the wet season, so powerful they felt solid: curtains of rain drawn across the end of each day. Italic rain. But no such rain has come, so he runs across hard and broken ground, dotted with scrubland bushes, their leafless twigs branching from the ground like burntout capillaries. The shattered shells of damba fruit scatter the path, the debris of hungry baboons. The hills are grey and purple in the distance.

He had left Enkeldoorn that afternoon following the service in the Dutch Reformed Church, giving himself at least five hours to run the thirty-seven miles to Umvuma before darkness. The congregation was small but familiar, the usual gathering of administration men and farmers' families. Wide-necked, sun-tanned men dwarfing their smaller wives, each wearing a frilling of young children.

Slipping away into the corrugated iron vestry he had packed his cassock and the dark bottles of medicine into a brown leather satchel before removing the stiff clerical collar, unclipping it at the back of his neck and folding it into a side pocket, so he could breathe. These were his rituals of preparation before a long run. Walking outside, he filled his dented steel billy-can from a standpipe by the supplies shop, listening to the deep gurgle rising in pitch as the valve strained to pull the water up through the layers of rock and dry earth. Then he bent to tighten the laces of his boots, and noticed the split between the upper and the sole had widened again. Standing up again, his thighs aching from another long trek a few days earlier, he secured his satchel across his chest, pulling it tight to reduce the rubbing that he knew would eventually leave him with a raw shoulder strap of red skin.

These preparations were important to him, and for more than just their practical reasons. They helped him to focus, to take a mental deep breath, like a diver filling his lungs before he tips off the cliff into the sea. In this way he would expel the thoughts that had occupied him for the last few hours – the stolen candlesticks from the church, the late mail from England, the worries and agitations of the farmers – and fill his mind instead with the space it required for the long run over the dustland of the veld. Or was it an emptying of the mind? To inhabit instead that place of no thought needed for the wide horizons that are never reached, for the distance between him and his endpoint and for the simple hugeness of the brooding sky above him. He needed this space, this mental clear sky so he could enter the landscape as part of it, and not as an irritation panting over its dry surface. It was only as a part of it that he could face such long runs at the speed he did.

It was growing dark. Not getting dark, but growing, the dark expanding, filling out, a living, corporal darkness. Veld darkness. The clouds that had been burning on their undersides were now bruising into night, and the evening light of long shadows had fallen through to grey. The sky was deepening, disclosing its first stars, and a cool evening breeze was discovering itself in the thick air.

He was worried he would be too late. Three children had already died in the village, and several others had been struck down by the fever when he was there a couple of days ago. It was then that he had promised to return with medicine, European medicine. He knew this would be unpopular with the local *n'anga*, but the people of the village were willing to accept his help, they had seen the children waste away and die, and each feared for their own family. But now it was a race against the darkness. Soon it would be no use carrying on, he would get lost, and would have to camp out for the night. But worrying wouldn't help. Thoughts of where he was going would only hinder him. 'Travel with nowhere to go' is what a Shona elder had told him last year, and it was good advice. Travel for the movement only, not the conclusion, that way you will be part of your journey, and not a victim of it.

So he concentrated instead on the minutiae of his sensations: on the wind that cooled the triangle of skin exposed beneath his neck by his open shirt, on the rhythm of his legs, on the tight beads of sweat that formed and evaporated on his forehead, leaving their residue of salt. He watched the orange and gold shimmer of the trees, their water-starved leaves flicking in this new wind, and he drew deeply on the lightness of his skin, which felt transparent, stretched to opaqueness by his fatigue. Listening to his blood tapping at his temple, he felt alive, painfully so, on the edge of existence. And above that there was the sound of his own breath, ticking in his throat in time with his steps. His metronome, keeping him in time with the sound of the veld, enormous, unapproachable, all around him; full with its own music of the ground shifting with unseen life, waiting for the rains. Full with its own song, a song he was still learning to follow, adjusting, fitting his life to the country. Slowly, he felt he was succeeding, absorbing the country and absorbing into it. On some of the shorter treks he had even gone barefoot when the heat made his boots unbearable. He had once arrived in Enkeldoorn like this, barefooted, skin caked in a fine covering of dust through which his sweat traced veins of dampness. A visiting dignitary had been there, a Bishop from England, and there had been words.

He was too late. He knew this before he even reached Umvuma, when he was still picking his way down the slope of the kopje before the village. Although it was nearly dark, the old light of the sun just a sliver of grey across the back of the land, he could still make out a cluster of bodies around one of the rondavels, shuffling and moving like an ungainly animal, unsteady on its feet. As he got nearer, he heard the wailing of the women. Long cries of grief from inside the thatched hut, three or four voices in a harmony of distress, weaving a song for the dead. The men remained outside, stern and serious. One of them leant on what looked like a hunting spear, the others held farming tools. They were waiting for the women to cry their grief dry, to empty their wells of sadness, so they could get on with the business of starting over again.

Arthur approached the rondavel, his skin cooling, the cotton of his shirt sticking to his flesh. His breath was coming back under control, drawing back into him, but his heart kept up its wild beating, banging out its pulse within his ribs which felt fragile against its rhythm. The group outside parted in silence to let him through. There was no greeting. Nothing needed to be said. He felt sick with fatigue and thirst, and there was an irritation of doubt working at his mind. Should he have abandoned the service, left earlier? Had he arrived sooner might he have been able to help this boy lying on the floor of the hut, his cheeks hollow with the thumbprint of fever? No, he didn't think so. A few hours would have been of little consequence, the fever had too strong a hold already. There were others that would be helped. Not that this mattered to the boy's mother, who knelt over him now, holding his head in her hands, her fingernails digging into the skin of his skull as she rocked back and forth, her eyes screwed shut but with tears still finding their way through as she cried out, 'Tovigwa naniko? Tovigwa naniko?' Arthur went no nearer the boy, staying where he was, unwilling to break her flow of grief. So he stood there, stooped in the doorway of the rondavel, light-headed with exhaustion, his skin prickling in his sweat-drenched clothes, listening to the mother's repeated question. 'Tovigwa naniko?' she asked the night. 'Who will bury us?'

That night the sky listened, and the rains came, so in the morning they were able to bury the boy in newly wet earth, with the scent of new rain and honeysuckle in the air. Both of these smells reminded Arthur vividly of England, and particularly his boyhood in Kent, when the smell of rain on the dry, hot gravel of the driveway would entice him outside to play. These sudden memories of England were still frequent, ambushing him with no warning, arriving in an instant of recognition before falling through with a pang of homesickness in his chest. They disturbed him, these sudden memories. He had left England. There was nothing there for him anymore.

Despite the night's rain the men of the village still had to start early to dig the grave. The ground under the wet layer of topsoil was hard and stubborn, and did not give easily to their tools. They worked in pairs, outside the periphery of the village, cutting, digging and sweating, the growing heat like a slow-pressing palm on their backs. Arthur watched them work. The boy's father was a Christian, and had asked him to perform the burial service, and he had agreed, although he knew that others in the village would want to fulfil the traditional Shona customs of the dead as well. From his experience this was only to be expected, and he didn't mind. He watched the men finish digging the grave then gather together at its side. A woman came out from the village, naked but for a skin about her waist and a delicate black tattoo across her stomach. She carried a clay pot and a long-handled cup, which she handed to the man who had started the grave now gaping from the red earth before them. The man, who was young, not much older than the boy who had died, took the swollen-bellied cup by its long handle and dipped it into the pot, which was filled with beer, brewed from *rapoko*. He lifted the cup and began pouring the dark, pungent liquid over his legs and arms. The others waited patiently. The beer would protect him from the misfortunes he might suffer from burying the boy, from the scent of the grave. The scent of death. It ran over his body sluggishly, drawing itself out in long trails which snaked down his legs, over the bulge of his calf and down to the ground where it was absorbed by the soil. When he had finished he handed the cup to the next man who did the same.

Arthur watched them in silence, from a distance. They tolerated his eyes as they tolerated his presence. It was these traditional beliefs that wouldn't be submerged beneath Christian ritual, and again he didn't mind. Some of these ceremonies had already taken on a significance for himself, and if anything he felt they made him and his God a more acceptable intrusion. Part of the landscape. A new chapter in the myth of the country.

When the cup had been passed around full circle, and all the men had dowsed their limbs in beer, Arthur turned and began to walk back towards the village, its rondavels clustered together beneath the gran-ite-strewn kopje. He walked to the one where he had stayed the night, a kitchen hut, its uneven shelves moulded from the wall and polished to a black that managed to gleam in the darkness. Here he put on his cassock and fastened the stiff dog collar about his neck before picking up his Shona prayer book, kneeling onto the hard floor and preparing himself for his own rituals for burying the dead.

He gave the service and last rites in Shona. He wasn't yet fluent in the language but had learnt enough to perform his duties, memoris-ing the necessary passages. The language fitted him well, he enjoyed the sensation of its vowels and sounds on his tongue. The alien into-nation gave the words a music he had never found before, freeing them from immediate meaning, lending a rhythm and a metre he had failed to achieve with the broken syllables of English. As he spoke the sun rose behind the grey clouds, and the heat grew, expanded around them, closing them in a humid grip. The boy, who could have been any age between fifteen and twenty-five, the fever having drained him of his true appearance, had been lain out with care, his thin arms folded across his chest, and his body wrapped in pieces of white cloth. His skin had been oiled with groundnut oil, his hair washed with wild apple juice and his eyes cleaned. His mother stood beside the body, quiet and unmoving, her grief wrung from her throughout the night, leaving her hollow with mourning.

Arthur listened to the sound of his own voice shrink into the veld air and watched the shifting bare feet of the little crowd around the grave. When he finished he stood back to let the body be lifted into the newly dug hole, where the boy's ritual friend, the *sahwira*, was waiting to receive it. But then he saw something was missing. The blanket. The blanket beneath the deceased's head. There wasn't one. Dropping his prayer book, he slipped his cassock over his head and began folding it into a neat bundle. As the heavy cloth slipped off him he felt a welcome rush of cool air against his skin, an escape of trapped heat. Kneeling to the ground, he placed the improvised blanket under the boy's head, gently lifting him with his hand around the base of his skull, then lowering him again onto the white cloth. His head felt fragile, hollow, the bone beneath the skin as thin as a bird's egg. The people remained quiet, and the boy's mother looked straight ahead, out towards the mountains in the east. How many children had she lost in this way? How many more would she lose? No one could tell her, least of all him. He felt useless. He stood again and stepped back from the body. The men closed in and lowered it into the grave. Arthur looked at the mother. She was still, her face set, one tear that had outgrown the lip of her eyelid settling on her cheek instead.

The sky listened again, and as the *sahwira* arranged a few paltry belongings around the body – a cup, a catapult and a carved wooden necklace – and the boy's father and cousins scattered the first handfuls of soil into the grave, the rain began once more. Large drops, that hit the ground heavily, leaving wet dents in the earth and turning the red dust dark. Arthur watched as the men began to shovel the earth back over the body, the loose soil filling in the shape of the boy: the crease between his upper arm and his torso, the shallow basket of his crossed arms, the spaces between his toes, the sunken sockets of his eyes. Soon there was no boy, just a pregnant swelling of disturbed soil, and eventually Arthur turned away, finding it hard to breathe under the restriction of his collar. As he walked back towards the rondavels and smoking fires of the village the last spadefuls of earth padded into the grave behind him, following him like footsteps.

PART TWO

Rhodes House Library, Oxford, England

—◇—

I have come looking for you again. This time in the underground stacks of the Bodleian Library where I am hoping to find a seam of your life, a trace of you, running like an ore through the layers of books, documents, journals and letters buried beneath the streets of Oxford.

Making my way up Parks Road from the confusion of undergraduates and tourists on Broad Street, I pass the tall blue iron gates of Trinity College. I stop and look through their bars at the pristine lawns, symmetrical and level as the baize of a snooker table. An Asian couple are sitting on a bench at the edge of one of them. They have asked a passer-by, another tourist, to take their photograph. He sizes them up in the viewfinder, brings the camera down from his face, takes a step back, and tries again. The boy has his arm around the girl and both of them are wrapped in scarves. They smile, stiffen and wait for the click that will tell them this is caught forever, the moment confirmed. The passer-by hands the camera back and the couple thank him, then move on, cradling the camera and the frame of film inside it which holds the image in grains of silver, in fragile negative, that will, in years to come, be today: their memories of this town, of each other and maybe even of the passer-by who captured it for them.

I stay at the gates for a while, feeling their cold iron against my cheek, looking at the implacable passivity of the college buildings, stately at the end of the lawns. Trinity was your college and I suppose these are the buildings that you must have walked through when you were a student here: writing, boxing, rowing, acting, playing out the gentleman's life and preparing for a career in the law like your father and your brother before you. A half-blue, a runner, a member of OUDS, a poet who published his first pamphlet at the age of fifteen and then another here with Laurence Binyon. These are just some of the facts that I know about you, part of the scaffolding of names and dates that supports my idea of your life. But at the moment that is all I have, facts and the opinions of a few historians and theologians. But

I want more than this, I want more than facts. I want to know you, who you were, and that is why I am here.

Turning away from the iron gates, I walk on up the street towards the library, the leaves of the trees turning above me, a few of them falling to the pavement, a slow burnt rain. The gothic Pitt Rivers Museum rises to my right, collections of skeletons and other treasures housed within its patterned Victorian walls. I turn into South Parks Road and walk up to the green brass dome that sits above the entrance to Rhodes House Library. Pushing the heavy door open, I walk in, my shoes squeaking on the polished white and black marble flooring. Busts of thinkers and academics look back at me from the far wall and the whole place bears a weight of study about it. A weight of history and lives kept.

Walking into the atrium I feel a thrill of anticipation at the thought of being so near you, of meeting you outside the pages of Steere's biography, one to one. This sensation though, is also the excitement of investigation. Because I have not just been drawn here by the desire for more than facts. I have been sent here too, by a couple of lines in Steere's book about your decision to leave for Africa that caught my eye and snagged on my mind:

> There is an undocumented but persistent rumour of a love affair
> with a girl which might have changed Cripps' earlier drawing
> towards the celibate life. This was apparently terminated by the
> decision to leave for Africa.

The statement is so cursory, so fleeting, that I can't help but think it hides an undisclosed weight, like the tip of an iceberg that gives no sign of the bulk it carries beneath the water's surface. This may of course be an illusion, a self-inflicted intuition, because in a way this is what I have been looking for. Evidence of your life beyond your actions, something that will give me a handle on the man behind the history. These lines seem to offer a chink of light onto such a man, suggesting as they do, a capacity for individual and romantic as well as philanthropic or Platonic love. But they cast a shadow as well as light. At times your life has seemed almost penitential in nature, as if governed by a duty of atonement, and I can't help thinking that these two possibilities, an aborted love affair and the philosophy of your living, may be related in some way. That you had reasons to leave England as well as to go to Africa.

I walk up the dark wooden staircase to the right of the entrance hall and into a long narrow reading room, the walls floor-to-ceiling with books. Coats and bags hang in the corner to my left and there is a quiet hum of work. Down-turned heads, the click of fingers on a keyboard, the odd dry cough.

I type your name into the library's computer system and it turns out you are not so hard to find. The words conjure up a list of your publications: poetry collections, novels, political tracts. But these aren't what I'm looking for. What I want comes later: 'X106: Correspondence, manuscripts, misc. photographs. 7 boxes.' I fill out the reader's request form, and hand it in to the librarian at the front desk. She tells me I'll have to wait for a couple of hours; apparently you don't come so easy after all.

I pass the time outside, walking through the buildings of the University that draw the eye upwards, as they were built to do, their yellow Cotswold stone contrasting against the bright blue of a clear autumn sky. Carved grotesques crouch and leer from under the modern guttering alongside yawning gargoyles, their mouths full with dripping lead pipes. It is lunchtime and the pubs are packed close with students after lectures and tutors in armchairs, shielding themselves against the day behind their papers. I think about joining them, going in for a drink in the smoke and the talk, but I keep on walking instead, the city flowing around me, restless with thinking about what those boxes will reveal of you.

When I return the library's warmth is welcome after the cold of the day outside, an embrace of books and heating. I find a table alone, then go up to the desk and request your boxes. The librarian asks me which ones I want. She won't let me have you all in one piece, I can only have you two at a time. So I take the first two. Begin at the beginning.

Taking the split cardboard lid off the first box, I find a large brown envelope, stuffed full with your letters. They are bound with a thin cord, and when I lift them out and pull on the knot to untie them, they give a little and expand, as if breathing out the air you breathed over them a hundred years ago. I turn over the first sheet and there is your handwriting. Seeing it there, in front of me, I suddenly feel as though I am trespassing, invasive, as if the sheaves of paper I am touching are not your letters, but your lungs. I have read about you, talked about you, but this is my first physical contact with you, tracing the looping, slanting ink that ran back through the pen to your hand.

I begin to read, but it is not always easy. You often ignore the rules of writing: writing down, then across the same page, sometimes overlapping paragraphs and adding your own marginalia as you go, as if no piece of paper could ever be large enough to give you room for what you had to say.

As I work through your years in that library, you get even harder to read. The paper becomes cheaper, and sometimes it isn't paper at all, but the back of a school exercise book, a scrap of newspaper, a rough piece of packing material. Letter by letter, box by box, I span the fifty years of your life in Africa, tracing it in your handwriting; large and open when you are optimistic, smaller and constrained when you are angry or concerned. Year by year, letter by letter, I also watch the writing disintegrate, the strong line waver, the touch on the paper weaken, until, by the 1940s and 50s it is a child's hand, unsure and unsteady. A letter to your brother William dated 29 March 1940 tells me why:

> My Dear William,
>   My left eye, afflicted with ulcerated cornea was removed in Salisbury hospital March 27th. It may heal soon (D.V.). Please let Edith and Violet know.
>   My love for you always,
>   A. S. Cripps

There is another a couple of months later:

> May 5th, 1940
>   . . . My eye socket's muscles may yield to exercise, so I hope, in the course of the next three months or so – with a view to my replacing a shade with a less conspicuous (and fairly cheap) glass eye (D.V.). But apparently they are by no means up to it – do you (as being surely something of a specialist on eye afflictions through your work on the Kent County Council) know of any particularly hopeful help to weakened eye-muscles, apart from the exercise of shutting and opening one's eyelids?

And then, in a letter to your niece, my great aunt Elizabeth, dated 9 October 1951, your handwriting is gone altogether, replaced by another, confident and youthful. They are still your words, your voice, but speaking in another's hand. Scanning to the bottom of the last page I find yours again, in a wisp of ink, awkwardly pulled and dragged across the paper to form a rough *A.S.C.* It could be the first efforts of a child, or not even writing at all, just the chance falling of a pen over the page. After this signature there is a postscript, again in the stronger hand:

> P.S.
> I would like you please to pray for your uncle Rev. A. S. Cripps, for he is getting deaf and when reading to him I have to shout for the same word for many times. My best wishes to you!
> Yours in the Blessed Lord – L. M. Mamvura

The surname strikes a chord in my memory. Mamvura: this is the name of the man who became your secretary for the last twenty years of your life. A schoolteacher who rode across the veld on his bike to read and write your letters for you. Leonard Mamvura. I try to estimate how old he would be now – seventy? eighty? I wonder if he is still alive. For some reason the idea of a living connection with you is not one that has crossed my mind before, perhaps because you have always been history to me, an element of the past holding no purchase in the present beyond words on a page.

I try to read the letters you wrote after this date, but it becomes impossible. Either Leonard was not always on hand, or your stubborn nature defeated your own eloquence as you tried to write without the aid of sight. The old papers, thin as skin are covered in ink, but no words make it through. There is just chaos on the page, a desperate tangled clue of half-formed characters. But you do continue to write, fifty or more letters. I don't know if you ever sent them, but you never stopped the writing, as if even when you could not be understood, you still had something to say.

I reach for another box, an earlier one, and in this action I pass my hand back over a decade to where you are readable again. Here, there is the surprise of encountering events of history, suddenly intruding into your intimate correspondence. This to your brother on 15 June 1940:

> I heard yesterday that Paris had fallen. I am indeed thankful that the sacred and beautiful treasures of mankind may have been left in peace. That noble Venus (in the Louvre is she not?) may outlive our crazy times now – all being well. Last night I was reading at Keats's 'Grecian Urn', and seeming to learn something of the perspective of Religion and Art, of Time and Eternity –

'All breathing human passion for above,
That leaves a heart high-sorrowful and cloy'd,
a burning forehead and a parched tongue'
That Venus surely may preach on now the abiding Truth and
Beauty for many a long year to come,
'When old age shall this generation waste,
Thou shalt remain, in midst of other woe
than ours, a friend to man, to whom thou say'st
beauty is truth, truth beauty – that is all
ye know on earth, and all ye need to know.'
I kept the 71st Anniversary of my birth this week. My love for you
all always!!!
Yours ever Arthur S. Cripps

Most of the letters, though, are about your daily life, the pattern of
weekly and annual events that informed your days and years in Africa.

There were some rather enjoyable new year Sports and Horse
races on Saturday. I made no show or rather a very bad show in
the 100 yards (I tried running bare foot like one or two of the others as I had no proper shoes), and wasted my entrance money . . .
Gouldsbury, my R.C. friend in the native commissioner's office at
the Range, won the high jump . . .

I take your letters back to the front desk and carry two more boxes
to my table. The windows of the library are bruising into evening and
I can see the street lights outside have come on, illuminating the leaves
of the trees that hang above them. Opening the first of the boxes I find
a large brown envelope which I tilt onto the table, emptying its contents onto the dark wood. A cascade of photographs falls out, a scattered pile of white-bordered rectangular images, curling at the
corners. Moments of your life in no particular order. I feel a sense of
relief at seeing these photographs spread before me; somehow it is in
these images that I am convinced you will come even nearer to me.
The camera never lies, apparently, and I have come to this library with
a faith in its impartial eye. But the photos I find are awkwardly
abstract, their stillness robbing them of life, the arbitrary moment
existing in its own space only, with no before or after offered. The
photograph on the cover of Steere's book, however, is the only one I
have ever seen of you, so it is still a surprise to suddenly have so much

of you in one go: years and decades passing through my fingers as I sift through the pile.

In themselves they are ordinary photographs, sometimes badly framed or focused, of people standing and sitting, but their age, and their connection to you, makes each one a fascination. The faces of the people are modern, no different to those around me in the library. Yet I know the distance between them and me, of time and ideas. In the early ones the eyes that look back at the camera have no knowledge of modern warfare; the trenches of the Somme and the camps of Auschwitz have not happened for them, the atom has not been split. Inside their heads they inhabit a different world of ideas to the one I know, and that innocence is in itself beguiling.

I find one of you at Oxford, a posed studio shot taken by Hills & Saunders, your eyes impassive, looking out of the frame. You wear a high wing-collar shirt and cravat with a dark waistcoat. You look healthy, young, with full lips and neatly parted dark hair. I trace the resemblance of family members in your features: my cousin Andrew, my younger brother, and even me. The photograph next to this is also of you, but it is sixty years later and you are a different man. It is printed in a pamphlet-sized parish magazine, *The Link*, dated September 1952. You are sitting on an old trunk in front of two thatched rondavels, their mud and daga walls painted with patterns. Again you are looking out of frame, but this time in profile, and from behind a pair of dark round sunglasses. You wear an old panama perched on the back of your head, an oversized light jacket, books bulging from its pockets, and battered shoes. One hand holds the side of the trunk you sit on, the other a clay pipe, your elbow resting on your thin crossed legs. Your face is sunken, the cheeks indented, as if sucked in by a vacuum inside you, and your mouth is down-turned. I do not think you know a photograph is being taken. The caption beneath it reads simply, *Arthur Shearly Cripps – Poet.* I place the two photos next to each other, and again I feel uneasy. There is something voyeuristic in my ability to have the boy and the old man in front of me, a lifespan laid out on the table, the beginning and end of an untold story which has, over those sixty years, written itself on your face and your body. I put them down and pick up another studio portrait, taken in 1912 and given to the Schultz family, in which you are dressed in your safari solar hat, safari jacket and white dog collar. You look straight into the camera, your chin locked at a defiant angle and your eyes burning into its lens. I look back at them, and they seem to be accusing me, challenging me. Asking me what I am doing there in your life so long after you died.

I turn away to the other photographs, to the other stages of your life played out in the work of light on paper. You in your long black priest's cassock under the African sun. Your church, its five high-domed thatched roofs like a patch of giant termite mounds rising from the flat earth, a crude wooden cross topping their disorder. You aged seventy-two, your eyes obscured by the round medical sunglasses, standing beside E. Ranga, an African evangelist who stares solemnly into the camera, taut in his European suit, shirt and tie. A black-and-white postcard of a ship, the *Hertzog*, white spray about its prow and two lines of signatures signed above and below it, one in the sea, one in the sky.

One photograph in particular catches my eye. It is a wedding photo, taken outside the entrance to your church at Maronda Mashanu. You stand in the background, wearing a black hat folded at the sides and your long white, pleated vestments. Yours is the only white face, and the rest of the wedding party stand in front of you, just the bride sitting down, the groom, bridesmaid and best man flanking her. They wear suits and dresses that appear a brilliant white. The old camera cannot cope with the midday heat reflected, and all of you shine out against the grey of the church and the veld, an angelic haze surrounding you as if your bodies are on the point of diffusion, burning brightly in the brief dilation of the lens. In the corner of the photograph, hard to see on first looking, a ribbed dog slouches past, its shrunken belly pulled taut against its spine, its thirsty tongue hanging loose from its jaw.

There are other photographs not of you, and I find myself scanning the ones of the women, in their high lace collars and neat buttoned dresses, the line from Steere's book – '*a persistent rumour of a love affair*' – still repeating in my head. I do not really know what I am looking for, a face to attach to this suggestion perhaps. But I find none. There is a photograph of your mother, Charlotte, your sisters Edith and Emily, but no woman whose name has any reason to arouse my suspicion. And it is the same with the letters. You wrote to everyone: family, friends, societies, the Archbishop of Canterbury, the *Manchester Guardian*, even 10 Downing Street, but there are none to anyone who could be guessed at as a lover. There is over fifty years of your correspondence here. I have to assume that the rumour was just that. A rumour.

The windows of the library have passed through grey to a deep blue to black, and it is time for me to go. I place the fragments of you back in their envelopes, tie the boxes with string and hand them in to the librarian. As I walk out through the marble-floored hallway I pass under the huge stone head of Cecil Rhodes, set in a backlit alcove above the entrance. The light casts a long shadow from his angular jaw across the wall and the irony of your letters being kept here, in the library of the man whose actions you spent a lifetime working against, does not escape me. I carry on out into the street where autumn leaves are falling through the shafts of street lights and a line from a Yeats poem comes to mind: *'the yellow leaves fell like faint meteors in the gloom'*. Pulling my coat about my neck I walk on down the road, my breath fogging before me, wondering, as your photographs and letters make their journey back into the darkness of the stacks, if it is always this way: the light and the dark, the stone and the paper, the money men swallowing the spirit men in boxes.

On my way out of Oxford I pass my old college and I decide to go in and take a look. As I stand with my back to the street the library squats at the far end of the front quad, its lit windows casting long gold rectangles on the lawn in front of it. To the right of the library is the old bell tower and then the chapel, ornate in the corner. I walk towards the arches of its stained-glass windows, through a scattering of students leaning on their bicycles, talking.

At the chapel evensong is about to begin, so I walk inside. Epstein's anguished Lazarus stands bound and huge in the ante-chapel, its Hopton Wood stone pale in the dim light. He looks over his shoulder up the aisle towards the altar (or appears to – his eyes are closed) and there is something pained about his face. As if he is regretful, a reluctant waker, unwillingly disturbed from the dead.

Walking under the pipework of the organ I feel the beauty of the building shed itself over me, its distilled atmosphere entering the body like clean air. A carved reredos covers the end wall behind the altar and I remember how I once came in here alone, when the place was empty, and spent an hour up close with the saints there, studying their faces, the details of their fingernails and skin creases, each one an individual. I never took part in the religious life of the college, but this reredos had always drawn me. It made me think of *Jude the Obscure* and the craftsmen who made it, the dust on their hands as they coaxed each of these saints from the stone, as if they had always been there, waiting for the tap of the chisel to break them into existence.

I take a seat at the back, on the right, but first I check for a wood carving under a misericord that my grandmother once showed me. Lifting the folding seat, I find that sure enough, it is there. Two people caught having sex with impressive contortion, conker-coloured, hidden under the dark wood of the seat.

The choir file in, extravagant in their surplices, the ruffs holding their heads as if on platters. Boys as young as ten or eleven alongside the older students of the college. I catch glimpses of trainers and jeans under the heavy red cloth of their cassocks. They peel off into facing rows, and stand there serious, their faces lit by the candles that burn on tall holders before them. The students bear marks of their lives before and after this service – highlighted hair, the odd earring, travelling bands on a wrist – but the younger boys are more timeless, their neat haircuts parted like wet feathers across their heads. The whole thing seems a little ridiculous. But then the organ rouses itself and they sing, their mouths opening simultaneously, as if operating on one mechanism, and a sound disproportionate to its origin unfurls up into the rafters of the chapel.

I don't think I will ever have a relationship with a god in the way you did. Perhaps the modern imagination will not allow such a thing, or perhaps I know of too much harm done in the name of gods. As I sat there, however, with that singing uncoiling into the air, something happened: a tuning in of the mind, a spiritual awareness, a consequence of sound and place – call it what you will, but there, in that evensong, I felt a connection with a presence larger and greater than the present and the self. Perhaps it was the clarity of the notes clearing my consciousness, but I was aware of it, whatever it was, out there, beyond the thick stone walls, past Epstein's pale Lazarus, outside the hushed cloisters. History, the collective soul, I still have no name for it, and I didn't then either. I just knew I wanted to be part of it, always pitched at a higher note, and I knew that would be impossible, and that is why I wanted it.

Shutting my eyes I rest my head back against the wood of the pew and let the music envelop me while I try to think about what I have learned of you today. But it is hard, you still come in fragments. I do know though, that you were not, as I had once thought, a child of your time, but rather a child outside time. Today, reading your ideas, your hopes, your aspirations, I realised that your talent was one of disassociation: an ability to stand aside from the ideas and codes of the day and see them in the long view of humanity. Despite the prejudices of those about you, you maintained the capability to see anyone as everyman and it is this, above all, that has impressed me, and once again I feel I want to know more about who you were, about how you lived and why. Because now I have disturbed the dust of your life, I know it will not settle until I do.

Fort Salisbury, Southern Rhodesia

◇

Mrs Cole was disappointed. When Bishop Gaul announced after the service last Sunday that the young priest relieving Archdeacon Upcher at Enkeldoorn would pass through Salisbury on his way to the mission, she had immediately offered to lay on a dinner of welcome. Since then, she had been looking forward to the visit of Father Cripps. For the first time in months she woke with a sense that there was something on the horizon, an event to prepare for and anticipate, rather than the familiar dull ache of lethargy she usually associated with her cramped bedroom. Her husband had been away at the Boer War for over six months now, and the pioneer spirit he once so valued in his wife had dwindled even further in his absence until she found each day merely something to be endured, rather than embraced as a challenge. The basics of living, shopping, preparing meals and washing had become daily trials that drained her of energy and enthusiasm. It was not a change in her character that Mr Cole would have liked to see. He was, as he would remind anyone who would listen, 'one of the originals', one of 'Rhodes' Apostles' who had trekked up into Charter territory back in the 1880s. A bullish man, who placed high value on 'backbone', 'spirit' and 'mettle'. As a member of Dr Jameson's staff who had risen to the post of Civil Commissioner for Salisbury he believed completely in Rhodes' dictum on the life and duty of the pioneer: '*Those who fall in the creation, fall sooner than they would have done in ordinary life, but their lives are the better and the grander.*' Mrs Cole's life did not feel better or grander. It just felt harder, and empty. And she did not really cherish the idea of falling sooner than anyone else either, or indeed, falling at all.

The sound of the maid clanging pots in the lean-to kitchen roused her and she looked about from where she sat in the corner of her brick dining room, lit by the one flickering candle on the dining table. She dreaded to think what her husband would say if he could see her now – his proud pioneer wife, drenched and despondent, the debris of her welcome dinner party spread before her, wincing at the sound of hyenas howling on the outskirts of town.

Mrs Cole had been the first European wife to enter Mashonaland. Mr Cole had sent for her from England as soon as Rhodes lifted the embargo on women in 1891. He met her and his two-year-old daughter at Fort Tuli with two mules and a battered old ox wagon, in which he took them a further 400 miles into the country to Salisbury. The wet season had not longed passed, and the journey was laborious and stilted as a result, with whole sections of the track simply washed away or turned into impassable mud. But Mrs Cole loved her husband, and she was pleased to see him again, and was even more pleased for him to be with their daughter, Anne. It was the first time he had seen her since her birth. Mrs Cole remembered with some irritation how her husband had departed for Africa again only days after she was born, just staying long enough to impose a name upon the child and to display a hint of dissatisfaction that she wasn't a boy. On that journey, however, she'd watched him grow familiar with Anne. At first he handled her as he might a lion cub, with interest and slight trepidation, but over the nights that followed Mrs Cole observed her husband's manner change towards their daughter. After the first week of their journey she often found him cradling her on his lap by the camp fire at night, telling her about the wonderful life of farms, crops, lakes and animals he would build for her in their new country. Perhaps Mrs Cole was seduced by these night-time tales her husband told, or perhaps she had lent too much credence to the picture painted of Rhodes' blossoming young country at home in London. Whatever the reason, she could not help but feel the emptying of disappointment when they finally rounded a small kopje three weeks later and Mr Cole proclaimed, 'There she is! Fort Salisbury, our capital!'

She had followed the line of her husband's finger, and at first thought she must be looking at the wrong part of the landscape. But there was nothing else to see. Just what her husband proudly pointed at: a line of tin shacks, their roofs glaring in the sun and a scattering of pole-and-dagga huts, cut through by a swamp that divided them from another, smaller scattering of huts. There were no other permanent buildings, just groupings of canvas tents, more huts under construction and collections of wagons covered with buck-sails. She had been travelling for over two months to get to this place, this town which promised so much on the map, its letters not only bigger and bolder than any other town's, but underlined too. She had endured the concern of her mother when she told her she was leaving for Africa and the scorn of her mother-in-law when she expressed her doubts. She had travelled through storms at sea and through hundreds of miles of inhospitable country, all with her young daughter in her arms. She had lain awake at night, in ships' berths and in the rocking wagon, dreaming of when the travelling would stop, of when they would reach their new life. And this was it. A frontier outpost of shacks and huts, the centre of their new world.

As Mr Cole chivvied the mules before them and proudly rode his family into town, men appeared to greet them, their moustaches and beards trimmed, pulling on their best jackets in honour of their arrival. A woman had come to live among them, and with her, like Eve to Adam, she brought the hopes of new lives, companionship and a civilising influence. The small crowd threw their slouch hats in the air and cheered as the wagon drew up beside a long rectangular hut, larger than the others. It looked like a cattle shed but a newly varnished wooden sign told her it was the town's police station. Mrs Cole smiled down at the crowd, holding Anne tighter than ever to her bosom and feeling a sharp stab of regret as she thought of her home in London, small and neat with furnishings, a world of culture outside its door.

That night, for the first time since their reunion in Africa, Mr Cole made brief and awkward love to his wife on a bed of sacking cloth, then slept a deep sleep while she lay awake once more, listening to the crack and swallow of the frogs in the swamp and wondering what she had done. But she did not cry, not once. Instead she woke the next morning and rose to the challenges of her new home. She set about making curtains out of old wagon canvases, instructed the cook and the maid on the times for lunch and dinner, and rearranged the basic out-house kitchen. The next day she got the boy Marufu to help her start digging a vegetable garden at the back of the two-room pole-and-dagga house that was now hers to call her own.

Many of the plans and projects she embarked on in that first week were to frustrate her in the months to come. The heavy curtains lessened the already slight breeze that the house badly needed and gave the rats another surface to climb. Both the cook and the maid left the same night after they had again been told that what they did was wrong. Until she adapted her gardening to the local method the vegetable seeds she had brought from England were either washed away with each heavy rain or perished and died under the heat of the African sun. But she continued to support her husband in every way possible, feeling that as the first woman in the community something was expected of her. If she showed weakness, it would be a sign of failure, and no one in Salisbury would let that word be spoken let alone admitted to. So when the total population of women in Salisbury numbered just seven, it was she who gathered them together to organise the town's inaugural dance. Despite the lack of material or clothes shops she led them in making evening dresses out of limbo, the local calico, and made do with yellow leather working boots as dancing shoes which flashed into view every time Mr Cole spun her in the Lancers.

She cared as best she could for Anne, though secretly she dismayed to watch her daughter growing up in such a rough environment. Anne, meanwhile, took to the country better than her mother, and was happy to play in the dust with the native children until one of her parents would find her and scold her, shooing away her playmates as they picked her up and carried her inside. As she grew older Anne's increasing ease with the country and the pioneer lifestyle fed her mother's corresponding unease. Eventually Mrs Cole persuaded her husband to send his daughter back to England; there she would live intermittently under the care of her aunt and the stern regime of a girls' boarding house, where she and her fellow classmates saw out their months as discarded children of the empire, waiting for the precious sea mail letters that told of their lost lives abroad. And that was when Mrs Cole eventually cried: six years after her arrival in Salisbury when she saw the wagon carrying her eight-year-old daughter shrink in the tall grass and slip away behind the kopje that stood on the edge of her restricted world.

Until then she had withstood it all: the lion attacks at the edge of town, the drunken behaviour of the prospectors back from the bush, the ongoing struggle with the natives to understand and be understood, and even the petty attempts to maintain London society in a ramshackle town of six hundred souls. This 'society' came complete with the hierarchies necessary for its existence. Administration men and their wives naturally assumed themselves a step above the prospectors and farmers, and did all they could to keep themselves there. Mrs Cole knew of wives who had starved themselves for weeks, eating only bully beef so as to be able to lay on the most enviable dinner in town, if only once every two months. But the departure of her child (her only child, she and Mr Cole did not produce any more in Africa, and she was not surprised, her womb felt as arid as the summer veld) was the trial that eventually broke the cast of her perfect pioneer womanhood. She did not, however, allow Mr Cole to see her cry, composing herself until she had walked around the back of the house to the new lean-to kitchen she had built. And it was in here, sitting on a sack of mealie meal with the white ants crawling over her broken yellow boots, that she finally wept. The tears came from six years deep, and each sob felt as though her soul was turning inside out. With the tears, something else left her as well that morning. Whatever it was that had been holding her up from the inside began to dismantle and fragment, as if she had been carrying a fragile egg within her which now was breaking, cracked as it was by the leaving of her only daughter.

So as Fort Salisbury grew and assembled itself around her, as her own house expanded from mud hut to wood then brick, Mrs Cole did the opposite. As the dirt tracks became tar macadam roads, so the lines of communication with her husband disintegrated. With every new brick building and every new public office that asserted their civilisation a step further into the veld, she felt the veld counterattack in her, edging itself an inch further towards her heart. It was a sensation that was exacerbated by her husband, who disapproved of this change in his wife. Maybe he didn't realise that he held the power to stem this flow away from herself. His kindness, his love, that she now had to convince herself had once existed, would have been enough to bring her back. But instead, he grew more distant, throwing himself even more into his work in Dr Jameson's administration and the foundations of Salisbury, which continued to grow towards the promise of its name just as Mrs Cole continued to shrink from the promise of hers.

And that is why she was disappointed tonight. Because it had been the first night in such a long time that she had felt herself abate this movement away from herself. It had been the first time for months and maybe even years that she had felt that movement reverse, felt herself wake and move again towards the Mrs Cole she recognised in her memories. She was not disappointed because the evening had gone badly, but rather because it had gone well, and because now it had simply gone. Passed. She wanted it and that feeling back.

She had to acknowledge, also, that there had been anticipation beyond just the meal itself, and the relief it offered from her boredom. There had also been the anticipation of meeting Father Cripps. Over the last few months she had heard various reports about the young priest. He was up in Umtali living at a mission, undertaking language training while assisting the Anglican priest there. The opinions and views of him that trickled in with travellers coming in from the east were varied and confusing. That there were any at all was a mark of the man. Few would have much interest in another missionary picking their way through the country, but Cripps had attracted attention, and that in itself was interesting. Many of the men were impressed by him when they met him. He was a straight talker, and a physical man, like them. He seemed to be a suitable church man for the country, and they admired the distance and speed of the treks he undertook through the country of the Eastern Highlands. But then others thought him a trouble-maker, a liberal and a negrophile who let his ideas obscure the realities before his eyes. He was talented with the Africans, but too lenient. They thought he would soon be hoodwinked by the wily Shona. And then there had been the dispute with some farmers outside the town. Cripps and another elderly missionary at St Faith's mission, Rusape, had been accused of moving the boundary pegs of a farmer's land, little by little, over a period of nights. When he was confronted by the farmer, Father Cripps had openly admitted to moving the pegs, claiming the farmer was encroaching on land reserved for the natives. It was this story particularly that had caused a stir in the rumours and gossip that blew between the settlements like a trade wind. Nobody wanted an interfering missionary in their territory. For her part, Mrs Cole found the image of two priests moving land pegs under the cover of darkness an amusing one. But the story had caught somewhere deeper in her as well, as if a long-buried concern had been accidentally snagged and disturbed.

The third view of Father Cripps that had excited her curiosity did not come from general gossip or opinion, but from one person, a woman. She was the wife of a travelling doctor who had met Cripps up country when he was on one of his treks. While her husband was setting up his stall in the high street, she recounted quite openly to

Mrs Cole over tea in the hotel (a long open-fronted shack with a bar) the deep impression that Cripps had made on her. She spoke about his eyes a great deal and left Mrs Cole in no doubt that for a woman, beyond any other reason, Cripps was a man worth meeting.

His arrival was quieter than she had expected, though why it should have been any other way she couldn't think. Maybe anticipation had led her to expect something else, a shift in the air when he entered her world, a noticeable change in her environment. But it was all the same, all so familiar. He had come in from Umtali that day by wagon, and had not long left his case at the Bishop's lodgings when the two of them turned the corner of her house and walked up onto the wooden veranda Mr Cole had left half-finished when he departed for the war. She was sitting under the shade of the convolvulus that twined its way around the corner pillar, holding a glass of whisky and soda and reading a novel that had somehow found its way from England into her dusty outpost life. The sun was low in the sky and the light of the day had softened. She wore a red dress, her only evening dress, and a large opal pendant that her husband had given her on his first return from Africa. Out in the veld the under-murmur of twilight was rising to meet the encroaching darkness. It was her favourite time of day, and although the town had grown since her husband claimed this plot, there were still no other buildings to obscure her view. The ground beyond their house was too swampy and marshy to support the weight of foundations. She looked across it now, through a quivering cloud of flies suspended above the patchy grass and took a sip of her drink, feeling the tightening around her lower jaw that she always felt with the first touch of alcohol. And then they were there, silhouetted against the light of the dying day, the diminutive, stocky Bishop coming up to the taller man's shoulder.

She rose to welcome them, moving around them as she did to get the light out of her eyes, which is when she saw his, and when she realised what the doctor's wife had meant. He looked down at her as the Bishop introduced them, and Mrs Cole looked back at him. They were blue, but she had seen blue eyes before. Her husband's eyes were blue; but his were nothing like these. It was as if Cripps had been facing a low sun which had somehow left its evening light in his irises: an opal iridescence with flecks of fool's gold around the pupils, floating, deep and black, adrift in their mineral waters.

Mrs Cole had also invited the Reverend Holt and his wife, who arrived shortly after the Bishop and Cripps. She had never liked or trusted Holt, who was another missionary, but of a different breed to the Bishop or, she felt, Cripps. His work in Africa was funded by a group of religiomaniacs back in England whom Holt kept informed with a regular supply of exaggerated and skewed tales of Rhodesian life in return for his healthy income. He expressed his successes in figures: 800 Bibles distributed, 370 baptised, sixty more of those confirmed and 2,000 on the roll for mission schools. It made Mrs Cole suspicious of him, a man whose spiritual work read like balance sheets, but she could not have avoided inviting him tonight.

They took their drinks on the veranda, Cripps taking a lime juice instead of a whisky and soda. Then they retired to the small brick dining room, where Mrs Cole's maid and house boy served impala steaks that she had bought from a hunter just that week. To her surprise Cripps politely declined the steaks on the grounds of being a vegetarian, and accepted a hastily-cooked cob of mealie corn instead. Mrs Cole was momentarily thrown, her careful preparations shattered on the rocks of this bizarre preference, but she did take some enjoyment in the Holts' raised eyebrows and shared disapproving glance. To follow, the maid served sweet wine and sour apples, which, Mrs Cole was relieved to see, Cripps did accept despite his earlier refusal of a drink.

They ate, drank and the evening went as evenings like that always had done. A swing of conversation and silences, politenesses, compliments, a lot spoken, little said, and almost nothing which was not tempered by the situation. Father Cripps did not keep within these boundaries as much as the others, but he did not speak often either, and when he did it was with a soft, halting voice that did little to assert itself beyond the words that it carried. His thoughts appeared to come at him from many directions; he often stopped a sentence midway and jumped onto another and he peppered his speech with the phrase 'I mean', although he never seemed in any doubt about exactly what he meant.

Mrs Cole observed him as they all went through the motions. He was not what she had been expecting at all. She thought him somewhat untidy; his khaki suit was crumpled and worn, and looked as though it needed a wash. He himself looked as though he needed a wash, although his clerical collar was a clean, brilliant white. Physically, he was obviously fit, and she noticed his strong neck, its mobile muscle and veins under a taut skin. And yet he did not seem at ease with his body, as if his arms and legs were just too long, and he did not know where to put them when still. The Bishop had said he was thirty-one years old, only four years younger than herself, but he could have been even younger again. His face was clean-shaven, and sometimes, when he was listening, it betrayed a youthfulness not apparent on first meeting. And he seemed shy. He was neither the trouble-maker nor the zealous priest he had been painted as, but appeared rather to be simply an earnest man who was still working things out.

Mrs Cole sensed a mothering instinct rise in her when she thought of him like this. Or maybe it was another instinct, because she still saw, despite his shyness and his dishevelled appearance, what the doctor's wife had also noticed in him. A certain magnetism, an interest about him that held the eye, unlike someone like Holt, whom the eye slid off as easily as if he were just another stone on the ground. She also found an attractiveness in his serious nature that could suddenly break to a smile and laughter, in the conviction of what he said, and of course in his eyes, which seemed to speak of a longer life than he could possibly have yet lived. He was obviously close to the Bishop, and this friendship was in itself another attractive quality. Mrs Cole liked the gruff little Bishop, and she liked the way the two men worked together, almost like a father and son, with an unspoken understanding passing between them even when they were silent, listening to Reverend Holt recite his numbers game.

Above all, though, Mrs Cole liked Father Cripps because she liked herself when she talked to him. Once she had broken through his shell of reticence they had talked quite freely, and she found his views refreshing. There was none of the anxious arrogance she had encountered in other missionaries, the conviction that godliness was won through a white man's way of life, and all the taxes that went with it. He seemed new, yet open to Africa, and especially open to her people. Mrs Cole found herself engaging parts of her mind that seemed stubborn and rusted with misuse. He made her think, and talk, and he listened to her. It was something a man had not done with her for such a long time, and for the first time in years she recognised herself again.

And that is why she was disappointed. That is why she had stood outside her house and looked out into the darkness long after they had all left, and why she stayed there as the clouds opened and brought the rain, sheeting down over the tin roofs of Salisbury. Not because the evening she had looked forward to and prepared for was over. Not because she would miss the Bishop or Father Cripps, or the general company. But because Cripps had made her recognise herself once more, and unless she could retain that feeling, she would miss that woman. She had enjoyed having her back.

Enkeldoorn Charter District, Mashonaland, Southern Rhodesia

———◇———

Arthur watched from a distance as the young Mashona man gathered the loose skin of the bull's throat. He pulled it taut with one hand while firmly pressing a thin-bladed knife into the hard hide and muscle of the animal's neck with the other. As he did this he bent close to where the knife's point made contact with the skin, his face fixed in a concentrated frown while his friend, who held the animal's large, angular head in a rope halter, looked on. Its wet nostrils fumed in the early morning air. All three of them were still for a moment in this position, a frozen tableau, but then the elbow of the young man's arm jerked forward a fraction and the bull flinched and raised its head in response. A pearl of blood grew at the apex of metal and skin. The young man kept his pressure on the knife, gently twisting the handle from side to side, as delicately as if he were piercing a loved one's ear. Arthur could see the tendons and stringy muscle of his forearm working over the bone with each turn of his wrist. As he twisted the knife he bent down even closer to where the blade entered the skin, turning his head to the side as he did so, listening for the almost inaudible hiss which would tell him he has gone far enough. It comes, and withdrawing the tip of the blade in one smooth action he picks up the calabash bowl at his feet just in time to catch the first arc of black-red blood spurting from the punctured vein. He keeps his other hand at the wound, coaxing the blood through the skin. It is early morning and cold, the mists that have lain on the ground all night are still dispersing and the blood steams in the bowl as it fills.

Arthur has seen this cattle-bleeding before, but it still fascinates him. He likes to think of it as a kind of African Eucharist, a literal translation, although he knows it is more practical than that, performed for the body not the soul, gleaning the animal's protein while keeping it alive for another day's work. After a couple of minutes the bull's eyes waver in their sockets and its knees give then recover like those of a dozing midday sleeper. The young man holding the animal's head says something to the calabash holder. He speaks quickly and urgently. The other man places the large bowl on the ground in response. As he does this he tries to follow the pulsing arc of blood, which rises and falls with the bull's heartbeat, until the bowl is at his feet again but still catching the hot liquid, which gulps and falls down the animal's neck, red against its dun hide. His hands free, he bends and picks the leaf of a plant which he places over the wound, pressing it to the puncture in the bull's neck with both his hands. The sound of the blood flowing into the bowl stops. A bird calls from one of the trees and somewhere a woman is singing. Only now do the two young men turn to Arthur, as if it is only in this new silence they have noticed him. They are both naked except for scraps of blue limbo tied around their waists covering their genitals. They must be no older than seventeen or eighteen. The young man pressing the leaf to the wound takes a hand away and waves to Arthur. '*Mangwanani ishe.*'

Arthur raises his own hand in reply. '*Mangwanani. Makadii?*'

'*Ndiripo makadiwo.*'

Arthur nods and smiles. '*Ndiripo.*'

The young men look back at him. Both have a little blood spattered on their arms and legs. They smile, and, in that way that Arthur has come to love, laugh and nod their heads, for no other reason than it is a good morning. Waving again, he turns away from them and continues up the narrow track that leads on in front of him, its pale dust cutting a ragged path through the patchy grass, boulders and low thorn trees of the veld and onto Enkeldoorn, ten miles away. Behind him he hears the chatter of the two men and the deep lowing of the bull. He likes the translation of that greeting he was given once. There is something in it that calls to the core of a very human need, the affirmation of one's existence in another's:

'Morning chief.'
'Morning. How are you?'
'I am here if you are here.'
'I am here.'

It is three years since Arthur disembarked at Beira Bay to find Bishop Gaul waiting for him, and since then being 'here' has often meant walking the track he is on this morning, between his mission station at Wreningham and the small Dutch town of Enkeldoorn. The track is rough and narrow, no wider than the span of a hand. It has been made over the years by the feet of the people who walk this way, wearing away at the soil with their hard soles. It is an unremarkable track, a common footpath, and, to the infrequent eye, anonymous, like any of the thousands and maybe millions of similar paths that cross and intersect over the velds of Africa. But to Arthur it is his track, his path which he has claimed over the three years he has walked it, with his feet, his sweat and his aching muscles, twice every week. It is a journey that he has made so many times, in so many weathers, that now he can travel the path in the pitch dark of an African night, walking by instinct and familiarity alone. His feet know every bend and swell, his eye recognises every misshapen rock that looms out of the darkness towards him. Only his ears are still surprised by what he can meet on it: an unfamiliar breaking of twigs or undergrowth often bringing him to a dead stop, motionless, listening to his own breath loud and clumsy in his ear. Several times now he has thought he has heard a lion rolling a growl in its throat, and it has left him standing still for minutes, waiting for the sound again, hopefully receded, or, as he so often feared, louder and closer to him again. But now, after three years walking the track, he is even getting used to these noises. The howling of the striped hyenas, the static of the cicadas at dusk and the whooping of the baboons in the trees are all as much a part of the veld for him now as the endless horizon and the towering clouds piled up in the sky. With every day spent out in its barren beauty he was growing into it, and so far it had not harmed him. Blisters and sweat rashes, not lions or rhinos, were his only regular discomforts.

He stops by a boulder and leans against it, feeling its pitted hardness against his hip bone. Bending his right leg, he holds it by the ankle with his right hand and, pulling down his woollen sock with his left, he examines his ankle, like a farrier passing his eye over a tricky hoof. The skin on his heel is hardened and calloused, but this morning it has bloomed again into a patch of rosy pink, laced with the darker red of broken skin. He spits on his left hand and wipes away the dust that has been sanding away at it as he walks. As he pulls his sock back up he notices that the piece of bully-beef tin he had nailed to the sole of his boot is coming loose again. There is little he can do about it here, so he just stamps his foot hard on the ground a couple of times, raising little puffs of dust from the path. Adjusting his satchel about his shoulders, he looks up into the sky. It is clear blue and cold. He watches a tawny eagle launch itself from a white thorn tree on a kopje off the path and slow-glide a spiral in the air. It beats its wings just once, the movement reaching Arthur with the sound of a breath. He follows its slow tour of the sky. Then he carries on.

Behind him, the track leads back through the scrubland to Wreningham mission station, where he started out at first light this morning and where he has been stationed since he arrived in the area from Umtali three years ago. In 1891 Bishop Knight Bruce, the first Bishop of Mashonaland, passed through this country, maybe on the same track that Arthur is walking this morning. The Bishop walked 1,300 miles through the veld that year, looking for ground on which to stake his spiritual claim for the Anglican church. At Wreningham he introduced himself to the chief of a nearby village, and requested an area of land. The chief gave him some, and the Bishop's native boy marked the place with a tall white cross, planted on top of a kopje. Then the Bishop and his boy left, to find another chief and another area of land. On that trek Bishop Knight Bruce met more than forty-five Shona chiefs. All of them gave him some land and in all these places the Bishop planted a white cross until there was a chain of white crosses stretching out across Mashonaland. Over the next ten years these crosses attracted more white men and with their arrival, they grew, like magical seeds, into mission stations. Wreningham was one of these stations, named after a school in England of which the first priest to serve there, Archdeacon Upcher, had particularly fond memories.

The station itself occupies a low kopje that overlooks an expanse of tall yellow grass through which the wind, when it comes, blows shifting waves of shadow and light. Outcrops of granite and the odd thorn tree are the only features to break the immediate view on all sides, although just over the horizon there are scatterings of Mashona kraals, their conical rondavels dotting the ground down towards a dip in the land where a sluggish river ebbs and flows with the seasons. At the top of the kopje two huge gum trees stand on either side of a small compound. In front of these is the square thatched hut that serves as both church and schoolroom, and behind this another hut of a similar shape, but smaller, which is the priest's quarters. The store room and kitchen stand a few yards further off again. Across from the church a ragged line of rondavels back onto a patch of scrubland vegetation that falls away down the east flank of the kopje. Their walls are made of a crude wattle and daub and their mud-clotted thatches reach almost as far as the floor. Goats, dogs and chickens wander freely about the area between these huts and the church, and the air is often languid with the heavy smoke of open or smouldering fires, lingering like incense.

Arthur stops again, this time by an acacia tree that he knows marks the half-way point on the track. Digging in his satchel between the books and the letters, his fingers find the cold steel of his water bottle. Pulling it free with a metallic swill of the water inside, he untwists the cap, and brings the bottle to his lips and drinks. The water is still cool despite the growing heat of the day and he feels it run down his throat into his stomach, tracing the route of his gullet with a chill sensation, coming to rest in a dark cold patch in the pit of his belly. He resists the temptation to drain the bottle, although he knows he needs the water. He has not long recovered from a bout of malarial fever, and he still carries the residue of that sickness in the shape of a vicious thirst. But he is only half-way, so he places the bottle back in his satchel, buckles its one strap and carries on again.

Ahead of him is Enkeldoorn, the only other significant destination on this path apart from Wreningham. It is a small place, no more than fifty or sixty people making it their permanent home, and its history is one of chance and accident rather than design. Arthur is not alone in considering it something of a lost town.

Enkeldoorn was established hurriedly in 1896 when news of the attacks by the Matabele impis in the south of the country reached the area of low veld and vlei country in which the town now lies. The stories of butchery and burning were enough to rush a scattered collection of pioneers together to form a laager around the one existing farm. When the rebellion receded these pioneers remained, naming their new home after a prominent Kamuldoorn tree that stood sentinel over the settlement: Enkeldoorn, the Dutch for 'single thorn'. For a while they were the only white men and women to live under the tree's long evening shadow, but gradually more came to join them, lured south by stories of gold reefs, rich for the picking, that were spreading through the country and through Europe like a virus. One reef was said to pass right through the hills outside Enkeldoorn, a glittering band of wealth embedded in the rock, just below the surface of the thin soil. And so they came, with their dynamite and their dreams, and Enkeldoorn was born again as a prospecting town. Bank clerks and shopkeepers became miners overnight, setting out in ones and twos on wagons loaded up with explosives, mining tools and a couple of native boys riding on the back, their legs dangling into the dust clouds stirred up by the wheels.

After weeks in the bush these men would return, pale with rock dust, smelling of dynamite and the earth. They went to drink in Vic's Tavern, the only bar in town, but they weren't there just looking for drink, or even for an hour with one of the handful of whores who had come down from Salisbury. They were also looking for other men and, more particularly, for other men's dreams: for someone they could take aside into a corner after a few whiskies, and on whose shoulder they could lay their hand as they pulled out a lump of quartz from their pocket, which they'd spit on to reveal the specks and strands of gold hidden inside. With these waistcoat tempters many an administrator or traveller was persuaded to put up a share of capital in a mining enterprise. But all too often the prospector would then disappear, leaving them with their anticipation of riches dwindling by the day. Because the gold in the hills did not exist after all. But now Enkeldoorn did, and so it remained, washed up on its imaginary reef out in the veld, four days' wagon drive from Fort Salisbury and a week's at least from any other town of consequence.

In the years since Enkeldoorn's brief gold rush a spur of the railway had been promised to the town by Rhodes himself, but when Arthur arrived in 1901 Enkeldoorn was still waiting for it to be built, to come and lend a meaning to its lonely existènce. At least with a railway the town could claim to be the end of the line. As it was it was not even that. It was simply a full stop in itself, a stubborn outcrop of European life set adrift in the heartland of Africa.

The railway spur never came, but in its absence Enkeldoorn made the best of its lonely position. Destined never to be a destination in itself, the town became a trading post, a supply town, a stopping and going place, supplying the farmers that surrounded it and the travellers that passed through it.

The geography of the town, like its character, was uncomplicated. Widely dispersed dwellings, lean-tos and huts spread out from a tighter concentration of buildings that lined the one main street. This street was a wide streak of dust flanked by wooden and brick buildings with clumps of veld grass growing in between them. On it stood the post office, Vic's Tavern, the administration offices, the police station and a collection of shops selling pioneer equipment: tools, tents and general supplies. At the end of the high street was the town jail, a long squat iron-roofed block in which a dozen or so natives served sentences for offences that many of them never knew were offences, breaking, as they did, no code of their own. Early each morning a couple of native policemen overseen by a white officer escorted these prisoners out of town, chained neck and foot, to work on the Salisbury road. Apparently, somewhere to the south of Salisbury there was another group of chained men, also working on the same road, the idea being that one day they would meet, and Enkeldoorn would finally have a clean link to the capital. No one Arthur had spoken to seemed particularly convinced of this.

The only other building of any stature was the Dutch Reformed church, set back from the high street on the left as you approached from Salisbury. This is where Reverend Liebenberg preaches to the town's Dutch and Afrikaans population, and where he also lets Arthur preach to the much smaller Anglican congregation. It was an arrangement the two men came to not long after Arthur's arrival in the area, it being obvious to both of them that the question of denomination was a diminished one in comparison to the scale of the task they both faced. Liebenberg and his wife had since become good friends of Arthur's, and recently Liebenberg had even been kind enough to play the church's old piano in Arthur's services, banging out the hymns on the yellowing keys with such enthusiasm that he often drowned out the singing of the small congregation altogether.

These then, were the punctuation points of Arthur's life in Mashonaland. Enkeldoorn and Wreningham, white and black, commerce and church, lost and found. It was in these two locations that his contrasting parishes lay, and this is why he spent so much of his time on this track, passing between the settlements twice a week on his solitary treks, etching his mark on the country with his feet.

On the veld, alone, however, was where he felt he most belonged. After three years in Africa it was here he felt closest to the essence of the country, and to his God. Sometimes, on the longer treks to other towns and villages further away, he would sleep out in the open, lying beside his camp fire, tracing the myths and stories of the constellations, familiar and yet different in the southern sky above him. Waking in the morning, his red blanket covered with dew, he would perform a private Eucharist on a nearby rock, or on the bank of a stream, before packing up and carrying on again. It felt completely natural for him to do this, and it was during these solitary celebrations that he was at his most content. And in many ways he thought this was suitable: that he felt most complete neither in Enkeldoorn nor in Wreningham, but in between them. He was, after all, the in-between man, in every sense of the word. Between sky and earth, God and man, European and African. For although by skin colour and country he belonged to the whites in Enkeldoorn, he knew he could never feel himself a part of their pioneer lifestyle, and in return he knew that many of them were suspicious of him. His closeness to the natives and his attempts to live with and like them unnerved the Dutch farmers and the British administrators alike.

In the first few years he'd found it no easier with the Africans, many of whom also regarded him with suspicion. The people who lived on and around the mission recognised his good intentions but however hard he tried to serve them he was, for many outside the mission, just another European *mufundisi* bringing talk of a God and rituals that disturbed the stability of their own beliefs. Some of the Mashona elders in the surrounding villages feared he would upset the delicate balance of their ancestors' spirits while the *n'angas*, the local shamans, saw him as a professional threat and did what they could to fan this fear. Arthur had heard some had even warned the people that allegiance to the white man's God would anger the *Mhondoro*, the tribal spirit, and bring tragedy upon their families.

In those early years Arthur's lack of Shona was a further frustration. The young missionary girl who had been his tutor in Umtali, having been told so often that the white men were right, had been too timid to ever correct his mistakes, so he arrived in Wreningham with a more imperfect grasp of the tongue than he had hoped. For the first year at the mission he spent hours in his hut each night, bent over a Shona grammar and dictionary, painfully composing his sermons word by word and learning them by heart by the light of a candle. But his efforts at fluency on paper were all too often dismantled on his tongue as he stumbled through the subtle nuances of the language's tonal pronunciation. It was only when the young mission boys began running around the church hut with their knuckles on the ground in the manner of chimpanzees every time he spoke of *Shoko Kristu,* that he learnt he had been preaching for months not as he had thought on Christ's *message*, but Christ's *monkey*. There was only a breath and an upward inflexion between the two words, but it was enough.

The language, however, could be mastered, and in the meantime he had continued to try and serve the Mashona by doctoring, representing them in the colonial courts, assisting with their farming and helping in family disputes where he could. But there were other elements of his presence among them that were harder to overcome. Above all, there was the fact that he was white. The 1896 *chimurenga* had happened only eight years ago; the European settlers had killed over four thousand natives in revenge. The Mashona had not forgotten, and could not forget, these men, or the things they had done. Stories were still told in kraals and around fires of how the suspected rebels were hunted down and hung from trees and of how caves into which whole families had fled were dynamited by their pursuers.

When Arthur arrived in 1901, the relationship between the white settlers and the native Mashona in the wake of the uprising was uneasy and awkward, but he was still surprised at the extent of the settlers' ignorance and disinterest in the Africans around them. Interaction was minimal, restricted to the boys and women who worked for them as carriers, cooks or maids, and even in these situations the meeting of the two cultures was rarely successful. Either the Africans were mistreated or they stole from their employers, or, most commonly, they simply left and went back to their kraals. Because before the settlers came the Mashona had no need to work for money, and for most this was still the case. The settlers, however, needed labour to build their new world, and they were frustrated by the thousands of natives who refused to supply it. The Africans' apparent absence of wants stood in exact opposition to their own lives. They were here for gold, farming, trade. The Mashona were simply here.

This problem of the labour situation dominated discussion across the settler community. It had been a thorn in the side of the administration since the establishment of the British South Africa Company; in principle they were opposed to slavery but they were also desperate to engage the massive potential labour force they saw before them. The Company found an answer to the problem with the introduction of a 'hut tax' to be paid by every male native for himself and for each of his wives. The tax was required in cash, and cash could only be earned by working in the settlers' mines, houses or farms. It seemed simple. The Africans had an absence of wants, so in its place the Company had created a need. The need for money.

The hut tax further exasperated the already fragile settler-native relationship and its initial establishment had been at the root of the native uprising in 1896. For the Mashona in Mashonaland and the Matabele in Matabeleland the twenty years of rule by the white population had brought nothing but disruption to their way of life. Whole tribes had been moved from their ancestral land where their forefathers were buried, and foreign diseases were brought into the country killing both the people and their livestock. Herdsmen were forced to dip their cattle in the local streams to protect them against rinderpest and foot and mouth, only to find that the dipping chemicals polluted their drinking water. And now the hut tax was to be levied in every district to pay for the price of this disruption. It was a move too far for many, and encouraged by their spirit mediums they rose against the white men. Eight years later that uprising had been reduced to fireside myth, the rebel leaders were long dead, the Mashona's self-belief was crushed and the hut tax still remained. The men around Wreningham wore its brass payment tokens on pieces of cord around their necks. Arthur had noticed these necklaces were something of a status symbol for the younger men; the more tokens, the more wives, and the more huts. But for the older men he knew the necklaces were worn in another symbolic gesture. For them, who could remember life here before the settlers, the brass tokens threaded on a string of hide were a reminder, worn against their skin, of their new position in a land they had once called their own.

The hut tax angered Arthur and he had tried his best to undermine it at the Anglican Synod in Salisbury in the April of 1903. As usual he chose to walk the hundred miles to the capital, and he arrived with just minutes to prepare before presenting his case. He stood in front of the assembled clergy, his already threadbare khaki suit caked in the fine red dust of the veld and the sweat still fresh on his face. Clearing his throat, he proposed:

In view of the agricultural and pastoral character of the Mashona people, and of the fact that they have been only twelve or thirteen years in contact with civilisation, we consider that the most desirable form of taxation to stimulate their industry is taxation in kind.

He had worded his proposal carefully. He knew it would be seen as a stab at the British South Africa Company, but he also felt sure that in the eyes of the church his argument was strong. A tax in kind, he went on to explain, would diminish the disruption to the Africans' way of life in their kraals and villages. A tax in cash required the men to leave their homes in search of work. A tax in kind would at least let them stay. Surely it was in the interest of the Anglican Church to promote the idea of a stable family home among the native people? He sat down, aware of the murmurings of disapproval both his speech and his outfit had provoked among the clean pressed suits and vestments around him. The proposal was refused. As was his second request that the Synod delete a section of their 'Resolutions on the Native Question' which read: 'Neither individuals nor races are born with equal facilities or opportunities.'

The day after the Synod Arthur began his long walk back to Enkeldoorn, taking with him a dramatically altered view of his position in Africa. Although in theory the entire Anglican Church in Southern Rhodesia was missionary in nature, few of the other clergy were leaving for native postings that morning. Few of them even spoke the native language of the country or had tried to learn it, and he realised what he had already begun to suspect – that his view of the Mashona people and of the place of the missionary in Africa was not just at odds with many of the whites he met in Enkeldoorn and Salisbury, but it was also very different to that of the Church in whose name he was serving.

Bishop Gaul had seen him off that morning. Over the last two years the two men had grown closer. Arthur had often accompanied the Bishop on his treks, the Bishop riding a donkey and Arthur trotting alongside, sometimes even reading to him from his book of poems. He had got to know him well, as a man as well as a priest, so he knew that morning that the Bishop recognised his dissatisfaction, his dawning realisation of the divide between his own ideology and that of the Synod. When Arthur had taken him up again on his failed proposals the Bishop had been uncharacteristically apologetic.

'You must understand,' he'd said, stretching up to lay his hand on Arthur's shoulder, 'that many of the Synod don't share your intimate experience with the Africans. Their parishes are European – farmers, businessmen – and in their own way they carry the interests of those people as close to their hearts as you do the interests of your Africans.'

Arthur shook his head in reply, speaking softly, but still unable to disguise the tautness in his voice. 'But I still don't see how the Synod can stand up behind the Company and say that, that all races aren't born equal in God's eyes. That's a mistake, a terrible mistake.'

As he listened to the young missionary, the Bishop remembered something another priest had said about Cripps the previous evening, at the close of the Synod. 'When I hear Father Cripps speak,' he had said, 'I know in my heart he is right, but I still can't agree with any of his conclusions.' As Bishop Gaul looked up at Arthur now, he knew what that priest meant. His intentions were sound but Cripps was too fiery, too quick to condemn. He smiled, and patted Arthur's shoulder,

'The best thing you can do now is carry on your good work in Wreningham.'

Arthur looked down at the Bishop. He looked thinner than when he had last seen him. His skin sagged from his cheekbones and there were crescents of shadow under his eyes. He looked tired, and somewhat distressed. He thought he shouldn't press his case any further.

He took a deep breath and exhaled through a smile, 'Good work? I don't know about that. I suppose I manage to get around a bit but there's still so much I don't get done. And I'm sure most of Enkeldoorn think me quite mad, they certainly look at me as if they do.'

The Bishop began to laugh, but the breath cracked in his throat and rattled into a cough which bent him double, one hand over his mouth the other smacking his solar helmet against his thigh. Arthur went to him, putting his hand on his back. He could feel the ribs there, and the muscles around them contracting with each hacking breath. He made Arthur think of his old cat back home in Kent, its bones tangible under the skin.

The Bishop spat a thick gob of mucus into the dust at his feet and eventually took a deep clean breath. He stood up straight again, his cheeks red with burst capillaries and the veins in his neck standing proud above his dog collar.

'Malaria,' he said, breathing heavily. 'I'm taking enough quinine to poison myself ten times over, but I still can't shake the thing.'

Arthur nodded, although he recognised that cough and he knew it wasn't malarial. He'd seen both natives and whites coughing like that in Enkeldoorn, and it had always meant one thing: TB. He thought of his visit to Keats' room in Rome. How the poet's friend, Severn, had described the sound of Keats' consumptive breath 'boiling' in his lungs.

'Anyway Cripps, that was your fault,' the Bishop continued. 'Making me laugh like that. "Get around a bit" did you say? Never heard anything so ridiculous, man. Last I heard you were covering a hundred miles a week down there.'

'Well, yes, but it's good for me, clears the head, and,' he added, 'it's nothing to what an African might do, you know that, don't you?' He swung the strap of his satchel over his shoulder. 'But it suits me well, suits me very well indeed.'

When they had made their farewells and Arthur had left, Bishop Gaul did not turn and make his way back to the town but stayed where he was and watched the young missionary walk off towards Enkeldoorn, his characteristic long, rangy stride and his satchel bouncing on his back. He followed him until he could no longer make out the shape of his body, until he was just a dark speck on the dust road, and as he watched him he listened to his own thin breath, wheezing and falling in time with the younger man's steps. Only when Arthur had gone, dissolved into the heat haze above the road, did the Bishop turn and walk back into town, wondering as he went whether he would ever see Cripps again.

That walk back to Enkeldoorn was one of Arthur's hardest since his arrival in Southern Rhodesia. But it was not just the Bishop's health and the Synod's short-sightedness that concerned him. The ground he walked over was dry and cracked; a couple of years of late rains had made this a lean year, and he knew it was going to get worse. The spectre of famine was more than a possibility. Already the ground broke like dry plaster about the plough blades, and the early crops had failed. He knew that for many of the natives in his district starvation was a real threat, and he was aware that the mothers worried for their newborns with an anxiety beyond their usual instinctive fear.

Three days later he was sitting on the veranda of Vic's Tavern, sipping a mug of tea in the shade of a wisteria. He had his eyes closed and was enjoying the coolness the plant cast over him after his hot morning walking when a passing Afrikaans farmer told him the news that had come in to town just hours before him. The British South Africa Company had announced its decision to increase the hut tax on native men by fourfold, from ten shillings to two pounds. The farmer passed on, throwing a last remark over his shoulder, 'At least we might get some of those kaffirs working now, isn't it, eh, padre?'

Arthur didn't answer him. He had hoped the Church would provide a stumbling block for the Company on this issue. He couldn't see how it wouldn't. It was its duty to. But it had not, he had been wrong, and he saw that now. Wrong not to press his case with the Bishop harder and wrong to place his trust and the welfare of his African parishioners in the hands of an Anglican Synod, most of whom had never witnessed African living, let alone experienced it.

He responded in the only way he knew how: in writing. He had always written, since he was a schoolboy, and his coming to Africa had not stopped him. As he walked across the veld he composed poetry in his head. At night, he penned novels and short stories in battered school books and worked on his sermons. His only contact with home, with his brother, sisters and mother, was through writing letters. In this way he had lived by the pen for the last three years, always writing, setting down an epistolary and literary version of his life that shadowed his day to day living in Africa. But now he wrote with a different purpose and for the same reason he used to run. He wrote to release the energy inside him, as if his pen was a lance, and with it he would drain his anger and frustration. He wrote to the Chief Native Commissioner, the acting District Commissioner, to the papers in Salisbury and even the papers in England. He had no idea if it would be in the slightest way effective, but he felt he had to do something. He had already failed once, so further failure seemed nothing to worry about.

Along with the letters, which were mostly ignored, he wrote a poem, which was not. Over the weeks following the Synod he worked each night in his hut at Wreningham on a satirical piece which he titled *Ode Celebrating the Proposed Quadrupling of the Hut-Tax*. When he had finished he posted it for publication at his own expense in Salisbury, sending with it a letter informing the publisher to place it on sale as widely as possible, and to make sure it got into the hands of the administration. It was too unsubtle to be a true satire, but he hadn't written it for literary merit. He had written it to be noticed, to make an impact. The closing stanza made his point clear:

> Go glean in the fields of the harvest bare,
> From famine meat a four-fold share!
> Apply a text as best you may –
> From him that hath not, take away!

Arthur knew the poem struck a nerve in the capital a few weeks later when he called in at the post office in Enkeldoorn to receive a wire from Bishop Gaul in Salisbury. It was the stern message of a father to a son who had gone too far, and in deference to the Bishop Arthur withdrew the pamphlet from circulation. He was disappointed that Gaul had not let it live, but he was also satisfied that the poem had served its purpose, however briefly, as a voice of opposition on behalf of the Mashona, who as he now realised, were denied any public voice of their own.

Arthur had anticipated the reaction to his poem in Salisbury. He knew there was no way that such open criticism of the hut tax would be allowed. What he did not anticipate was the reaction from the other side of his life in Mashonaland, from the Mashona themselves. Unknown to him, news of his protest spread quickly through the 'bush telegraph', a network of African messengers passing on important news between the kraals and villages from the vantage points of kopjes and hills. It was the bush telegraph that told African workers in Salisbury about the massacre of British troops at Shangasi in 1893 hours before any official news got through, and after Arthur's protest against the hut tax its effectiveness was proved once more. In the months following the publication of his poem, Arthur's congregations swelled and he was visited by a number of headmen who either wanted to question him on the tax and other aspects of the administration, or who just wanted to see in the flesh the white *mufundsi* who had defied Salisbury.

It was not just the message but also the medium that struck a chord with the Mashona. Poetry was part of their lives: there was a poem for grinding the maize, a poem to speak to your ancestors and praise poems for great chiefs. It had been particularly painful that after the failed 1896 uprising the whites had celebrated the fall of their spirit mediums in song. The settler paper, *The Nugget*, had printed it in triumph, a long piece of doggerel ending on a threatening note of intention:

> As others have learned long ago,
> So the young generation must learn to know
> That the White Queen means to reign.

But now Arthur had spoken out against the White Queen and although his voice may have been silenced in Salisbury, it continued to resonate in the kraals of the Mashona, who in turn resonated their new-found respect for Arthur in the names chosen for him in the months following his protest. Father Cripps became *Baba Cripps*,

Baba Cripps became *Chapea,* He-Who-Cares-for-People, and then *Chapea* became *Kambandakoto*: He-Who-Goes-About-as-a-Poor-Man.

Arthur was nearing the end of his morning's journey. As he came over a lip in the track the buildings of Enkeldoorn appeared before him, a mile or so off and about a hundred feet lower than where he stood. He rested against a young tree, shifting his satchel strap away from a raw patch of skin on his shoulder, and looked down on the town. Its scattering of tin roofs reflected the sun in a white glare so the settlement shone in the shallow valley like a trace of diamond in base rock. On the near side of the town he could see people scattered out across a flat area of land cleared of the tall veld grass. They were making the final preparations for the annual New Year games. Ladies' white parasols and wide-brimmed hats stood out against the dun red of the earth, clustered together like the petals of oversized flowers where they stood in groups, chatting. In contrast to the stillness of these white islands their husbands and sons ran between them, pulling lengths of rope, guiding ox wagons into position and testing the ground with the heels of their boots. A temporary flag pole had been erected and the Charter flag, a Union Jack with a lion proud at its centre, beat and fluttered over the scene.

Adjusting his satchel again, Arthur set off towards the cleared field. He didn't want to be late, he had a service to conduct later that day and he wanted time to prepare after he'd competed in the games. He knew, though, that in Enkeldoorn he may as well concentrate on the sports, as it was there on the games field he was most likely to win the respect of his white parishioners, rather than later from the pulpit.

<><>

Charlie Anderson shielded his eyes with his hand and squinted at the figure making its way down the kopje path towards the field.

'Looks like the Devil Dodger's decided to join us,' he said, partly to himself but loud enough for the man crouching beside him tying a rag to the tug-of-war rope to hear.

'What's that?'

'The Devil Dodger, the peripatetic parson, that's him, isn't it?'

The other man stood up and looked where Charlie Anderson pointed. He was taller than Charlie and wore the bush uniform of a

District Commissioner, khaki short-sleeved bush shirt, long shorts to above the knee, white woollen socks pulled up to just below, and for the occasion of the games, an Oxford Blues tie and a khaki Wolseley helmet.

'Mmm, yes, that's him. Good, I was hoping he'd come. He's pretty fit, you know.'

'So he bloody should be,' Charlie said, turning away from the sun towards the taller man. 'All that fucking walking. I don't know why he doesn't get a bloody horse.'

'He did.' The taller man's voice was softer than Charlie's, less of Africa in his throat. 'But he never rode it. I saw him outside town once, leading the thing like a pet. It died. Tsetse fly I think.'

A couple of native boys carrying a trestle table caught Charlie's eye over the taller man's shoulder. 'Self-righteous bastard,' he mumbled, before yelling at the two boys, waving his arms in front of him. 'Ho! Daniel, not there you bloody fool! Over there, behind the tent, right back!' He paused, then said, 'Sorry Cul, better go and do it myself.' He walked off towards the two boys, shouting at them again, this time in stilted kitchen kaffir. '*Tsauka kuruboshwe! Shure! Shure* the bloody tent!'

The tall man watched Charlie's stocky, bow-legged frame stride off towards the tents at the side of the games field, then turned back to follow Arthur's progress down the kopje. A fly buzzed his ear. He made a half-hearted swipe at it and was surprised when he felt the tick of its body against his fingers. Looking down he saw where it had fallen: a dark currant, vibrating in the dust, one wing useless, the other flicking madly at its side. He lifted his right foot and brought the heel of his boot down on the fly's panicked dance, twisting it into the ground like the stub of a cigarette.

The tall man's name was Cullen Gouldsbury, and he was Assistant District Commissioner for the Enkeldoorn Charter area. Cullen had been serving in Southern Rhodesia for all of his first three-year tour and although still officially an assistant he'd taken on the duties of a full blown DC. Despite his age (he was only twenty-two) it was a promotion he had taken in his stride. He had an affable, easy manner, with enough of a public school education to get on with the officials and enough of a country childhood to get on with the farmers. His habit of flicking his blond fringe away from his eyes by blowing up into his hair made the kaffir children laugh, and he was popular with their parents too.

Cullen enjoyed his work. One day he might be overseeing native court cases and handing out licenses to farmers, another collecting taxes and holding an open surgery for the problems of the natives. Those surgery days could be some of the hardest, when fifty or sixty African men appeared out of the bush before dawn. A crowd of young and old, some in torn European clothes, most in the traditional scraps of limbo or skins, crouching silently on the ground before his veranda waiting for him to arrive. When he did, accepting them into this cramped office one at a time, their petitions often seemed endless. And sometimes seeing them there in the town was not enough. During his time in Enkeldoorn he had often been called out to preside over disputes in the local Mashona villages too, sitting as judge on cases as diverse as arguments over land and chieftainship to accusations of adultery or abuse. The extent of his influence often bewildered him, and it sometimes made him feel uneasy when the headmen called him *Shumba*, the Shona for 'Lion', or when he looked at the simple figures of his situation. Just him, aged twenty-two, a police chief and half a dozen native policemen governing over more than a hundred thousand natives and several hundred whites.

But Cullen had aspirations beyond his Colonial Office work. Since arriving in Africa he had written about his experiences on the continent in novels, short stories and poems, and his tales of pioneer characters and settler adventures had been as well received in London as they had in Fort Salisbury. He was hoping to build upon this fledgling reputation, and that is why he was watching Father Cripps today. That is why he observed the priest's every movement as he approached the games field, as he paused by the stone boundary and fanned himself with his old panama. Because the priest, he was sure now, would be the subject of his next book.

Cullen had recently finished his latest novel and had been looking for a subject for his next. It had struck him, as he sifted through the people he knew and his three years of memories in Rhodesia, that the missionary might well provide him with one. There was something about the man that fascinated him: the excessive nature of his pastoral care, his outspokenness, his empathy with the natives and his strange mix of contradictions. And there was something else too: a fissure in him, a fracture that worked upon itself, creating a friction that only ever reached his surface as an intonation, a tremor. Cullen could only surmise what this disturbance in the missionary may be, but he hoped that today he might get closer to finding out, that he might be able to talk with Cripps and get nearer to what lay beyond the priesthood that he wore so faithfully, like a blessing and a curse.

The 1904 New Year games had been organised by Charlie Anderson, a local farmer known more commonly in the area as 'Champagne Charlie', a moniker he'd earned as a miner in Kimberley ten years before. For a few days back then Charlie had been the embodiment of the dream that kept so many young men travelling south, and which kept them there, year on year, in the face of endless disappointment. Because Charlie had struck diamonds, and not just a couple of stones, but a rich seam, packed as tightly in his claim as bees in a hive. Rather than mine them himself he'd sold his rights to the Company and earned his nickname the same night he signed his deal. Taking his cash to the Belgrave, Kimberley's finest hotel, he'd treated as many men as he could fit in the bar and the billiards room to free drinks. Then he bought out the hotel's stock of champagne and booked himself into its most expensive suite, where he filled the bath to the brim with the drink, emptying the bottles, frothing and spluttering, two at a time into the white enamel tub. In the bar below the corks sounded from above like gunfire for half an hour and with each pop the men cheered, drunk not just on Charlie's generosity but also on the idea of his success, which in a way was theirs too, keeping at bay as it did their own doubts and fears, even if just for one night.

Charlie shared his champagne bath with a couple of whores from the brothel across the road who waited until he had passed out before robbing him blind. They left town that night, leaving Charlie still in the bath, a smouldering cigar perched on his lower lip, wagging in time to his snores.

The owner of the Belgrave found Charlie the next morning standing naked in the back yard behind the kitchen blowing apart the chef's chickens with a Rigby shotgun. Two dogs crouched and whined in the corner, the terrified hens flapped and squawked about the dusty patch of ground, and Charlie stood in the middle of it all, a belt of cartridges across his shoulder and his feet caked in a dough of earth and champagne. Downy white feathers were stuck all over his body, as if he had been caught in an innocent pillow fight and not with a smoking rifle in his hands.

That morning marked the end of Charlie's brief celebration and the start of a slide that took him gradually further and further north up the railway and eventually into Southern Rhodesia. Enkeldoorn was where he came to rest, blown in like so many others on the winds of their past lives. He bought a couple of hundred acres of land and a small herd of cattle, mostly jumped from native villages, and resigned himself to the life of a small-time farmer. But he never regretted that night and he still dreamt of it often. The proud moment of a man who had lived. The taste of women and champagne, flesh and drink, the stars of Africa through an open window and the thrill of success. He wouldn't change it now even if he could. That feeling of optimism, of possibility, had been too sweet to ever regret. At least he had felt it once, that's what he told himself, and it was this thought that kept him going, through the monotonous days of farming, drinking and remembering.

Today was a different kind of day, though. Today he was in charge, and the games were his to organise. Overseen by Charlie a team of native boys had cleared an area the size of four football pitches out of the bush grass that grew around the town. It was marked out at its four corners by a couple of opposing thorn trees and a couple of stakes, driven into the ground. A boundary of stones had been laid to further mark out his new territory. Along the town side two large canvas tents had been erected, for food, lime juice and ginger beer. Cullen wanted to keep this a dry games this year, and he'd made that clear to Charlie. One whole half of the square was roped off for the horse races and the longer running races, while the shorter sprints would take place right in front of the tents, where everyone could get a good view. Some Scotch carts had been brought in for people to stand and sit on, but many of the ladies had brought their own folding camp chairs, and some families had even brought their wicker veranda furniture.

Charlie looked around him from where he stood beside the food tent. It was filling up, a good crowd. Most of the townspeople were here. The doctor and his family, Pastor Liebenberg, Vic from the hotel, the Nashes and the Tullys, Majumder who owned the biggest supply shop in Enkeldoorn, and the usual crowd of British administrators, Company men, Dutch farmers and a few Portuguese traders. There was even a reporter from *The Nugget* down from Salisbury. A scattering of natives sat on the slope on the other side of the games field, drinking kaffir beer from clay pots. Charlie eyed them suspiciously. He made no secret of disliking the natives, especially this kind, who hung around the town in their ragged uniform of cast-off European clothes. He'd drafted in a couple of native policemen to keep an eye on them, but he'd be watching them himself too.

He checked his watch: ten o'clock, time for the games to begin. Picking up a milk churn resting against the tent he strode out into the centre of the field, carrying it in his arms like a groom taking his bride on to the dance floor. He placed the churn on the ground, and sliding a hammer from his trouser pocket began beating its sides with a rhythmical swing of his arm. The hollow clangs resounded across the cleared ground like the peals of a church bell calling the people to service, and it was with satisfaction that Charlie watched the entrance of the drinks tent switch from dark to pale as the crowd there turned to face him.

From the shade of the drinks tent Cullen Gouldsbury watched Arthur enter the first race of the day, the hundred-yard sprint. The games had started with some fun sports for the children – sack racing, an obstacle course and a mini gymkhana – but this was the first adult race. The priest had taken off his jacket and Cullen watched him walk out towards the starting line (a thin pouring of flour between two cricket stumps) with the other shirt-sleeved men. The entrants made a good cross-section of the settler types he had worked with over the last three years: stocky, tanned farmers in riding breeches, a Portuguese trader, a couple of store keepers and some administration officials. There were no Africans, although Cullen noticed that Arthur, like a few of the others, had chosen to run 'native style', taking off his boots and socks.

The police chief, McGregor, took the role of official starter. He was a barrel-chested man with the air of a sergeant major and an impressive moustache that obscured much of his mouth beneath his white Wolseley helmet. His call of 'Marks!' reached Cullen and the crowd around the drinks tent and the chattering hushed as he raised his arm and they waited for the report of his pistol. The men crouched into their starting positions. Cullen could make out a thin cloud of flies hanging above them, like starlings come to roost. The silence seemed on the point of breaking when McGregor eventually fired, the crack of his pistol resounding across the flat earth and a puff of white smoke emerging at the tip of his raised arm.

The noise of the pistol startles Arthur, and it is only when the other men around him surge forward that he starts running, pumping his arms in an effort to drag his weight up to sprinting speed. But it's a bad start, and already the Portuguese trader on his left is ahead of him, and one of the farmers, Jones, is hard up on his right. All around him there is the sound of breath and the flapping of flannel trousers and loose shirts. The ground is rougher than he thought and as he lands again and again on the stones and pebbles he realises it was a mistake to have gone without his boots. He can see the thin tape of the finishing line now, but the trader is well ahead, as is another man on the far right, although he seems to have lost the farmer. He is still sprinting hard when the trader breasts the tape ahead of him, his arms high, its ribbon giving about his chest then escaping the grip of its holders to curl about him in a brief, fluttering victor's embrace. It is already falling to the ground and coiling into the dust when Arthur crosses it, a disappointing fourth.

He stops, feeling the sun-heated dust burning the soles of his feet, and bends over, supporting his hands on his knees, a wave of sweat washing over his skin. The other men congratulate and commiserate around him. Over by the tents the trader's companion is whooping and waving his hat, shouting to his friend 'Ganhaste! Primerio Lugar!' A couple of hands rest on his heaving back for a second, accompanied by voices. 'Well run, Father', 'Good race, Padre.' No one calls him by his name.

Cullen had been waiting all morning for the right time to approach Father Cripps, trying to keep an eye on him between the tide of conversations and duties that events like these always brought his way. So far, however, he'd been unsuccessful and now he had been waylaid again, this time by Mrs Chesterton and her niece, Miss Haverly. Miss Haverly was fresh from England, come to Rhodesia to 'keep house' for her aunt, a common euphemism for looking for a husband. It was well known that in Africa the men outnumbered the women ten to one. Cullen knew he was one of a handful of eligible bachelors that Mrs Chesterton had in her sights, but although Miss Haverly was perfectly agreeable he didn't intend on getting within striking distance. As an aversion tactic he did his best to exaggerate the misfortunes of his way of life, giving the ladies a particularly grim sketch of Colonial Office living. He finished with a tale about another DC who had tried to end the despairing loneliness of his isolated position by cutting his own throat with his razor. He'd survived, but only because his African boy had found him and coaxed his master back to health. He'd returned to England now, Cullen told them, taking a whisper of a voice and a neat choker of scar tissue as mementos of his stint in the bush. He left the two women wide-eyed under their parasols, Mrs Chesterton giving the worried-looking Miss Haverly a squeeze of the arm with her white-gloved hand.

In an attempt to avoid any more run-ins with the overly sociable Enkeldoorn crowd, Cullen made his way around the back of the drinks tent to its far end, where, resting his shoulder against the tent's corner pole, he could get a clear view of the sports field. From this position he watched the riders preparing for the puissance while also hoping to catch a glimpse of Cripps, with whom he still wanted to talk.

A small group of men sat talking behind the food tent next door, and as he watched the games Cullen also listened in on their conversations and stories. They were sitting in a semi-circle, perched on upturned crates, stools and old kegs. At the moment only one of them was talking, an older man with a clear bald head beaded with droplets of sweat. Although the others listened intently Cullen had no idea what the man was saying. His voice was no more than grunts and moans, but this was of little surprise, given the state of his face.

The speaker's name was Bill Usher, an Enkeldoorn old-timer who'd been prospecting in the area when the 1896 uprising blew out of the bush like a sudden summer storm. In those days Bill was known for two things and neither of them was his skill as a miner. The first was his storytelling, which was the most engaging anyone knew in Southern Rhodesia, and the second was his wig, a thick head of real hair he'd had made for himself in Dar es Salaam. No one had ever seen him without the hairpiece and as far as they knew it was a permanent feature.

On a hot afternoon back in 1894 Bill was setting charges at the bottom of a thirty-foot shaft when he broke with the habit of a lifetime and removed his wig. The heat had made his head sweat, sending rivulets of perspiration down his forehead into his eyes, blurring his vision. He placed it in his shirt pocket, then got back to lighting the fuses before shouting to the native boys at the top of the shaft to wind him up on the windlass. Like everyone else, the boys had never seen Bill without his wig, and didn't even know what a wig was. No

Mashona had ever felt the need to cover their baldness with another man's hair. The boys were winding furiously, kicking up clouds of dust with their feet as they gripped for purchase in the soil when they saw Bill's bald head emerging from the mine. All Bill heard was a cry of '*Umtagati!*' (The Devil!) before the tension of the rope went slack, then gave altogether with a wild lurch that sent him rushing to the bottom of the shaft. The boys had fled, letting the windlass go, its twin handles flaying like a maniac's arms as they spun backwards, sending Bill down the shaft with a rush of air punctuated by a deadening thud as the basket hit the mine's floor.

When Bill came to the first thing he saw was the charges, sparking and spitting like wet candle-wicks in front of his face. Realising he only had seconds before they exploded, he frantically began pulling them from their plugs and biting at the fuses. He had the last charge almost to his teeth when it went off, blasting away the fingers of his right hand and part of his lower jaw, leaving a mess of flesh, tongue and shattered mandible hanging from his face.

Ten years later Cullen watched Bill sitting on the crate, talking with the other men. His right hand was hidden inside his jacket and a decade of healing had moulded the disaster area of his chin and mouth into a marble cast of scar tissue and bone. Most of the front of his chin had gone and skin had grown into the gap left by the explosion like ivy occupying the derelict remains of a house. His tongue had not survived, but his upper lip and jaw had, giving him a bizarre overbite above the diminished lower part of his face. He was lucky to be alive, though, and had the charges he'd bought off a scamming trader in Enkeldoorn been authentic and not mostly packed with sand he would almost certainly have been killed and wouldn't be sitting here now, telling tales and mopping his bald head with his handkerchief.

Bill never wore his wig again, but the accident didn't stop him telling stories. And people still sat and listened to them. Only his oldest friends had any idea of what he might have been saying, but that didn't seem to matter. The words went on in his head and his listeners heard the shape of them: the pace, the hand movements, the rise and fall in pitch, the tone of his eyes, the frowns, the nuances and the grim, deformed smile. It was a strange predicament, Cullen thought, watching Bill talk: a storyteller with no speech to tell his stories. If he was literate he would write, he supposed. But he couldn't, so he was left with this language of sound and movement instead. This resonance of language. But watching him now he understood why you might want to sit and listen to Bill for a while. Maybe the old man had struck something after all: if not gold, then at least the idea that maybe this is enough, this storytelling without words. As if the words had just been obstacles after all.

While Cullen watched the group watching Bill he also kept an eye on events on the games field, still hoping to catch a chance to talk to Father Cripps. Scanning the crowds he finally saw him, on the slope over on the far side. He was sitting with the Africans there and Cullen could see even from this distance how his body language changed when he spoke with them in Shona. His movements were more fluid and he tilted his head to one side when he listened, just as Cullen had seen the headmen do when they came and crouched outside his office. Some of the Africans wore scraps of material tied about their arms, blood red against the brown and greys of their torn and dirty shirts. These armbands were Cripps' doing, a mark of temperance he encouraged the men to wear as a sign of their sobriety. It was, Cullen thought, a gesture typical of Cripps: forthright, simple, direct and just a little ridiculous in its naivety.

A peal of deep laughter punctuated the end of a story behind him, perhaps one of Bill's, with all its words unsaid. The men got up from their makeshift seats and dispersed past Cullen, making their way into the food tent. As Bill passed he acknowledged him with a curt nod of his head and what Cullen thought was probably meant to be a smile. Cullen watched him walk away, massaging the white bud of his crippled right hand with the fingers of his left.

The beat of hooves made Cullen turn back to the field in time to see a rider canter his horse past the drinks tent, warming up for the puissance, the first equestrian event of the day. He felt a rush of tepid air as the animal passed, scents of hot horseflesh, disturbed dust and oiled saddlery blowing over him. Cullen was a keen rider himself and would usually have been entering this competition, but his own mare had thrown a shoe out in the veld last week and the ride back home had left her lame on the near fore. He didn't want to damage her any further so he would have to settle for being an observer this year. It was a shame, he thought, she was certainly as good as any of the horses cantering about the field now, and he suspected they'd have stood a good chance of being placed, if not winning the event.

His mare was called Daisy and over the last nine months Cullen had grown very fond of her; the idea of leaving her here when he returned to England saddened him every time he thought of it. The first time he'd ridden her in April last year was also the first time he had met Father Cripps. He was buying the horse from a local farmer and he wanted to test her on a long veld ride before parting with the eight pounds the farmer was asking for her. The communication he'd received from Salisbury requesting him to go and visit Cripps seemed like a good opportunity to try her out, especially as the round trip of twenty miles went across some good flat country over which he hoped he could test her speed. The mare, however, had only ever had the farmer as her rider and Cullen found the journey out to Wreningham somewhat unsettling, bouncing around in the unfamiliar saddle as the horse jittered and pranced beneath him, resisting the strange weight and balance on her back. On his arrival at Wreningham he soon found his visit to Cripps was to be no smoother a ride.

The request from Salisbury had come down from the Chief Native Commissioner's office in response to a letter from Cripps protesting about the recent increases in the hut tax. Apparently the priest had published a poem on the matter too, and for some reason it was this that had particularly annoyed the Governor. Cullen was to pay Cripps a visit and smooth things over with the missionary, set the record straight and explain to him why his protest was misguided. The tax, he would inform Cripps, was a crucial part of European governance in Southern Rhodesia.

Cullen was not a religious man. Although raised as a Catholic, in his early twenties he'd made a conscious decision to steer clear of the church. Reason, he had argued, was what separated men from beasts, and it was to the doctrine of reason, if any religion, that he considered himself a disciple. His experiences with the missionary system in Africa had further strengthened this view. He disliked the pious attitude with which so many missionaries he'd met treated the natives. The arrogance of their evangelism annoyed him. The church, he had discovered, obtained the best land, the best farms, supported itself with church fees of one pound per head per annum, and yet its involvement in the country was frequently more disruptive than helpful. He was in Rhodesia himself to develop the country economically and socially and he couldn't see the point in adding to this considerable burden by meddling with the natives' souls as well.

So it was with some degree of confidence that Cullen approached the twin gum trees of Wreningham on his new jumpy chestnut mare. Armed with his reason and unburdened by any sense of reverence, he was sure he'd have little trouble defending the administration's actions to Father Cripps.

From his position resting against the tent pole Cullen watches the first competitor approach the puissance fence in the centre of the field riding a thoroughbred bay mare, her hooves beating out a rhythm on the hard ground. A few strides out he checks her with a couple of twitches on the reins, bringing her hocks under her, the muscles in her rump bunching up with restraint. Three strides out she lifts her head, the slab of her neck muscle contracting. The rider holds her there for one more stride, then gives with his hands, opening the door to her jump. With a kick of dirt and dust she bascules over the single pole and lands with a snort of her nostrils. A ripple of applause runs through the tents on either side of Cullen like a handful of stones thrown into mud.

Cullen had discovered Cripps outside the long pole-and-dagga shack that served as the mission's schoolhouse. He was sitting on a wooden Shona stool reading from a Bible to a scattering of young children who sat cross-legged at his feet, fidgeting in the dust. While he waited for Cripps to finish his lesson he tied up his horse and looked around the compound. Unlike other missions he'd visited there was little to mark it out as a European settlement. Women passed between the rondavels and the raised kitchen hut carrying pots and baskets just as they did in the native kraals. Open fires smoked into the still air and a group of older men sat at a *dare* of stones at the far end. The only concession to the mission status of the place was the European clothing the women wore. Bright skirts replaced the usual skins and limbo wrapped around their waists, and homemade shirts covered their usually naked breasts and the filigree of dark tattoos about their waists.

Finished with his reading, Cripps welcomed Cullen, if somewhat formally, to the mission, offering him tea outside his quarters, another pole-and-dagga hut with a crude sheet of corrugated iron for a door. As they sat on a couple of upturned crates a young woman knelt before them and held out a bowl of water for them to wash their hands. Another woman brought the tea, together with a plate of dry biscuits. Cripps spoke to both of them politely and softly and always in Shona. A herd of goats were grazing below the mission and the percussion of their bells lent the morning a delicate quality. Cullen suddenly felt incredibly calm after his jittery ride and he noticed that even his mare was now grazing contentedly where he had tethered her at the edge of the compound.

The two men made polite conversation but Cullen could tell that Cripps was curious as to why he had come to visit him unannounced. So, blowing his fringe out of his eyes he eased himself into the topic of the hut tax, following a line of argument he had rehearsed on the long ride over from Enkeldoorn. Hoping to appeal to Cripps' academic past he presented his case as a form of thesis, explaining his historical perspective on the current situation. Did he, he asked the priest, know what the name Mashona implied? Cripps said he thought he did but Cullen went on. It meant blanket-draggers, dogs, a nomadic people whose women and stock had been threatened for centuries by the warrior-like Matabele impis. This, he explained to Cripps, was the kind of life the settler administration had saved the Shona from, giving them roads, medical supplies, courts, schools and above all, protection. All this had to be paid for and the hut tax was the most efficient way of doing so.

Cullen was doing his best to make this point in his most affable manner. He had, in his time, charmed farmers, police chiefs and natives with his ability to be liked and he saw no reason why he shouldn't prove as successful with Cripps.

Cripps listened, but he had an answer for every point Cullen made. He understood his position (if not his perspective on Shona history) but didn't he think, he asked, that his argument suffered from an asymmetry of indulgence on behalf of the philanthropic nature of European settlement? Hadn't there been as much taking as giving? And anyway, he pointed out, the roads only go to where Europeans want to go, and the courts judge crimes and impose sentences that didn't exist before the settlers arrived. Cullen would have to forgive him if he still considered the hut tax too high a price to pay for the disruption already caused to the Africans by the settler influence.

Cullen was wrong-footed. He hadn't expected such an eloquent, heart-felt response. He remembered looking hard at Cripps as he considered how to reply, trying to work out what type of a man he was, trying to find a foothold in his character that would help win him over. He also remembered thinking how old Cripps looked, old beyond his years. The Native Commissioner had said he was thirty-three, not much older than himself, and yet his tanned face already seemed too thin for the bones that supported it. His manner was athletic but reserved and his skin was lined with deep creases around his eyes from squinting over the glare of the midday veld. But the eyes themselves were not of an age with this face. His eyes, which stared unblinking at Cullen as he waited for his response, were young. Bright blue, penetrating and more than a little unsettling.

Cullen cleared his throat and tried another approach. Weren't the church fees that the natives paid to the missions just like the hut tax? A necessary income to keep the work of the church going in Africa? Yes, Cripps agreed, and Cullen remembered thinking here was his turning point, here was the matter on which he would win ground. But Cripps went on, quietly assuring him that he had never charged such fees at any of his churches or mission stations, nor at his mission schools. He was in fact at that moment engaged in discussions with the Synod on this very point.

Another horse approaches the puissance fence, which now stands at over five feet. A chestnut Arab, much like Daisy, the martingale and reins working up a lather of sweat flecking across her shoulders and neck. Cullen watches her jump, her darkened muscles straining to clear the pole. It looks as though she's over when she hits the pole with a trailing hoof, sending it rattling from its cups and falling to the ground with a solid thud and a long cloudburst of dust. The crowd let out a collective gasp, then applaud anyway.

As Cullen and Father Cripps continued their discussion outside Cripps' ramshackle hut that day back in April, Cullen became increasingly confused and frustrated by the missionary. Cripps possessed a remarkably harsh view of the BSA Company's administration which seemed unshakable. When the priest quoted Shelley to him (*'What more felicity can fall to creature/ Than to enjoy delight with liberty?'*) Cullen had quoted from the 'Dual Mandate' in reply, arguing that in following this mandate (to help existing forms of government develop and evolve), he was bringing law to the country. Law, he had said, feeling his composure slip, which is designed to bring liberty to all. Cripps dismissed this assertion, as he did so many of Cullen's points that day, with a wave of his hand, insisting the Dual Mandate was thwarted by the Company's self-interest. Cullen shook his head first in disbelief, then in mild amusement. It was clear that whatever he said he would not change Cripps' view of the hut tax as anything other than a form of forced labour. By now, however, he didn't even have to talk to evoke Cripps' opinion, and Cullen sat by, listening to the goat bells and winking at the pot-bellied young children standing at a distance viewing him cautiously as Cripps expounded his theories on everything from race relations to agricultural techniques.

As Cullen sat and listened to Cripps speak the contradictions that the priest revealed in himself both fascinated and irritated him. From what he could tell, like most missionaries Cripps was strongly opposed to many of the traditional practices of Shona witchcraft. He had no time for the superstitious fear of curses and he didn't allow polygamists to live on mission land. And yet in the same breath he appeared greatly in awe of the Shona capability for faith, of their highly developed spiritual intelligence. Cullen found himself being given an impromptu lesson in the Shona system of belief, which, as Cripps said, was much more than mere animism. He was, Cullen remembered, especially taken with the Shona's relationship with their dead ancestors, the sprits of dead grandfathers, grandmothers, uncles, mothers and brothers that governed over the fates of the living. As he got more excited it seemed to Cullen that Cripps was even making parallels between the Shona belief system and his own. He referred to the practice of *chisi*, the Shona day of rest, and each tribe's *Mhondoro* as an example of worshipping one deity. One comment in particular, though, had stayed with Cullen, and had perhaps given him his first insight into what drove Cripps' character. Taking a sip of his tea (which Cullen was sure must have gone cold while he was speaking) Cripps had said in his quiet manner, but firmly, as if it was his final statement on the subject: 'You know, there are many Shona out here who are better Christians without knowing it than some of the settlers who call themselves such. They may not go to church like the Europeans, but believe me, spiritually and in their practices, they are the more mature Christians.'

Cullen was aware that despite his views he was warming to Cripps. There was something refreshing about the passion with which he argued his case and there was no doubt that his love for the African was real. He spoke about the Shona as other men might speak about their brother or cousin. As if they were adults, not children. Cullen had never heard that before, in Rhodesia or England.

What Cullen could not ignore, however, was what he considered the most crucial contradiction at the centre of Cripps' situation. The missionary's vision of the African world seemed Arcadian in nature (indeed, he had admitted as much when he confessed to Cullen that the Shona lifestyle reminded him of Theocritus' *Idylls*), and threatening this vision was the white settlers' corrupting influence. All of his ideas, his arguments, pointed towards this desire to defend the African way of life from the European. And yet, here he was, a missionary, bringing an alien faith to the Shona, performing a role that in its very nature was evangelical, exerting influence and change. However much he lived as an African, Cullen felt that Cripps could not escape the facts of his situation. But he didn't press the point. It was getting late, Daisy was restless and he needed to return to his office. He also wanted to leave Wreningham on a good note, so, engaging his ability to please again, he took the opportunity of a lull in the conversation to ask Cripps about his writing instead.

Literature was a subject on which the two men shared more common ground, and Cullen ended staying later than he had meant, discussing poetry, his own writing and some short stories that Cripps was working on. The missionary seemed especially pleased that Cullen had been writing about his African experience. 'That's excellent,' he'd said. 'Places like this need to be written about. Until they are, some people don't seem to think they exist.' Cullen thought he knew what Cripps meant and he agreed, remembering how Rider Haggard's *She* had lit his own interest in Africa all those years before.

By the time Cullen had mounted Daisy and Cripps had accompanied them down to the bottom of the hill the sun was already low in the sky, the clouds blood red on their undersides. After wishing him well and promising to come out again Cullen bent from his horse and shook Cripps' hand before beginning his ride back to Enkeldoorn; but he found himself thinking about Cripps long after Wreningham had disappeared behind him, and particularly about the priest's parting comment.

He couldn't tell if Cripps had been joking or not. He thought probably not; he had been smiling, no doubt thinking about their earlier discussion, but there had been a serious note in his voice as well. They were making their way down the kopje, Daisy picking her way between the granite rocks and Cripps sucking on his clay pipe, when suddenly he'd said, 'People talk about the need for medical missionaries in South Africa but in a country like this, you know what the Africans really need?' Cullen waited for Cripps to continue. 'Legal missionaries, that's what we need here. Not Christian, not medical, but legal. That'd put the cat among the pigeons, wouldn't it?'

Cullen had no choice but to laugh and agree. It really was late now and he had to get Daisy back to her owner. So he'd left without contesting Cripps' point, but in many ways, as he rode back to town, he wished he had. Then perhaps he would have resolved what Cripps was getting at, and maybe resolved the comment in his own mind too instead of pondering on it all the way home. At least Daisy had been calmer on that return journey. Her trip into the veld seemed to have tempered her and it was on that day, when Cullen finally saw the first lights of Enkeldoorn in the distance, that he'd resolved to buy her. Damn the eight pounds he couldn't afford; she seemed settled with him, and he with her. It would be a shame to say goodbye to each other now.

A well-built grey gelding ridden hard by a farmer canters towards the puissance fence, tossing and throwing its head. Cullen watches as it straightens its forelegs a couple of strides out, scuffing up the ground with its hooves, bringing its hind legs sliding under its belly. The farmer lurches out of his seat, losing a stirrup which flips over the saddle behind him. The crowd lets out another gasp, more urgent this time, as the farmer clings on around the horse's neck and the gelding hits the wing of the fence before spooking and galloping off across the field, the farmer clasped to its side like a child to its mother.

Cullen shifted himself away from the tent pole and stretched his arms above his head. The day was getting hot and he could do with a drink, but thinking of that day with Cripps had made him even more anxious to talk to the priest today. Since April they'd become much better friends than could have been expected after that first discussion, but he still didn't know him well enough to ask him the questions he had really wanted to on that first meeting. Did he get lonely out there on his own? How did he defend his position as a missionary? What did he think about on those week-long treks of his across the veld? No, he hadn't asked those questions, but today, if he could catch him, then maybe he would. After all, if he was going to write about Cripps he had to know what made the man tick. What he knew at the moment, the facts, how he acted, what he thought, wasn't going to be enough.

Another horse approaches the puissance fence, a bay thoroughbred ridden by an army officer. Again Cullen watches as the animal gathers its energy a couple of strides before the pole, now standing at over six foot, then launches itself into the air. With a twist of its hind legs it clears the fence, landing heavily on the other side in a cloud of earth and dust. Distracted by his thinking about Cripps, Cullen has only been half watching the event, but the loud cheering and applause from the crowds indicates this horse has won. The officer swings the thoroughbred around and canters up to the front of the tents where he brings her to some kind of a halt, the mare's veins standing proud beneath her sweat-darkened coat. Her blood is still pumping hard and she jogs and fidgets under him as Charlie pins the blue first place rosette to her bridle.

After the puissance Cullen watches Cripps compete again, this time in the one-mile walk, lining up with a string of other men, distorted by the midday haze as if they were reflected in a fairground mirror. On the crack of the starter's gun the line breaks and the men begin striding the three laps of the horse track. A mounted judge trots beside them, moving up and down the line, keeping watch on their stride lengths. Cripps seems in his element and is far out in front when another man suddenly gains on him in the final straight to pip him at the post. It is clear to Cullen that this man had broken into a jog to catch up with Cripps, and sure enough he watches as the mounted judge trots up to Cripps, leans down to speak to him, then canters up to the tents where he brings his sweating horse to a halt and announces Father Cripps as the winner. Cripps walks up to the tents, obviously pleased, to receive his trophy from Charlie. Charlie shakes the priest's hand vigorously and leads the crowd in a round of applause. As the clapping dies down Cullen thinks this is probably a good time to corner Cripps for a chat, but as he begins to walk over towards him he is stalled by Charlie's voice booming across the field, followed by more clanging on the milk churn.

'Last call for entries for the high jump!'

The high jump is the only event Cullen is entering today. He stops by the drinks tent, where he sees Cripps sitting with a glass of lime juice in his hand. The priest acknowledges him with a wave of the hand and Cullen is about to approach him when Charlie's voice cuts through the chatter again,

'High jump, Cul! Where the bloody hell are you?'

Managing just a brief smile to Cripps, Cullen turns out towards the field and jogs over to where Charlie is standing with a group of other men, shouting ahead of him as he runs towards them,

'All right Charlie! Calm down, I'm here.'

Cullen won the high jump, as he had expected to, and it was as he was receiving his own trophy from Charlie, its metal smelling of new polish and two thin blue ribbons tied to its handles, that the screams started.

First a woman's, a primitive scream of fear, and then others, men and women, two, three, a fourth, joining in like a macabre chorus. The crowd around the tents stands frozen, a painting of the day, looking above each other's heads as they listen for the next sound to reach them from the town. But it is another voice they hear, a man's, an African's, shouting and getting louder as he gets nearer. The first time he shouts, no one can make out what he is saying, but then the words find themselves on the air and they hear him crying out, over and over, '*Shumba! Shumba!*'

The word ignites the crowd like a flame to touch paper. The men begin herding the women and children into the two tents, fathers picking up sons and daughters under each arm. Others drop their drinks and their food in the dust and sprint to meet the man running from the town. A large Boer farmer shouts at his boy, his booming Afrikaans voice laying itself down over the panicked chatter like a slab of granite over ants, 'My gun! Get my bloody gun! *Kurmidza! Kurumidza!* Quick now!' The boy runs off, his pale soles flicking up behind him, puffs of dust touching off the ground with each sprinting step. The army officer is struggling with his horse, hanging off its bridle with both hands as it wheels around showing the whites of its eyes, panicked by the rush of people into the tents and the men into the town.

Arthur reaches the edge of the town shortly after Cullen, who he follows down the side of a house and through a gap between two stores where a group of men are already standing on one of the stoeps. They are all staring at the far end of the high street. Arthur joins them and follows the line of their pointing fingers.

At the other end of the town, no more than 300 yards away, a lioness is padding down the empty high street, golden against the dun road, her head slung low between her powerful shoulders. She is thin and Arthur can see her angular hip-joints protruding, working mechanically under her skin as she prowls down the street and circles to face the post office. She stops and Arthur feels the group of men hold their breaths. McGregor, the police chief, whispers 'Stay calm everyone, Charlie's bringing a gun now, just stay still.' As he speaks the lioness turns her head to face them. Her movement is fluid, slow, careful. Their smell of sweat, cloth and urine has reached her on the breeze and her impassive face breaks into a snarl, her upper lip retreating to bare her white teeth and the fleshy black skin of her gums.

Arthur hears footsteps behind him, someone running towards them, and someone else say, 'Here he is, here he is now, clear a space.' But Arthur doesn't turn to look at Charlie. He is transfixed by the lioness, by the dreadful ease of her body, the amber of her eyes and the way she moves, pneumatically, sliding under her own spine. She should look so strange, there in the street which is normally bustling with people. But to Arthur it is the buildings around her that suddenly look strange, out of place. He watches her move a little further down the street, and however unfamiliar the sight is, unnatural, disjointed, he cannot bring himself to see her as an impostor. She is of the veld, and she is reclaiming her territory, moving between the clumsy buildings of brick and wood, marking them ephemeral with every print of her paw in the dust.

As she gets nearer, he can see that her coat is shabby and flea-bitten and she is short on one hind leg, as if she has injured her hip. More than likely, he thinks, another victim of the drought, forced to hunt for food in a town emptied of people for the day. She turns towards the knot of men standing on the stoep once more, her ribcage expanding and contracting as she breathes, then she looks away again, moving her head with the same slow deliberation. Movement behind Arthur indicates the arrival of Charlie. He can hear his heavy, panting breath and the sound of a gun breaking open.

But now the lioness is moving again too, stalking towards the veranda of the post office. And it is then, as he watches her slouch nearer the post office steps, that Arthur sees the dog. A bull terrier, tied by its lead to a pole on the stoep. Until now it has been quiet, crouched back in the shadow of the awning, but as the lioness approaches, her shoulders hunched high in hunting position, it begins to bark, pulling its lead taut and letting out explosive yelps of fear.

'OK, stand back, give him room.' McGregor again. Arthur feels someone push him to one side.

'Shoot, go on, shoot!' someone else says, and then Charlie's voice, clenched, quiet, 'I'm waiting for a clean shot, you idiot. I want that skin.'

But now the terrier's yelps have become whines, and its lead has slackened as it retreats from the edge of the stoep. It's what the lioness has been waiting for and with one sudden push of her hind legs she lunges forward onto the squealing terrier, crashing her heavy front paws, black claws extended, down on the dog's body. In the same movement she clamps her jaw about the back of its neck and with one sharp tug breaks the lead from the pole. Spinning on her hindquarters she runs off the stoep and up the high street, the terrier in her mouth, its legs still kicking, and the broken end of the lead trailing in the dust behind her.

As she turns a rifle cracks from behind Arthur and one of the post office windows blossoms into shattered glass. 'Shit.' Charlie's clenched voice again. Then another man's voice: 'The second barrel, the bloody shot!'

The lioness keeps running as Charlie fires the second barrel of the combination hunting rifle, firing a twelve-bore cartridge instead of the first .303 bullet. The lioness, at full gallop with the terrier limp in her mouth, corners around the last building in the street as the gun explodes again. A second later the rush and crackle of pepper shot streams through the branches of a tree like a plague of locusts. But the lioness has gone.

And then there is silence. Just the echo of the gunshot reverberating between the wooden buildings, and the dust, blowing up in eddies of wind in the empty street. And on the stoep of the post office, a splash of blood and a broken lead tied to nothing but air.

That evening, as Arthur prepares for his evensong in the Dutch Reformed Church, he hears the men of the town outside making their own preparations, organising and setting off on a hunting party to track down the lioness. A rogue lion will not be tolerated, and he listens from his vestry to the yapping of the dogs, the clutter of ammunition belts being strapped on and rifles being shouldered. They are going to war with the veld, an invasion party to revenge the invasion of their own bolt-hole of civilisation.

Later, he preaches to a small congregation of women, children and old men only. He tells the parable of Daniel and the lion, and Pastor Liebenberg bangs out the hymns on the old piano. The singing is not as lively or joyous as his services in Wreningham. None of the women here shut their eyes when they sing, sway, break from the pews and shuffle a dance. But it still lifts his spirits to hear the hymns sung, each note marking out a territory of his own.

The men return with the lioness as Arthur is shutting up the church and padlocking the door to the vestry. The light has almost faded from the day and a streak of sunset lies across the horizon, setting off the trees and thorn bushes in sharp silhouettes. They return triumphant, the dogs barking at their heels and the body of the lioness slung across an old Scotch cart which they pull themselves, four at the front holding the shafts and two on either side, like a royal procession. Except in this procession, the queen is dead, shot through the heart, the stomach and the hip, dried blood caked on her golden coat. Her eyes are still open and her tongue hangs from the side of her jaw, a slab of pink flesh, shaking with the movement of the cart.

As the men pile into Vic's Tavern taking the body of the lioness with them, Arthur can't help feeling that he is witnessing a defeat, not a victory. He shoulders his satchel, and begins his walk out of town back to Wreningham. Walking down the street he passes through the gold bars of light cast across the road from the windows of the hotel. From inside he hears the chatter of happy men, the clinking of glasses, a tune winding up on a gramophone, and, as he walks on into the darkness, the faint click and heartbeat of billiard balls connecting and rebounding off the soft baize of the table.

Wreningham Mission, Mashonaland, Southern Rhodesia

◇

Although he is only eleven years old, Tendai has been waiting outside Baba Cripps' rondavel all night, ever since the *n'anga* appeared out of the thick bush behind the schoolhouse and announced he had come to see the white *mufundsi*. Tendai's mother told the *n'anga* that Baba Cripps was in Enkeldoorn, but the *n'anga* said he would wait, striding over to Baba Cripps' hut and crouching on his haunches at the side of the compound where the beaten earth became bush.

Tendai had seen the *n'anga* before at his aunt's village. He'd once watched from outside a group of older men as he divined with bones and on another occasion he'd sat outside a hut where the *n'anga* was talking to a spirit that had possessed his uncle. The spirit had asked for goat's blood and the *n'anga* had sent for a he-goat. Tendai remembered the white of its hair in the dim early morning and the sound of the blood gulping from a slash in its throat into a calabash bowl. Despite these occasions, he still couldn't stop himself staring at the *n'anga* now: at the silver-grey baboon skin slung over his shoulders, the beads about his neck and the bangles round his ankles, his walking staff adorned with ostrich feathers and the skin pouches tied around his waist that jiggled on his hips when he walked.

His mother had told him not to stare, and giving him a gentle tap around the ear she'd taken him inside their rondavel to wash. But later, when she pushed him out again to go to bed, Tendai saw the *n'anga* was still there, sitting motionless beside Baba Cripps' rondavel. So he did not go to bed, as his mother had told him to, but crept over to Baba Cripps' rondavel and sat against its wall, just on the other side where the *n'anga* couldn't see him. He would wait there for Baba Cripps to come back, and when he did, he would tell him the *n'anga* was there to see him.

Tendai and his mother had been living at Wreningham for nearly as long as he could remember. In fact, there was only one clear memory

Tendai had that was not of his life at Wreningham. It was his first and it was of his father dying.

He must have been just three years old. It was after the uprising and he and his mother were hiding with other mothers and children in a cave in the kopje near their village. He remembers the dark, wet smell of the rock that had never seen sun. The flapping and screeching of the bats above them. And then hearing the explosion. No, feeling the explosion in the cave next to them. Like a giant hand through the rock, pushing them away from the wall. The explosion in the cave next to them, in the cave where his father was hiding with the other men.

But that is not really where Tendai's memory begins. That is just where he thinks it does. Really it was his mother who told him about the dark, wet rock, the bats and the giant hand of the explosion. His own memory begins afterwards, outside the cave, in the searing mid-day sun, when he feels his mother's scream through her chest. Then looking out from behind her arms to see his father, crawling out of the other cave with his hands clawing at the ground and the red, red blood, like the blood of the goat, gushing where his legs should have been.

His father was a proud man. He made brass in their village, melting the spitting, sparking metal in his furnace. He was the only father who knew how to make brass and that is why he was a proud man. But in Tendai's only memory of him he is a begging man. Begging the white men who stood over him to shoot him with their rifles. But they would not, so Tendai watched him die slowly instead, his mother holding his head in her hands and crying, screaming along with the other women who held their own husbands in their arms, already dead or dying.

Since then Tendai has lived with his mother at Wreningham, sleeping in her rondavel, helping her with her farming and going to Baba Cripps' school. But now he is not allowed to sleep in his mother's ron-davel anymore. The elders have told her he is too old and he must sleep with his cousins in another rondavel instead. And that is really why Tendai has not gone to bed tonight. Not because he wants to wait for Baba Cripps, but because he doesn't like sleeping with his cousins. They are older than him and roll on top of him in the night, or kick him out of the way, or claw him with their toenails. He misses sleeping with his mother. The warmth of her body, the smell of peanut-butter oil on her skin, the way she sings him to sleep, quietly, so only he can hear. But even she says he must sleep with his cousins now. That he is too old to sleep with his mother, that he must become a man.

So instead of going to bed Tendai has decided to wait for Baba Cripps and tell him the *n'anga* is here to see him. He waits there, outside the rondavel, as the sun sinks and the light drains from the day. Every now and then he creeps to the edge of its wall to look at the *n'anga* and he is always there, in the same position, motionless. Crouched on his haunches, his elbows inside his knees, staring across the mission compound at the sky through the trees. Even in the dim light Tendai can see the black empty sockets of the baboon's head, and the sharp teeth of its upper jaw, crowning the *n'anga*'s stern face. The baboon skin terrifies him, but there is something pleasurable in the fear and he finds himself looking at the blank eyes, the sharp teeth, again and again.

It is dark by the time Baba Cripps returns and Tendai, who has been falling asleep against the rondavel wall, his chin dropping to his chest, again and again, only sees him when he is very near. Rubbing his eyes he watches the shadowy figure approaching. He looks hard, checking it is indeed Baba Cripps, then gets up and jogs towards him, saying softly, 'Baba, Baba, the *n'anga* is here to see you.'

Arthur is surprised when Tendai comes running out of the darkness towards him, but he is tired after his walk and he says nothing as the boy tugs at his jacket, pulling him towards his rondavel. Once there, however, he understands the child's excitement. Gufa the *n'anga* is sitting on the ground waiting for him. He has never spoken to Gufa before, but he has seen him and he has heard about him from the villagers around Wreningham: a diviner and a chemist, a herbalist who, for the right price, will cure most ills.

Arthur pulls his stool out of his rondavel and places it before Gufa. He sits down, feeling exhaustion wash through him like a swelling tide, and tells Tendai to go to bed. Then, turning to Gufa, he asks how he can help.

Gufa speaks but Arthur cannot understand him. Arthur asks him to speak more slowly, '*Taura zvishoma,*' but it does no good. Even when the shaman articulates his words as if he is deaf, still he cannot understand him. He turns around. As he thought, Tendai has lingered at the edge of his rondavel. Arthur calls him over.

'*Handinzwisisi. Unoti chii neChiShona? Ungadzokorere here?*' ('I don't understand. How do you say this in Shona? Could you repeat?')

Tendai frowns, comes closer and crouches beside Arthur. He looks intently at the *n'anga* as he speaks, then slowly, he begins to translate, whispering into Arthur's ear in the pauses between the *n'anga's* speech.

As Arthur listens to Tendai's steady translation he suspects he knows why he could not understand Gufa. The *n'anga* can speak perfectly good Shona, but he does not want Arthur to be able to understand him. He wants him to feel like an outsider, and so he has chosen to speak in a local dialect instead. Arthur listens as Tendai continues, his lilting voice soft as ash in his ear.

'He says he has seen the white *n'anga* lying in the bush in his red and black, like a rain spirit, but the white man is not a real *n'anga*. The white *n'anga* cannot make magic from the plants. He cannot read the bones. He cannot make lightning strike a rondavel. He cannot stop the sun setting with stones. He cannot test a wife with water or speak with the spirits or know the land. He says he has seen the white *n'anga* walking the paths that bend like the river and that everyone knows *n'angas* do not walk on these paths. Real *n'angas* go in straight lines. Like the birds that fly and the elephant that walks.'

That night, after he has watched Gufa's baboon-covered back disappear into the darkness, Arthur falls asleep fully clothed on the mattress in his rondavel. His body feels light and yet heavy; the blister on his heel burns and his shoulders ache, but he sleeps a deep sleep. And all night he dreams. Of *n'angas* walking through trees, of the sun setting like a stone, of flannel trousers flapping in the breeze, of lions jumping out of flags and prowling through towns, of wives with their hands in water, of light across roads and of the sound of a gramophone, impossibly far away, playing the scratched record of a dead queen's waltz.

Maronda Mashanu, Mashonaland, Southern Rhodesia

—◇—

'*Zwinorwadza papi?*'

Fortune is washing him. Through his one good ear he can hear her hand dropping into the calabash bowl of river water and swilling the cloth around, then the run of drips from the cloth into the bowl, fast then slower as she lifts her hand out. Then from sound to sensation as she slaps the cloth to his body, squeezing it so the water spreads and rushes over his skin. It is cold, but the shock of its coldness is good. It wakes his flesh, brings it back from the stupor of the night's heat. Her hands are gentle but thorough, scrubbing across his naked back, sending the water running down his spine like a cool, dark shadow.

He is sitting on a low stool outside his rondavel. He can feel the morning sun reflected off its pale walls onto his back, and a slight tingling on his skin as the water evaporates.

'*Zwinorwadza papi?*' she asks again. 'Where does it hurt?'

He knows she is probably speaking loudly, but her voice comes to him through a fog of thickened sound. Some things he can still hear well, but voices seem to get lost, and he has to work hard to make them out.

He points to his stomach. '*Zwinorwadza apa,*' he says. Then he points to his head, '*apa*', and his legs, '*apa*', and his back, '*apa*'. He starts laughing, still pointing all over his body. '*Apa, apa, apa.*'

Fortune knows now he is making fun of her, and he hears her laugh and admonish him all at once. '*Aya, Baba!*' she says, slapping him extra hard with the cloth again and rubbing it vigorously up and down his legs. When he has stopped laughing, he says to her, more quietly, '*Ndiripo kana, wakadiniwo?*', 'I am fine, how are you?' A splash of hand in water, a cold explosion on his shoulder, her fingers, massaging his skin, and her voice, matter of fact, full of song, '*Ndiripo kana, Baba.*'

Fortune has lived at Maronda Mashanu ever since Arthur pulled her from her grave thirty years ago. Her parents had asked him to perform the last rites for a pair of premature twins who had not survived their early birth. When he arrived at the kraal a few miles outside Enkeldoorn she was already lying next to her twin sister, both of them wrapped in the one blanket, in the one grave. The family was poor, so there would be no coffin. And there were no other mourners either. Twins are not seen as good fortune among the Mashona, whether they are Christian or not.

The babies' father was throwing the first handfuls of soil over his dead daughters when Arthur saw Fortune move. No more than a tremor in her fingers, but enough for him to reach into the grave and lift her out. He brought her to his ear and listened at her tiny chest. A heartbeat as fragile and faint as a butterfly's wings fluttered irregularly under her skin. He didn't wait any longer, and carrying her as she was, wrapped in his vestments, he ran back to Enkeldoorn and the hospital.

When she was ready to leave the hospital Fortune's parents did not want her back. They said a child brought back from death is not a good omen. She had been to the spirit world of her ancestors, and some of those spirits may still be with her, from when the white *mufundsi* pulled her from her grave. So Fortune came to live at Maronda Mashanu, where Arthur put her into the care of another family who lived on the mission. He christened her Cecilia in the river that flowed below the church but she rarely answered to that name and everyone called her Fortune instead: because she had been so lucky to be born twice, once from her mother, and once from the earth.

Now, thirty years after Arthur wiped the dust from her face and the dirt from her ears and ran with her at his breast to the hospital, their roles are reversed, and Fortune carries him instead. Not miles to a hospital but a few feet from his stool to his bed in the cool of his rondavel. She lays him on the mattress and pulls a blanket up to his chin, stroking it smooth across his body. As her hand passes over his chest she feels his heart there, its beat as soft and irregular as a butterfly, flitting about the cage of his ribs, brushing its wings against the paper of his skin.

He is sure it is Thursday, but he wants to check, so he asks Fortune, '*Nhasi Chingani?*'

He feels her hands on him again, soothing and fresh over his body, and her voice, with a laugh in it. '*Nhasi China*,' she says, 'It is Thursday today', then she adds, in English, 'VaBrettell, he comes today.'

Arthur lies on his back and listens to her pick up the calabash bowl from outside and walk away, singing quietly to herself. Fortune was always singing. When Arthur once asked her why she sang she had explained to him that she was singing with her sister, who went everywhere with her. They liked to sing together because their voices were the same and the songs sounded like they were sung with one voice twice; like when the *Mbira* player plucks two frets with his thumb at the same time and they make one note.

A light suddenly turns on in the darkness of his right eye. The sun has edged higher in the sky and slipped its beams inside the frame of his door. He lies there, enjoying the heat on his face and he drifts again, into his memories and his dreams.

All morning the fifty years of his life in Africa have come flooding back to him: forgotten faces and names, moments in time as clear as photographs in his mind, all carried on a tide of recollection. Loosened by his sickness, his mind has unlocked the floodgates of his past, left itself vulnerable to memory, filling with the years he has lived, the people he has met and the things he has seen. Through all his memories, though, one act and the shadow it throws wells up like a dark lava threatening to break the surface of his consciousness. But he will not mine it, and so he tries to bury it instead with other memories, other events, although he knows in his heart it will not go away. Because it is the one act of his life that both made and broke him, that has both denied and given him liberty, and as he rises and falls through his half-dreaming state he knows that the memory of it is circling above him: a vulture, waiting until he is weak enough for it to land and begin its undoing of him.

The sound of a bicycle's wheels whirring with grass in the spokes brings him back to the day around him. He must have drifted again, his consciousness, loose from its moorings. Time has become fluid. Was it the afternoon already? Had Brettell arrived?

'*Mangwanani Baba.*'

But the voice is not Brettell's. Arthur smiles. '*Mangwanani Leonard, titambire.*' The words crack in his throat.

'I have brought you some letters, Baba,' Leonard says, preferring to practise his English rather than speak in Shona.

'Thank you,' Arthur replies. 'I wasn't expecting letters for another week at least.'

'The post is very quick now Baba,' Leonard explains. 'One of these letters came on an aeroplane.'

'Really?' Arthur thinks of the planes he had sometimes seen or heard above the veld, catching the sun with their silver bodies, like lonely angels in the empty blue sky. 'Will you read them to me, Leonard?'

He hears the scraping of a stool across the bare floor and the faint tearing of paper as Leonard opens the first letter.

Leonard Mamvura is the teacher at Arthur's school in Maronda Mashanu, and has been there ever since Arthur extradited him from a police training camp in Salisbury fifteen years ago. Leonard's mother had come to Arthur complaining that her son had been forced to join the police, that he did drill all day in a hot parade ground surrounded by wire when all he wanted was to train to be a teacher. Arthur wrote a letter to the police chief in Salisbury, requesting Leonard for the post of teacher in his school. He got no reply, so he sent another letter, and then one each day for a month until eventually he got a response, not in the form of a letter or a telegram, but in the form of Leonard himself who arrived at the door of his rondavel with a suitcase in one hand and a bundle of his letters in the other.

'The chief said to bring these back to you, and to take myself while I am about it,' Leonard had explained.

Over the last ten years Leonard has added the job of secretary to his post as teacher in the school, writing the letters that Arthur dictates and reading the replies that still come in from societies, family, friends and publishers. Arthur insists on signing his letters himself and he makes Leonard read them back to him several times before he lets him seal them in an envelope and address them. When the letters are to Arthur's family though, Leonard secretly writes his own postscript, telling them how Arthur really is and sometimes asking for money to feed him. The letters are fewer now than they used to be, so many of his friends have passed away, but Leonard is still the bringer of news for Arthur, releasing him from his confinement with each letter he reads just as Arthur released him from the police camp with each letter he wrote.

He lies back on his mattress and listens to Leonard's clear voice. His well-defined words placed one after the other, carefully, building the sentences like a bricklayer laying his bricks tenderly in the wet cement to build himself a wall.

The sun rises higher and its heat falls over Arthur with the words; words written thousands of miles away and sounding on his ear from different countries, different lives. The words of the world, resting in their envelopes, flown and shipped to Africa, carried by rail, donkey and finally a barefoot boy down the dust road from Enkeldoorn to Maronda Mashanu, where Leonard sits beside Arthur reading, bringing them to life on his careful, considerate tongue.

PART THREE

And there went out another horse that was red: and
power was given to him that sat thereon to take peace from
the earth, and that they should kill one another.
Revelation, 6:4

Rev. L.M.T. Mamvura,
Maronda Mashanu
P.O. Box 62
Chivhu
Zimbabwe
5th October, 1999

Dear Mr. Owen,

I hasten in replying your kind letter received today with open arms dated 28th September, 1999. Thank you very much for writing.

I will be only too pleased to be meeting you and if I could be helpful to you for your Research work about your uncle, our 'Hero' the late Beloved Father and Noble Friend, the simple Missionary Poet, Father Arthur Shearly Cripps.

We will only be too pleased to be with us at our Shelter if you approve of it for any time you wish to be with us and stay with us at our Shelter. We are KM. 9, from local town Chivhu. It will be cheaper for you to be with us than to stay in our Town Hotels for they are very expensive.

You can come with and friend or friends and stay with us for any time you so wish to stay. Life is very expensive in with the prizes of things rising every day. The cost of living is indeed very high here.

Please do write and phone me when you arrive in Harare and tell us when you are coming to us after your arrival on the 10th of November, 1999.

Yours very thankfully for writing and expecting you your arrival with red eyes!!

Leonard Mamvura

Harare, Zimbabwe

The Blue Arrow coach service leaves Harare for Bulawayo via Chivhu at seven-thirty every morning. Even at this time the heat in the city is oppressive, and handing my rucksack to the driver to store in the hold I feel rivulets of sweat run down my back. I reach around and pull the damp shirt away from my skin. Inside, the coach is air-conditioned cool, icy in the nostrils when I breathe in. There are not very many of us on the Bulawayo via Chivhu route today. Some women carrying bulging canvas chequered laundry bags, a younger girl with her head in a novel, some silent men, two of them in suits, shiny black leather folders on their laps, a young man in glasses who looks nervous. Another young man in a suit, wearing a brown trilby perched on the back of his head and with his foot in plaster is cracking kumquats between his teeth, one after the other, sucking out the flesh and spitting the rinds into the plastic bag on his lap.

The coach judders to life and reverses out of the parking bay at the front of the Blue Arrow offices on Speke Avenue between Jason Moyo Avenue and Robert Mugabe Road. With a crunching of gears and a couple of revs of the engine it pulls out into the Monday morning traffic of downtown Harare, edging onto the main street between the private cars, the farmers' trucks and the packed commuter taxis, minibuses so full they race through the town with arms hanging out their windows and the conductors hanging from the sliding doors, wads of greasy Zim dollars stuffed into pouches on their belts.

We drive west out of the city on Samora Machel Avenue. Past the Zanu PF Headquarters which a few days earlier a Rixi taxi driver had told me people call the 'shake-shake' building because it resembles a carton of 'shake-shake' beer. Past the Zimbabwe Agricultural Society Showground and then out onto the road south which ribbons ahead of us across the veld, a single tarmac strip, straight but undulating like a ripple caught in time.

The Volvo coach picks up speed and soon we are doing seventy along the pock-marked road. Smaller vehicles get out of our way. I watch them through the back window as they tip and tilt back onto the tarmac behind us, as if they are riding the waves of our wake. The Blue Arrow hostess serves complimentary biscuits and tea and soft drinks. With one hand she carries the plastic cups shaking on a tray down the aisle, holding the seat heads with her other hand to keep her balance, walking the tightrope of the coach's rocking and swaying. *From Russia with Love* plays on the TV screen bolted to the roof at the front of the bus and I watch Sean Connery despatch SPECTRE agents as the veld rushes by my window, expansive and monotonous, broken only by the odd gathering of rondavels off the road, lines of flapping bright washing strung in between them.

I first saw this veld twelve days ago when the 747 that flew me here dipped its nose and banked, making the country rise in the window as if it had been poured into an oval glass, filling the Perspex with its yellow and red earth and a rash of green bush trees. Since then I have been staying in Harare, in the city, so it is only now, as the bus cruises south, that I get a chance to see the veld at first hand, to see the country you made your own, and which, in turn, made you hers.

Harare has no trace of the veld. Its grid of wide concrete streets interlock at a centre of tall glass buildings, offices, banks, shopping arcades and hotels. Traffic lights hang on wires at the intersections like in an American city, and 4x4s and open-backed trucks wait beneath them, shaking on their exhausts. Newspaper boys weave between the stalled vehicles, hawking *The Herald* and the *Daily News*, and at the side of the road cobs of corn roast in their leaves over the smouldering coals of oil-drum barbecues. More oil drums mark the end of the street where President Mugabe lives, but these are painted red and stand upright, dented and patched with rust. Soldiers stand beside them, wooden-stocked AK47s at rest across their chests. Ever since a drive-by rocket attempt on Mugabe's house this street is closed between six in the evening and six in the morning. The soldiers are ordered to shoot anyone seen on it during that time. They have already killed two people.

Mugabe has governed Zimbabwe since the end of the War of Independence in 1980. As you suspected a hundred years ago, issues of land ownership lay at the root of this war, but its conclusion has not seen these issues rest. Land continues to be both the country's fault-line and its foundation. When I arrive in Harare Mugabe is playing a dangerous balancing act between his promised redistribution of white-owned land and the consequences this would bring: disenfranchising the commercial farmers and thereby losing up to 42 per cent of the country's annual national export income. What redistribution has already occurred has been marred by corruption, the giving and taking of land by Mugabe to favour his supporters or punish his opposition, black and white.

The acacia and jacaranda trees that line the residential streets of Harare are one reminder of the veld that still exists in the city. Each year they blossom into bright reds and purples, but here their roots split pavements, not earth. In the centre of town crowds of people, black and white, stream through the arcades, drinking in cafés, talking on mobiles. On the corners craftsmen hawk their wire trinkets: birds, motorcycles, planes, all bent from the steel with a pair of pliers. Booksellers line the pavement with their second-hand paperbacks and months-old magazines, and every street has its army of Shona sculptures standing on parade for sale: green, white and grey fluid forms, reminiscent of Henry Moores, but African through and through.

On First Street department-store dummies look out onto the lunchtime workers sitting in the sun. White dummies, looking onto black people. Some of the blacks, though, are white or the whites black, depending on how you look at it. Albinos, walking down the street in wide-brimmed hats to protect their sensitive skin, blinking the fair lashes of their pink-rimmed eyes. 'Unlucky,' a Rixi taxi driver tells me. 'I would not like to be one.' He laughs, 'You are black, but you are white, so you belong nowhere. Nobody likes you.'

Further out of town shopping centres punctuate the long, straight streets and rows of flats and houses. Out at the Avondale Centre middle-class whites and blacks meet in the Italian Café for espressos, croissants and the latest news of strikes, farmers' disputes and stoppages up at the university. In the Fife Avenue shopping mall the same crowd meet again later, on the open terrace of the Book Café, where saxophonists play into the warm night and small-press poets read their work. In the suburbs large low houses nestle on well-kept lawns behind tall wire fences. Signs tell passers-by the speed with which the armed response unit will come to the house if the alarm is triggered. Further out again, after the suburbs, it is still city, but new city. Sprawling estates of high-density housing, rows and rows of unpainted breeze-block bungalows, some with aerials and satellite dishes on their roofs and cars parked in their driveways. But here the city's domination of the veld is not so complete. The streets are covered with a dusty earth that shifts across them in the wind, and tall grasses grow between cracks in the concrete, prising through like an old habit that will not die. Here, families all sleep in the same bed, the parents partitioned by a hung sheet from the children. It is the city, but the ways of the village have not been forgotten. There are chickens in back yards. Nervous, sullen dogs, and if you need him, a *n'anga* nearby who will tell you if the snake at your door was sent as a blessing or a curse.

The house I have been staying in is in Rowland Square, north-west of the city centre on Prince Edward Street. It belongs to a white Zimbabwean called Jeremy Brickhill. At seventeen Jeremy deserted the Rhodesian Army while fighting in the War of Independence and went to join the ZIPRA guerrillas in the Zambian bush. The war ended and he returned to Harare, as did his wife, who had been exiled from the country for protesting against Ian Smith's regime. Zimbabwe was now an independent state led by Robert Mugabe, who on coming to power had announced a policy of reconciliation. 'If yesterday I fought you as an enemy, today you have become a friend,' he told Zimbabwe's whites, 'and if yesterday you hated me, today you cannot avoid the love that binds you to me and me to you.' Encouraged, many whites did not 'take the gap' and stayed; but for some people the war was not over and they could not forget. One day as Jeremy turned the key in his car door he unlocked an explosion that blew him apart, embedding parts of his car into his body. The bomb may have been intended for him or his wife, he doesn't know, but as he walks around the hot house in just a sarong he still displays its mark, a cross-stitch of scar tissue, running the length of his torso. It reminds me, together with the photos he keeps on his wall of the decommissioning of weapons at the end of the war (rows and rows of missiles, machine-guns and armoured cars lined up in the bush), of how recent the conflict is here, lying shallow in the memory of this young and old country.

Jeremy is often away, so most of the time I share the house with his housekeeper, Richard. Richard is twenty-four, black, quiet, softly spoken and gentle-mannered. He lives in a one-roomed building behind Jeremy's house, with a single bed, a radio that is nearly always on and posters of Manchester United on his walls. He will be getting married next summer. On Sundays his cousin comes and calls for him after church. Wearing a long white deacon's stole and holding a Bible under his arm, he gently rattles the chain on the gate at the bottom of Jeremy's drive to call Richard out from his room. Richard appears in long trousers and his Sunday shirt and together they walk off through the square towards town.

I am in Zimbabwe looking for you again. In libraries, in archives and in the memories of people. I thought I had stopped following you, but you didn't go away, so I have come to the country you lived and died in, following in your footsteps, hoping that somehow I will find more of you here. Because I still think I don't know your whole story, and I feel instinctively that what is missing is the keystone I need to understand you. Before I left for Zimbabwe I visited my great aunt Elizabeth, your niece, who knew you and who wrote to you through those last quiet, isolated years in the veld. She told me that when she had come here for a memorial service years ago, she had been introduced to a woman who said she was your granddaughter. It had been quick, cursory, but she was sure she had said she was your granddaughter. If you have a granddaughter, you must have had a child, and a child must have had a mother, but in your letters, in the books written about you, there is always just you. So I have come to Zimbabwe, nearly fifty years after you died, to look for you again, and to look for your story, your real story that has been covered by the dust of time and history.

But 'real' is not such an exact word here as it was in Britain. Harare is all city – cinemas, Rixi taxis, cricket grounds – but like the grass that grows between the cracks in the concrete, the older Shona histories of myth, magic and superstition are always showing through the city's surface. Reality and myth and fact are not so definite here, but feed off each other to create a culture in which myth is no less 'real' than fact, just another way of telling the same story. There was a report in the paper yesterday about a prostitute who is being charged for cursing a client who refused to pay. The man woke the next morning to find that his genitals had disappeared. A doctor has given evidence to support the man's case, swearing it is true that the prostitute's curse has deprived him of his manhood, leaving a space between his legs, a blank page of skin. And there are other stories in the paper, about *tologashes*, spirits of the veld playing havoc with people's lives, about witchdoctors, about black magic and politics. Myth, reality and fact, in black and white, hand in hand in hand.

With you too, it has been hard to extract the real from the myth, but you are still here, in the city you first stood up to then stayed away from. I have been following your name around the city. There is an orphanage outside town named after you, and your books and letters are in the university library and in the National Archives. I thought I found a street named after you but found out later that it was not you, but another Cripps, a pioneer called Leonard Cripps. Most people I meet know your name because of a diary, the *Shearly Cripps Recipe Diary*, which is sold as an annual fund-raiser for the orphanage. I find a copy in a bookshop in town. It has a lurid rainbow cover with your name across it, and inside there are quick recipes, adverts for Dazzle Hair Design and Enbee Schoolwear, dates, school calendars, weights and measures. There is a section called 'Time and Trouble Savers': 'Emergency funnel – Use corner of brown envelope. Dropped egg – sprinkle heavily with salt to absorb the moisture.' When I meet people here many are surprised you are a man and a missionary. They thought you were a woman and a cook, a pioneer's Mrs Beeton. Fact and fiction, hand in hand.

Others, though, know you intimately, and these are the people I have come to talk to in Harare. They are the people who like me have traced you in history and tried to understand you, who have already tried to tell your story. After the time I have spent with your letters, with your life on my mind, meeting them is like meeting the ex-partners of a lover. What we have in common is you. They know and re-tell the same stories I have uncovered, they have touched your writing, had their minds enquiring in yours. At first there is instant contact, the shared interest recognised, then a period of mild competition, scoring off each other's knowledge of you. But then we settle into an exchange of ideas and theories, before the examination of you widens to take in their lives and mine, but always through the prism of yours.

Betty Finn's house is on Bradfield Road in the north-east of the city, number 33, a modest bungalow with an open garage on the side with wisteria trailing over its roof. The battered blue Rixi taxi drops me in front of a large black iron gate. I buzz the intercom and speak into it and soon there is the dog, as there is in every house in Harare, barking and baring its teeth at me through the bars beneath the armed response sign tied to them. The dog is joined and subdued by an older African man called Gregory who opens the gate with one hand while bending down and holding the dog by its collar with the other. The front door of the bungalow opens and Betty Finn welcomes me, apologising for the dog, the gate, the buzzer – 'But,' she explains, 'crime has got so bad now I have to be careful.'

I spend that afternoon with Betty, who has written academic articles about you, your poetry and your legacy. She is old now, in her seventies, but her interest in you has been a long-standing one. She shows me the unpublished manuscript of a book she wrote about your life; another person trying to pin you down with words. She says it doesn't work, though, that you slip from under them, reclusive, ungiving, unwordable. We have tea and she tells me what she knows and thinks about you. How she thinks you were an impractical man who couldn't even ride a bike, forced to live a practical life, your buildings and your body collapsing around the iron foundation of your faith. She says that in the last years people in Enkeldoorn said you were dirty, that you smelt, but that you always wore a clean white cravat. Above all else, she says she thinks you were lonely, unbearably lonely, despite your African friends and followers. The way she talks about your life in the bush, she makes it sound like a voluntary exile, rather than the finding of a home. I ask her about your child, if she knows the child's name or where they lived, but she dismisses the idea, convinced that there can be no child. There was no wife, not even an African one, which, she says, was common among missionaries out in the bush. No, there was no love affair, and no daughter.

As the afternoon fades Betty's subject of your loneliness spins on its axis until Betty is talking about her own isolation, and I wonder if there isn't something of the mirror-man in you. That people can't help seeing the ruling qualities of their life reflected in you. But then perhaps this is not a quality of yours exclusively, just the nature of relationships across history, between the writer and the written. The pursuer looking for something in their subject that they recognise in themselves. For Betty this seems to be loneliness, abandonment. She came to Rhodesia to be with the man she loved, Hugh Finn, a scientist and a poet, and married him here. She had always wanted to marry a poet ever since her childhood friend had announced dramatically while they were picking strawberries that she had discovered a great poet and that she would marry him. The friend was only twelve years old then, but years later she did marry the poet. His name was Tom Eliot, and hers was Valerie.

Hugh has been dead for some years now, and Betty is marooned in

Zimbabwe, the country to which her love brought her and in which it has now left her, washed up on her own grief, which is deep and solid, echoing as it does the dimensions of her love. She explains to me, simply and determinedly as if explaining a complicated equation to a child, that love does not go away with death, does not diminish, and anyone who says it does has not been in love. Instead, she says, it grows daily, fed by memory and its own nourishment, increasing in depth and volume and casting an equal shadow of grief as it does so.

Gregory serves us an English Sunday roast. The sun is hot through the barred window behind the table, a bird caws extravagantly from a tree in the garden and Betty cries for a while, holding her fork in one hand and her head in the other.

The Blue Arrow coach is still reeling in the long road across the bush. Out of the side window I follow the fluid dip and rise of the slack telephone wires hung between their wooden poles, a long black rhythmical wave against the dull grey sky. I have been in Zimbabwe for twelve days, and I have tried to call Leonard every day, to tell him I am coming, but I have never got through. Looking at these wires now I understand why. Many of them have been brought down, cut open and stripped of their valuable copper, and this is probably why my voice never reached this far out of the city, and this is why I am having to come unannounced. In my shirt pocket I have the last letter from Leonard, dated over a month ago, and I only hope the words of welcome written there are still valid.

A rash of half-built breeze-block bungalows signifies the edge of a town. It has started raining, hard, soaking rain. I look out the front window of the coach to see Chivhu appear in its frame through the clear arc of the one long wiper sweeping waves of water off the windscreen with each swing of its arm. The coach slows, crunches down a couple of gears and pulls into a small square with buildings on three sides. The driver calls 'Chivhu'. I am the only person to leave the coach. Outside, the rain is cutting up the dusty ground, unlocking the smell of the earth. I collect my rucksack from the hold then run to the shelter of the nearest building, a cream wooden hotel with green window frames and guttering and a swinging sign that says 'Vic's Tavern'. Along with a couple of men standing on the covered veranda I watch the Blue Arrow coach leave, then take my bag to a table, sit down, and order a toasted egg sandwich and a cup of tea. A waistcoated waiter brings my order out from the empty hotel and I watch the rain sheet off the sloping roof, spilling from the guttering, waterfalling to the ground, distorting the world beyond.

When the sound of the rain on the roof begins to ease I ask one of the men if he knows the way to where Reverend Mamvura lives, Farm 16 in Maronda Mashanu. He raises his eyebrows, smiles and says in a deep voice, 'Yes, I know where Reverend Mamvura lives,' he indicates with a flat hand. 'Up here, then left and then right.' He pronounces his English carefully, each syllable given its due weight in the Zimbabwean manner. 'It is about nine or ten kilometres,' he adds; then, tilting his head to one side, he asks, 'But how will you get there?'

'I'll walk,' I tell him. Because that is how you would have got there from this town, on your feet, and I don't want to follow you any other way.

The rain is light now, so I shoulder my rucksack, which feels too new in this town, and start to walk the way the man had described. I pass the post office on my left then continue up a long wide dirt street of shops, their entrances shaded by a wooden awning over an open walkway. The walkway and the shops' faded, once colourful signs remind me of an American Western set, lending the street a pioneer feel beneath the African trappings of the town. *Zvichanka Chete*, *Dikita Eating House*, *Fish and Chips*, *Chivhu Music Centre*, *Prop. D. J. Sithole*, *Zvoushe G. Dealer*, *Budget Boutique*. A broken neon sign writes *Enkeldoorn Garage* in dull letters against the grey sky, reminding me of the town's original name, and looking around now I find it hard to believe that it looks much different to when you were alive. Except, of course, today the people in the shops, walking on the walkway, driving in the beat-up trucks are all black and when you were here nearly everyone was white.

I turn left up a smaller street. A series of corrugated lean-tos line the left side and a squat, hexagonal rusted corrugate church stands on the right. The sun has come out now and a barber is outside his lean-to, shaving a path through the thick black hair of a customer who sits on a couple of upturned Pepsi crates. The long flex of his clippers leads back into the dark of the shed, where a small boy stares at me, his stomach distended and one finger in the corner of his mouth. I wave and he ducks back, further into the dark. The barber laughs and waves instead.

This street bears right, past the Chivhu hospital, a complex of low wooden buildings behind a wire-mesh fence with scrubland grass growing in between them. Some orderlies smoke under the shade of a large open thatched shelter that stands apart from the main buildings. At the corner of the hospital the road ahead of me peters out into veld grass, a narrow track and trees, so I turn left and start walking up the road I was told will lead me to Leonard's farm at Maronda Mashanu. It stretches ahead of me, a long, straight, rust-red dirt road that narrows into the horizon like a textbook perspective diagram. Slightly cambered, its centre has been driven smooth by truck and bus tyres, scattering the larger pebbles into small banks and dips at it edges in which the rain water has collected in long thin puddles. A strip of grass flanking either side develops into thick bush away from the road: low green trees punctuated with rounded granite boulders. The wind has whittled some of these into standing stone sculptures, one stone on another, and many are rashed with orange lichen. Sometimes the words 'Bus Stop' are painted on them in black writing. A line of telegraph poles margin the road on the left, their single wire a dark pencil line against a sky that is still portentous with rain.

I pass the hospital, where a man is sitting outside the entrance with his young daughter. The left side of her face is swollen, shutting one eye and blowing out her cheek. Her father wears an old suit jacket over a jumper, flannel trousers and battered slip-on shoes. He raises a hand and asks 'How are you?' in the Zimbabwean way, with the emphasis on the 'you'. As he does so his daughter turns away from me and hides her face behind her father's jacket. I tell him I am fine and walk on, my rucksack pulling at my shoulders and my water bottle swilling at my side. Occasionally the alarm of an insect trill laces the quiet, but otherwise the road is silent, just the sound of my own breath and my feet on the stones. Just once a man on a bicycle appears at the road's sharpened point on the horizon and cycles towards me, rising and falling over the undulations like a boat on a gentle sea. He gets nearer, until I can hear the whirr of his wheels, passes me, then is gone.

After about two miles I pass a battered farm sign on a pole, white paint on black, 'Farm no. 4, Cripps Road'. This is your road, then, the one you walked for forty years, made with your own feet, from Maronda Mashanu to Enkeldoorn and back, carrying your letters, your manuscripts, your grievances, your hopes and your memories. Many roads and streets in this country have changed their names since independence. Windsor Way is now Makombe Way, Stanley Avenue is Jason Moyo Avenue, but this is still your road, Cripps Road. Long, straight, unforgiving, it seems suitably yours, and now I am walking up it to find you in your grave, carrying my questions about your life and why you lived it the way you did.

Ray Brown is another person who has asked these questions before me. An English professor at the university in Harare, he has studied your poems and your stories for traces of you and like Betty Finn he is long familiar with your life. I sat in front of Ray in his house on The Chase, a wide Harare street with rows of jacaranda and Australian silver oaks obscuring the houses that line it on either side, and listened to him talk about you. He is a professor to the bone. Embraced by his huge armchair, he clenches his teeth on a pipe and thinks in silence for a long time before speaking. A wayward fringe of white hair falls across his forehead, beneath which a pair of large square glasses dominate his narrow face. He is a man of literature, and it is your writing that fascinates him: an English nineteenth-century poetic sensibility brought to bear on an African landscape at the dawn of the twentieth. A Keats scholar himself, it is maybe the mirror-man at work again, but he stresses the juxtaposition of your love of Keats, the physical sensualist, against your life of spiritual ideal and physical privation; the romantic nature of your writing against what he calls your 'muscular Christianity'.

When I ask him if he knows of a child, he is silent for longer than one of his usual pauses, then says, 'No, I doubt it.' He does tell me, however, of an occasion years ago when a girl stood up at a symposium held at the university and claimed to be your granddaughter, but he says that he and the other academics dismissed her as an impossibility. When I tell him that my great aunt also met a woman who said she was your granddaughter, and that I have an intuition that it was a specific event, something like a love affair that first sent you to Africa, he is quiet for a long time again. Eventually he stands, and goes to look for a book on his bookshelf. He brings back a selection of your poetry and prose, thumbs the pages, finds what he has been looking for, leans forward with his elbows on his knees and says, 'See what you think of this, it's from a poem called "To the Veld".' And then he reads:

> Take my love and praise . . .
> Most of all for thy weariness –
> The homeless void, the endless track,
> Noon thirst, and wintry night's distress –
> For all tense stretchings on the rack –
> That gave me my lost manhood back.

He looks at the page for a moment, then looks up at me again, peering over his glasses that have slipped down his nose, and says, 'That last line has always troubled me, "my lost manhood". Why lost, do you think?'

After two hours' walking, my water bottle is empty and I can sympathise with your vision of the 'endless track'. The clouds are bulking out above, darkening with rain and I'm worried that this is somehow not your road after all. I decide to carry on until the next farm at least, and walk on down a dip and over a little bridge. The land on the banks of the river that flows under it is covered in a lush grass that rises up into meadows on either side. A jacaranda tree hangs over the road, heavy with its lilac, bluebell flowers, and in the distance I can see a man carrying a spear and walking with two hunting dogs. I stop and rest, realising why you could have thought Mashonaland an Arcadia. Its country is unoriginal for miles, but then every now and then it offers up a place like this, where the simple beauty is all the more striking for rising out of the monotony of the veld.

I am about to turn around and find some shelter before the rain, which I can see sweeping across the land over in the east, reaches me, when I see the sign for Leonard's farm. It is a wide hoop of round metal painted white, with two dark-blue stripes like an old-fashioned life-guard ring. Leonard's name, the farm number and the P.O. Box number are written on it, also in blue, the words invaded by patches of rust. It hangs on an old metal gate, which I push open and walk through, following a rough track that curves up to a homestead scattering of huts on slightly higher ground.

As I walk up the track I take stock of the place. On my right is a single brick rondavel with a neat thatched roof and a line of washing hanging quietly in the still air outside it. Past this, there is a cattle kraal, not made from regular planks or fencing wood but from whole branches planted in the ground with other branches woven in between them to form the horizontal rungs. It gives the impression of intricate planned disorder, part natural, part artificial. Inside, a couple of short-horned cows shift from foot to foot in the mud. Past this, still on my right, there is a squat concrete well with its metal bucket pulled up short to the winding axle and a thin short-haired dog lying at its base, pole-axed by the humid heat. Ahead of me is the homestead proper, a rough square of dusty ground flanked by a whitewashed iron-roofed bungalow on the right, and a couple of thatched rondavels, raised on bricks, to its north and its south. Inside the centre square there is a wooden maize holder, constructed like the cattle kraal from undeveloped wood, an ancient green plough being reclaimed by the earth it once disturbed and a corrugated-iron drying stand on which a pile of red, green, blue and white pots and pans show up brightly against the background of yellow veld grass. A scattering of thin chickens, their red wattles trembling as they walk, strut the dusty ground, pecking for food. Just outside the square is a plain concrete block, its corrugated roof pinned down by stones, with an entrance at each end. White arrows painted on its walls point to each of them, and written above them in English and Shona are the words VARUME GENTS and VAKADZI LADIES.

I am just past the well when a young boy appears from behind one of the raised rondavels. He stops, stares and runs into the hut, calling to someone inside. I stop too, worried that I have intruded. I am suddenly aware that if this is Leonard's farm, then it is the first time I will meet someone who actually met you, who lived with you and knew you as a person, not as a subject written on a page. I wait, feeling the first heavy drops of rain land on my rucksack and my arms, and the sweat cooling on my skin. A woman wearing a brightly patterned skirt, a dark cardigan and a scarf wrapped around her head, and an older boy wearing a white shirt and black trousers, appear from the rondavel. I walk nearer to them, explaining I am here to see Reverend Mamvura. She smiles, says '*Aya!*', bringing her hand down in a gesture I don't quite understand, while the boy walks towards me, smiling, and shakes my hand. He leads me towards the bungalow and goes inside its darkness, calling softly 'Baba, baba!' He says a few more words in quick, quiet Shona and from inside I hear a man's voice, older, deeper. 'Come in, come in, yes, yes.' I step inside and hear the sky open up behind me as, like the drawing down of a blind, the sweep of rain reaches Leonard's farm, crashing onto the iron roof of his bungalow and splashing in the dusty square outside.

Inside there is an older man sitting in an armchair, wearing a dark-green short-sleeved shirt and a grey tank top. On seeing me he raises his eyebrows, lets out an 'Ahhhh!' and, pushing himself out of the chair embraces me and my rucksack in one. He smells of sadza, earth and mothballs. When we pull apart he keeps his arms around me, saying 'Welcome, welcome, Owen', smiling and shaking his head. This is Leonard Mamvura, lively, passionate, eighty years old but looking only fifty. I realise he is crying, and then that I am too.

The boy who met me, who Leonard introduces as Sabethiel, takes my rucksack while Leonard takes my hand and leads me to a small table in the centre of the room, at which we both sit down. As with the others I met in Harare, any distance is broken by our shared knowledge of you. Leonard introduces me to his cousin, the woman I saw earlier, who now brings me a white enamel bowl with blue trim, some soap and a towel to wash my hands, while Leonard makes a pot of tea before sitting down with me to talk about you.

The room is small and dark and simple. The shaky table we sit at stands at its centre with a sofa and an armchair against two of the walls on which free advertisement calendars and printed quotations from the Bible vie for space, along with photographs of Leonard's family and one portrait of Robert Mugabe.

Leonard himself fascinates me. Enthusiasm runs through him like an infection. He is almost completely bald, just a dusting of white hair circling the back of his head. His eyes are heavy-lidded and his face is lined, particularly in two diagonal grooves that run from the side of his nose to above the corners of his mouth. This gives his passive face a solemn look when he is not smiling. But that is rare, because he is often smiling, and laughing a characteristic laugh that peels off into a squeal. When he speaks to me his head nods and waves, as if it is this motion that powers the words which he marshals in the air in front of him as he talks. His language is clear, a careful, formal English, peppered with repeated *yes*es and *uh-oh*s when he is listening or responding to a question.

Leonard removes the white mesh fly-cover from a plate of biscuits and we talk. He tells me that your church, the original Maronda Mashanu, is not far from here, and that you are buried in its nave. Then he talks about when you were alive, referring to you in turns as

'Our hero, Father Shearlycripp', 'the most beloved Father Shearlycripp' or 'our noble friend, Father Shearlycripp'. Many times he says with a shaking head and in a high yet serious voice, 'He was a very good friend of the Africans, yes, yes.'

It is clear that Leonard has taken it upon himself to be the guardian of your legacy and your memory out here in the veld. He goes into his study, a tiny room with sagging shelves piled high with papers and folders, and brings out several books and articles that have been published about you. The words of more people who have come here to question Leonard about the old missionary poet he read and wrote for. Soon, however, it seems that my welfare overtakes the welfare of your memory, and Leonard sets about arranging my welcome, shouting orders at the silent Sabethiel, talking quickly to his niece. He shows me my room at the back of the bungalow, a mattress laid across two huge sacks of mealie meal, a wooden side table and one small window looking out over the track and the road I walked this morning. Then he tells me I must wash, and leads me down to the concrete toilet block where his cousin has already prepared a small blue plastic tub of warm water. The toilet itself is a simple construction of a raised hole set in concrete with a wooden board lain across it. A metal hook hammered into the wall skewers a sheaf of neatly torn squares of newspaper. Leonard leaves me with a bar of soap and I strip off beside the toilet, step into the tub and give myself a body wash, listening to the flies humming and tapping under the wooden board over the toilet hole and looking out of the one small window at the sky, already clear of the morning's rain clouds.

That afternoon Leonard shows me around his homestead, the neat ploughed areas of mealie corn, the kitchen hut with its open fire in the centre and highly polished black shelves moulded out of the earth walls, and the cows, still shifting about their wooden pen. He introduces me to his son, Horatio, who lives with his wife and children in the rondavel I passed on my way up the track. Horatio is fifty and speaks excellent English. He must have been born about the time that you died.

The headmaster of the local school joins us for more tea in the late afternoon. His name is Moses Maranyika, and where Leonard has told me stories about your missionary work here, Moses is keen to tell me about your supernatural powers: your ability to control the bees and, above all, your prowess as a rain spirit. He says that wherever you walked there might have been a band of rain either in front of you or behind you, but never over you. You always walked dry. Leonard laughs and says that Father Cripps must have been with me because it only started raining today when I came inside the house. Moses plays along, nodding, wide-eyed, and says, 'Yes, he is your ancestor, so his spirit will be with you here.' Moses is also a sub-deacon at the church, and he and Leonard segue seamlessly from this supernatural conversation into organising a church service for tomorrow to let everyone meet Father Cripps' great, great nephew.

That night, after a supper of chicken legs and sadza, I write notes from the books Leonard has about you by the light of a single candle while he snoozes in his chair, piping up to conversation every now and then. His talk drifts from you to the land situation to AIDS, which he worries about a lot. He calls the virus 'Slim' and tells me that in the last month he has buried twenty young men, all hollowed out by the disease. He shakes his head, looking sad, and says, 'They go to work in the towns, but then they come back here and they die.' Outside the cicadas are at full drill, and the night is a deep black. Later, I fall asleep on the mealie sacks, my legs aching from my long walk. As I drift towards sleep I think about tomorrow, when I will visit your grave, and about how to ask Leonard about your granddaughter, who seems to have already been everywhere before me but whose name and existence no one can tell me about.

Maronda Mashanu, Mashonaland, Zimbabwe

———◇———

The cock starts crowing early on Leonard's farm, around five-thirty, but it isn't this that wakes me the next morning but the tap, tap of Leonard working on his typewriter in his study next door. Sitting down to a breakfast of fried eggs and toast, Leonard hands me a slip of paper across the table that explains his early activity. It is the schedule for my stay with him, meticulously typed out and numbered, day by day:

```
FARM:- 16/54 ; Maronda mashanu S.S.C.F :-
Our Valuable Mr. Owen Sheers: Programme:-
1.    Tuesday : 23rd November, 1999:-
      Visit : Cripps' Shrine : 9: A:M -
2.    Wednesday : 24th November; 1999:-
      Mass at Maronda Mashanu Church near
      School, 9: 30 am -
      Visit All Saints Wreningham ;
      Acompanied by Subdeacon M. M. Maranyika
      and Others.
3.    Thursday : 25th November, 1999:-
      Leave for : Masvingo .
            Thank you :
            L.M.T. Mamvura .
```

After breakfast five of us leave Leonard's to walk to your grave at the old Maronda Mashanu church, taking the road I walked yesterday away from Chivhu. I walk with Leonard, who is wearing a pin-stripe suit jacket over his jumper and cardigan and a dark felt trilby-type hat. He walks with a stick, which he swings out in front of him at every step. On my other side is Horatio, wearing a woollen hat and a woollen jumper with a pattern of knickerbocker glories repeated over it. He walks with his hands behind his back, asking me about life in Britain. He wants to know what we ask for there: do we ask God for rain? No, I tell him, where I come from there is no need to ask, the rain just happens. Horatio's wife, Faith, and Leonard's cousin walk behind us, carrying a selection of waterproofs and bright umbrellas in case the rain happens again here. However much I try to slow down or wait for them the women always remain a few steps behind us. The morning is cool, but warming up quickly. A school bus passes us, and Leonard waves to the children packed in its open windows. Horatio kicks at some damba shells left on the road by baboons, who have cracked them open to scoop out their insides.

Your church lies off the road, down a narrow track through bush trees and a cluster of euphorbia. As Leonard pushes through the branches with his stick I feel a mounting sense of anticipation. My relationship with you started a long way away, in books and libraries in Britain. Then you inhabited me, the idea of you, incongruous and foreign to my surroundings while I worked in London. Travelling on the underground, driving to work on a breakfast TV show at four in the morning through the city's lamp-lit streets, you were always there somewhere. And now I have come to find you at last, in the patch of Africa you made your home for fifty years.

The ruins of your church stand in the middle of a clearing at the base of a small tree-covered kopje. They have been halted mid-disintegration, their stone walls held together with new cement, so they stand at head height, one large rough stone circle leading into another, smaller circle. I recognise its shape from the photographs I saw in Oxford, even though the precariously sloping thatched roofs have long disappeared. I follow Leonard into the clearing, past a tiny rondavel which must have been yours and into the church, through a gap in the larger stone circle. The remains of three rough pillars rise from the soil, like menhirs or standing stones, and then past these, there is you. A neat, smooth-bordered rectangle sculpted from the soil with a simple white cross at its head and bright blue plastic flowers in clay pots settled in its red earth. I stand above it and imagine you there, a long key in the lock of this grave.

Above the grave there is a concrete canopy, peeling a confetti of white paint. Horatio tells me this was built because the rain never fell on you, so when you were buried here, the rain stopped and the country suffered a drought. They built this canopy shelter so you would bring the rains. He swears that as the last pole supporting the canopy was made secure in the ground, the rain came and didn't stop for three days until the ground had recovered from its thirst.

Leonard and Horatio leave me alone with you for a couple of minutes, but Leonard is soon back, anxious to show me the rest of the area. From the church we go into your rondavel, which has been preserved, complete with its conical thatched roof. Inside the floor is smooth, a mixture of polished mud and cow dung. I feel the walls and remember a line from one of your letters about helping the Matabele workers build the school at Wreningham: '*Slapping sloppy masses of wet earth on a wall made of rough timber is rather agreeable.*' Leonard stands against the wall opposite me and a dappling of sunlight falls across his face from the hole at the top of the roof. He points to it and explains that you always left a hole in the roofs of your buildings so the birds could fly in and out of your churches and your huts. He goes on to describe what was in this rondavel when you lived here. Your mattress, a large trunk stuffed with your letters and your books, a wooden cross and a picture of your mother propped in the one slit window. Nothing else. I look at the floor and try to imagine you here. The rondavel is tiny, and a tall man like you could probably touch both sides of it when lying down. I wonder how you coped in here after the openness and freedom of the veld.

Leonard continues to guide me through the physical landscape of your life. He shows me the patch of ground where you grew your own pipe tobacco, the river in which you baptised him and hundreds of others, and the place on top of the kopje where you came to meditate. Then, looking very serious, he says we must have lunch, and we leave your church and your grave and walk back up the road to his farm. On the way back I am quiet, thinking about what happened when I was alone at your grave. While I was there I found myself speaking to you. I hadn't expected to, and thinking about it now as we walk back to Leonard's I realise that this speaking was perhaps a form of prayer. I can hardly remember the last time I prayed in earnest. I think probably when I was sixteen and my grandfather lay downstairs, dying. Since then the idea of it seemed redundant, a childish fancy, but now I had found myself praying again. It is what I did when faced with your grave, above anything else. Speak to you, ask you questions and listen to the silence of your reply.

Over the course of that afternoon and the following day Leonard guided me through what remained of you here in Mashonaland, the physical and the metaphysical. I visited your school in Maronda Mashanu where the children filed out into the central square to line up under a huge baobab tree, singing as they marched 'We walk in the light of God'. Leonard was tired by now, so he left Moses and Horatio to accompany me to your other school beneath the two huge gum trees of Wreningham, waving us off from the gate of his homestead. As soon as we were out of sight a change came over the two men, like schoolboys away from the teacher. Moses asked me about women in Britain and Horatio about my job. After half an hour walking along the road we stopped at a beer hall, a bare concrete building with faded Coca Cola signs painted on it. Inside was a crude bar, stacks of Scud beers and crates of Castle Lager. Moses and Horatio bought a couple of bottles each, opening one with their teeth and stuffing the other one in their pockets, giving me a wink as they did. At the school hundreds of children stared at me cautiously before rushing up as one to shake my hand and ask 'Makadi ni?'

On the Wednesday morning a mass was held at the new church in Maronda Mashanu. I walked there with Leonard while Sabethiel went on ahead of us with a canvas bag of altar objects clanking over his shoulder and his too-big Wellingtons slapping against his shins as he ran across the fields.

The church itself is a simple block building beside an ancient tree with a milk churn hanging from its lowest branch serving as a bell. Inside, Leonard changes into his preaching stole before carefully preparing the altar and supplicating himself in front of it, on his knees, his forehead resting on his hands and his hands resting in turn on the concrete of the altar step. A tail-less lizard runs a slalom between the silver paten, the candlesticks and the communion cup.

The church that morning is completely full. The women of the Mothers' Union line the pews in their uniforms of bright blue head-scarves and aprons, and the old men in dark suits and deacons' stoles play tall drums and shake maracas. Your name is mentioned again and again, in songs, in the sermon, in thanks and in prayers. The harmony singing is beautiful, weaving into itself and building to a crescendo until some of the women break from the pews and dance in front of the altar. I think of the reserved choir boys in Oxford. Leonard looks over it all, beaming and stamping his feet in time to the music.

After the service Leonard introduces me to some of the congregation, often in terms of their relationship to death rather than to other people. 'This is Mary, her husband died two years ago, she had four children and lost three.'

Old edentate men and women introduce themselves to me according to whether you married them to their spouse, baptised them in the river, or did both. One woman's back is bent with age and her face is obscured by a shawl over her head and a coloured cloth tied across her forehead. She grips my hand in both of hers and speaks to me in a hoarse whisper. Leonard bends to her mouth and then looks at me and says, 'She says she loved Father Cripps like her own father.' I ask him why her face is covered and he says simply, 'Because leprosy took it away, yes.'

Flash bulbs of lightning at the open windows that line both walls of the church signal the coming of a storm, which is soon above us, the thunder cracking so hard that I feel it in my ribs. The downpour sheets the sky dark, filling in the windows with panes of rain. Those who were outside come running in, and are joined by groups of other people who had been driving on the road in open trucks, bundling in through the main door, their shoulders hunched and their clothes soaked tight to their skin. The church is packed, and the storm continues raging about us, flinging rain through the windows and exploding its thunder in the clouds. The noise of the water on the roof is so loud we have to shout to talk to each other, but then above it all I hear one woman's voice start to sing. The shuffle of a maraca joins her and soon the congregation and the drenched refugees from the road are all singing, meeting the storm's hymn with their own.

◇

Four days after walking your road to Leonard's farm, I am walking it back again, although this time I am not alone. Sabethiel walks beside me, as Leonard insisted he should, to take me to the bus stop in town where I will catch a bus south to Masvingo. Sabethiel speaks no English, and I speak no Shona, so we walk together silently under the growing heat of a morning sun and a clear sky, your red road crunching under our feet.

In the space of these four days my idea of you has changed from an elusive ancestor I pieced together in photos, letters, poems, to a remembered man, fleshed out with the stories and memories of Leonard and the others in Maronda Mashanu. The manifestation of your life in these memories has made you clearer to me in many ways, but more of a mystery in others. My intuition that you lived partly as a pursued man in Mashonaland has deepened, I feel more strongly than ever that your life of sacrifice was also somehow a life of personal penance. I know from the histories and the accounts I have read that the men and women who came to Africa a hundred years ago all had their reasons to come here: riches, God, hope, health. But for most there was often a reason to leave their homelands too, and it is this other reason I am looking for in you. I know why you came here, but why did you leave? I can't be sure, only knowing what I do, but I am increasingly certain that your shadow granddaughter, who even Leonard said he knew nothing about, is a residue, a living proof of that reason.

And there is a name too. A new name that has fed my curiosity, one I have not previously encountered in your story. Before I left for Maronda Mashanu I spent two days in the dark wood reading rooms of the Zimbabwe National Archives, all the time I was allowed without the necessary permit from the Ministry of Information. In the archives I found more of your history. More letters, more manuscripts, more photographs (even one of my father aged four sitting on the knee of your brother, William). In one folder, between a map of the Sabi Valley and a school exercise book with your poems written across its grid of blue squares, I found your Last Will and Testament. It was in this will I found the new name. The will is short, sparse and simple, and the name appears in a codicil, added at a later date. It is the only name on the paper other than yours.

It is this name and the will that contains it that occupies my mind that day as I take a rattling bus from Chivhu further south to Masvingo, then a battered taxi from the bus station on to the medieval ruins of Great Zimbabwe, where I set up my tent inside the huge walls of the ancient stone complex. I am still thinking of the name and your will the next morning when I wake before sunrise and walk up to the imposing structure of the ruins' Great Enclosure. Entering into its circle through the west entrance, I sit on a pile of blue-grey stone beneath the tall conical tower at the heart of the edifice. I am alone. It is early, quiet, and for once the air is cool, empty of the heat that fills the day. I wait for the sun, which comes, blood-orange red, rising from behind the outer wall, picking out in silhouette the thin shards of stone planted like battlements, and the tops of the trees that have found root inside the shelter of this African castle. The sun rises higher, clearing the walls altogether and lighting the ground inside the enclosure. With it comes birdsong, long, urgent calls and higher signature tunes, played again and again on the clear air, and heat, which finds itself on my skin until the flesh on my forearms warms and the first pinpricks of sweat tingle between the hairs.

I sit there, at the centre of the ruins, almost ninety years after you sat here taking in the quality of these circles, pillars and domes so you could echo them when you built your church in that clearing beneath the kopje in Maronda Mashanu. In travelling here I have made that link complete in my mind. The shape of these ruins, and the shape of your church, Great Zimbabwe passed on into Maronda Mashanu, and then replicated again and again in the mission stations you built across Mashonaland. The pieces of your life coming together, more fragments joining to make your history whole. But now there is another fragment: this name, printed clearly in your will. The only name other than yours. The woman it belongs to is another part of your story, but one which echoes nowhere else in your life as I know it. Unless, of course the name is already an echo, a resonance of your past, and it is the cause of its existence there, not any consequence that I should be looking for.

I leave the Great Enclosure and make my way back to my tent lower in the valley. Coming over the lip of a hillock I disturb a baboon eating in a tree. I stop and it hangs for a second like a dark question mark, one arm hooked around a branch, before dropping to the ground and hunch-running over the horizon, leaving me looking at nothing but the swaying leaves where it has been. And that is how it is here, following your story in Zimbabwe one hundred years too late, picking up the fragments, uncovering your tracks. Fact and fiction, myth and history. Glimpses of things, suggestions in the corner of the eye which disappear or dissolve when you try to look at them head on.

1915
The Last Will and Testament
of Arthur Shearly Cripps

I desire to be buried without a coffin or monument on
the hill Makirri Maure on the farm Muckle Neuk.
The farms of Money Putt and Maronda Mashanu shall be
preserved as mission locations, free of any rent or
labour tax to native tenants residing thereon.

CODICIL

I the Reverend Arthur Shearly Cripps, do hereby give
and bequeath to <u>Mrs Ada Neeves</u> of <u>Icklesham, Rye,</u>
<u>Sussex</u>, England free and unencumbered by any death
duties, or should the said Ada Neeves predecease me,
then to her husband, or in the event of his death, to
her children in equal shares the sum of £25 Sterling.

Signed with his own initials when he was blind.

Maronda Mashanu, Mashonaland, Southern Rhodesia

——◇——

In the church at Icklesham. At her organ practice. Was that the first time he had seen her? Was that the first time they met? No, he doubts it. They must have met before. At services, in the village, when Reverend Churton took him on a round of the farms to introduce him.

'May I introduce Mr Cripps, our new deacon?' Then aside, usually to the man of the house, 'A graduate of Oxford, and a blue to boot, you know?'

So no, not the first time they had met. But now, remembering, more than fifty years later, he thinks of it as the first. He remembers the light through the five frames of the chancel window. The way it fell over her where she played at the organ. And her singing . . . No, he doesn't. He remembers she *was* singing, but he does not remember her singing. That has gone now. Now, in this rondavel, blind, he lives in a world of sound but he is deaf to the sounds of the past. Words, songs, they all pass so briefly. So few burn or brand on memory. But she was singing, he knows that. At the top of her voice, thinking she was alone. But she wasn't alone. He was watching her, one hand still on the iron handle of the porch door.

Ada Sargent. But of course he didn't know her name then. Just that he had disturbed her at her practice, and that he was as shocked as she was by their sudden meeting. By the silence in the church after the organ's last note and by the other's face, surprised, wide-eyed, staring at him through the frame of the chancel archway, the two stone tablets of the Ten Commandments laid in the wall above them.

Then they had spoken, introduced themselves. He probably made apologies for disturbing her, he can't remember. He knows she called him 'sir' and the sound of that word on her lips made a hollow in his chest. He didn't want her to call him *sir*, he wanted to be close to her, even then, and that word *sir* did nothing but set them apart. But that is all. He can remember little else of what they said.

She was beautiful. Seventeen years old. He can't see her young face now, but he knows she was beautiful. Blue eyes like his and blond hair;

skin the colour of the ivory she kept her fingers on, as if to let go of those keys would mean disaster.

He'd left her to her practise that morning. Gone and busied himself in the vestry. But in the end he had just sat there, in the darkness, listening to her play and sing to herself, trying to decide whether to go out and speak to her again. He hadn't; there had been no need.

Falling in love with her had been so easy. It happened over that summer, and again he can't remember how: the words, the expressions, even their first kiss. All he knows is that there *were* words, expressions and kisses. He knows they happened but not how. He knows he had been happy, but not how. Perhaps it is always this way. Perhaps to be able to recall happiness in all its sensation would be too painful, even at the distance of fifty years. But it frustrates him that he cannot recall, relive, just remember. Vaguely, softly: a dull ache rather than the sharp stab he desires.

He had been lonely in Icklesham. It was his first posting, deacon at the town's stocky Norman church. He liked the country, the low thorn hedges, the patchwork of arable land, the off-set roofs of the oast houses. The pearl-white sky that bore the light of the sea and the way the gulls came squalling in to the freshly ploughed fields, spattering the brown with their white like dashes of milk spilt across a table.

He had done some good walking there. To the hospital in Rye, along country lanes stumbling upon obscure peasants' cottages, stone boxes with straw lids (not unlike his own rondavel, he realises). And he had enjoyed the work too. But he had been lonely, he remembers that. And that is why she had been so perfect, penetrating his solitude with her beauty and her smile.

To her, he supposed, he must have appeared quite exotic. Educated, a Trinity man. But to him, it was she who was exotic. And to think he had accepted so easily the matching of her love with his! As if it would always be that way. Only the young can meet such fortune with casual ease, he knows that now. Only the young can be unsurprised by love. If he had known then, when he was young, what he knows now, old, then maybe it would have been different. Maybe it would have happened differently and maybe his remembering would not be so painful, a dull ache, throbbing behind his blind eyes and beating in time with his heart.

She liked him to read to her, he remembers that.

'*Beauty is truth and truth beauty – that is all ye know on earth, and all ye need to know.*'

A book's shadow across his face which he takes away, letting the sun into his eyes which he shuts. Flashes of orange motes on the inside of his eyelids, the sound of a river beyond his feet and her hairpins, digging into his skin beneath his shirt as she rolls her head to look at the sky.

He lies on his back, the grass tickling the back of his neck with his arms out, palms up. The heat of the day collects in his hands until he feels as though he is holding two glowing balls of sunlight, an orb of warmth in each, tingling in the bowls of his fingers.

They talked about his grave, Keats' grave. How they would visit it together one day. She'd said she would be able to tell it was a poet's grave, she'd sense the words in the soil. Then his hand on her head, stroking down towards her temple, the heat of the sun in her hair. His other hand, free of the book now, on her chest. Her skin beneath her blouse and her heartbeat beneath her skin, distant, as if arriving in her body from deep in the ground.

The sun is lower, the light less dazzling in his eyes. The buzz, stop, buzz of bluebottles over the picnic and the sound of her tearing blades of grass, scattering them in the wind. Rooks, cawing in the branches of a tree. Then a watch, his watch, opening the silver case, opening the day to time which runs on and on like the river below them.

And then she is by the river and he is watching her bend to its water, washing her hands. It divides about her wrists and she lets out a sigh of shock at its coldness. Then she is shaking her hands above the water, the droplets catching the last of the sun as they fall.

And his happiness is fragile inside him, humming, laced with a fear of its ending; a thin ice of joy grown across the cavity of his ribs.

> She dwells with beauty – beauty that must die;
> And joy, whose hand is ever at his lips
> Bidding adieu; and aching pleasure nigh.

And as she turns from the river, the sun's light corposant about her shadowed body, he decides he will take joy's hand from his lips and he will ask her to marry him.

She walks back towards him and holds out her hand. He speaks and she replies. Her mouth moves, the lips move, but he hears nothing. Already the image is fading. He cannot remember what he said or what she said; the sounds have gone and now the vision has too. Only feeling remains, the memory of sensation: the cooling of the breeze, the imprint of the grass on his arms, the river's coldness resonating in her hands, lapidary, like marble over her skin.

British Lake Force Camp, Kisumu, British East Africa

———◇———

Captain Richard Meinertzhagen angled the point of his sheath knife under the little toenail of his left foot and worked the blade in tiny movements, left and right; he brought the foot nearer with his left hand, bent to the toe and tried again. There was a jigger flea buried in there, a dark dot beneath the opaque nail, and he wanted to dislodge her before he embarked on one of the four steamers sitting low in the lake under their loads of artillery, supplies and braying mules. This harvest of jiggers had become something of a daily ritual since his arrival back in Africa. He'd already extracted more than twenty today, working the sore red spots out from under the skin like stubborn winkles from their shells. A couple of the officers had lost most of their toes to the parasites and hundreds of the soldiers, European and askari, hobbled about on raw, infected feet.

With a sharp prick of pain the flea came free, bringing with it a little pus from the hollow it had made in his toe. He examined it briefly on the point of his knife, just able to make out its hinged legs and its bloated body, spots of his own blood on its underside. Flicking it away, he wiped the knife on his shorts and looked up at the scene on the shore below.

From where he sat on a raised patch of ground above the lake, the small port town at his back, the embarkation process was mapped out beneath him. Immediately in front of the squat steamers the 28th Mountain Battery had lined up their two 75mm field guns ready for loading. Further along the shore the depleted 29th Punjabs and the worn-looking Loyal North Lancs were both preparing for battle, assembling their packs and cleaning their rifles. Nearer to where he sat, set back from the shore, the bizarre collection of men that made up the 25th Royal Fusiliers were also moving about their camp, noticeably older and larger than the other soldiers, even from this distance.

Beyond these regiment camps the open stables cut two straight lines into the tall blond grass, black quivering patches of flies shuddering above the heads of the mules and packhorses. Past these, order finally gave way to chaos with the tattered sprawl of the carriers' encampment spreading out along the shore, tapering northwards into the distance. Here, the hundreds of porters and their families carried on their daily lives in their temporary homes and shacks, a squalling, littered tag of civilian life attached to the military camp. Closer to where he was sitting on the hill, stacks of ammunition and food supplies lay in piles, cooks' fires smoked into the still evening air and a sullen heap of sandbags was being passed along a chain of askaris to the nearest steamer, where a pair of British officers packed them around a Vickers machine-gun positioned on the foredeck. To the left of where the steamers were docked, beyond the train track and its stalled wooden carriages, the field hospital tent was overflowing with sick cases, rows of men lain out on the ground on canvas stretchers. More than half the force in the hospital and hardly a bullet or a bayonet wound among them. Disease had wiped them out, not the enemy. Blackwater fever, dysentery and guinea worms, not bullets, shrapnel or shells.

As a professional soldier who had served in British uniform since 1899 Meinertzhagen had found this particular war displeasing. The conflict was just over ten months old, and as yet, all he had experienced was failure, incompetence and frustration. Not his own personal failure, which he would never have allowed, but failure by association. The British army in Africa had spent seven months at war with the much smaller, less well equipped German *Schutztruppe* led by General Von Lettow, and yet Von Lettow and his troops remained undefeated and German East Africa remained just that – German.

This was Meinertzhagen's second time in Africa. Thirteen years ago he had served as an officer with the 3rd King's African Rifles, during which time he'd distinguished himself as a vicious bush fighter against two particularly stubborn native tribes. In 1906 he transferred back to India and he was at the Staff College in Quetta when this war was announced. A few weeks later when the War Office in London decided to send the Indian Army to deal with the German colonies, Meinertzhagen, as the only member of the Indian Force with previous African experience, became the Expeditionary Force's Intelligence Officer. He was thirty-six years old, experienced, still fit and at the height of his military powers. He could, he felt, look forward to a challenging and rewarding campaign. Seven months on, he thought as he sheathed his knife, pulled his woollen socks up his calves and reached for his boots and puttees, he could not have been more wrong.

It started with the selection of the troops in India. Perhaps unsurprisingly the cream of the Indian Army had been despatched to France and the Western Front, and when Meinertzhagen saw the regiments collected on the docks at Bombay he realised that they, Indian Expeditionary Force B, had been left with the detritus. The ten regiments, battalions and detachments that boarded the ancient troop ships swaying drunkenly on the swell of the harbour were a rag-tag bunch, a rush job thrown together by desk clerks who he suspected had never seen an Indian soldier, let alone fought with one. On the two-week voyage across the Indian Ocean to East Africa, Meinertzhagen, writing from the relative comfort of a converted P&O liner, noted in his diary that the sepoys lying and retching in the holds of the other transports were '*the worst in India*' and that their '*senior officers are nearer to fossils than active leaders of men*'. He tried to bolster his hopes by admitting to himself that at least some of the other regiments in Force B had a degree of military spine. The Loyal North Lancs were as good a British fighting regiment as any, the Kashmir Rifles and the 101st Bombay Grenadiers had both seen good service, and he hoped that the KAR regiments they were joining in Africa had drilled their askaris to a decent level. These native soldiers would at least, he thought, have knowledge of the bush and the country.

On arrival in Africa Meinertzhagen's dismay at the quality of Force B's troops was soon matched by his frustration with their ineffective commanders, including General Stewart, who was in command here at the lake. The general was a tall man with a gentle face, an ineffective chin and a habit of clearing his throat before he spoke that reminded Meinertzhagen more of a scholar than a soldier. Meinertzhagen reached for his diary, a battered leather-bound book lying beside him which he kept on his person at all times. Pulling a pencil from his shirt pocket he added a note to today's entry:

Throughout my service I have always regarded a war with Germany as a certainty and as the climax of all training.

He paused, looked up at the preparations below him, at Stewart's well-meaning, charming but ineffectual manner, and bent his head to the book again. Licking the pencil, he finished the note:

And here I am in the rottenest side-show imaginable, rotten troops and rotten leaders and in a colony where from the Governor downwards there is no feeling of patriotism.

With a short sigh he pocketed the pencil and the diary, buckled on his Sam Browne and stood up. Standing with one hand on his hip and the other scratching the stubble on his chin, he gathered a glob of phlegm at the back of his throat, brought it up into his mouth with a growl and spat heavily onto the grass before making his way down the slope to make his own preparations for the activities of the coming night.

Meinertzhagen's early misgivings about Force B's prospects proved to be well-founded. The combination of poorly prepared soldiers and equally poor commanders had provided the perfect overture to the disaster that was the battle of Tanga last November. The battle was the first decisive British attack in the African theatre, and, Meinertzhagen thought as he strolled down towards the lake and his tent, would very possibly go down in history as their most embarrassing failure too. From the outset he thought it was bound for catastrophe. The confident clinking of brandy and whisky glasses in the smoky saloon of the command ship following General Aitken's eve-of-battle speech had done little to cheer him. Neither was he convinced by the officers' shared assurances to each other that the Hun wouldn't put up much of a fight, that the town might be won without a single shot fired and the whole thing over before Christmas.

Having failed to convince Aitken of the need to scout out the deep mangroves on the landing beach, and having listened to him refuse the help of his old company, the experienced 3rd KAR, Meinertzhagen had retired to his cabin and confided in his diary once more: 'I tremble to think what may happen,' he wrote, 'if we meet with serious opposition.'

They did meet with serious opposition, and over the following three days Meinertzhagen experienced the lowest ebb of his military career. It began with a misplaced exhibition of British fair play. Aitken, deciding to honour a naval truce of coastal neutrality, allowed the naval commander, F. W. Caulfield, to sail into the port of Tanga a little after dawn on 2 November to inform Governor Auracher that hostilities would commence unless he surrendered within the hour.

Three hours later, looking through the flat view of his binoculars, Meinertzhagen could still see the Imperial Eagle fluttering over the neat whitewashed houses of the town. A pointless British mine-sweeping exercise gave the German commanders another twenty-four hours to bring in reinforcements from up the line at Moshi, and Meinertzhagen despaired as his troops only started piling off the transports and wading through the warm water of the landing beach the following night. Sitting on a mangrove root on the beach, he had turned to his diary again, writing by the full moon which also illuminated the massing British troops and their transport ships:

> So here we are, with only a small portion of our force, risking a landing in the face of an enemy of unknown strength and on a beach which has not been reconnoitred and which looks like a rank mangrove swamp.

Three days later the entire British convoy steamed away in retreat from that same beach, leaving behind them the arms of three companies being inventoried by the German quartermasters and more than 700 British dead and wounded. Officers, sepoys, porters, the British corpses scattered the streets of the town, the plantations and the surrounding scrublands like a cargo of discarded dummies dropped from a passing plane. Meinertzhagen had killed two of these British dead himself. They were both 13th Rajputs, who along with the rest of their company had bolted at the first sign of heavy German machine-gun fire. With the enemy's bullets whining in the air about him and kicking up spurts of dust at his feet, Meinertzhagen had tried to stem the panicked retreat, first with his boot and then with his pistol. A terrified Rajput had drawn his sword when Meinertzhagen ordered him to advance, so he shot him through the head. The second wasn't even able to stand, but was crouched like a child behind a wall, crying into his hands. Meinertzhagen was so disgusted he shot him there and then through the back of the neck, more out of anger than in punishment.

The rest of the battle was equally disastrous. At one point the firing disturbed a colony of bees nesting in African hives, hollow logs tied to the trees. The advancing British soldiers were scattered both by the swarm and then by the German machine-guns that sprayed their retreat.

It was all over a couple of days later and on the morning of 5

November Meinertzhagen found himself suffering the ignominy of being treated to a breakfast by officers of the *Schutztruppe* as he visited their headquarters to negotiate the British surrender and withdrawal. The Germans laid on beer, eggs, cream and asparagus, and talked over the battle with him as if it had been a football game. Meinertzhagen, however, could not see it in quite the same way. He'd had to walk to the German headquarters through streets littered with the British wounded calling out to him for help, speaking in their native tongues of Hindi, Swahili, Xhosa, Urdu. In their distress, though, they'd all sounded the same; pain, as he had learnt long ago, was a language that crossed all borders.

Entering the German compound he'd seen what he first thought was a row of bamboo planting poles stuck in a deep furrow of earth. He'd looked again, wondering who would be planting here. But then he saw the furrow was sown not with seeds, but with men. The bodies of fifteen British sepoys, lying face down, each with his own bayonet stuck in his back.

Once the details of their withdrawal had been agreed Meinertzhagen left the German officers to their breakfast. He was on his way back to the British beach when he was surprised by the crack of a rifle report, then a second later by his sun helmet flying sideways from his head. He spun around and saw a German askari who, not recognising his flag of truce, had shot at him from point-blank range. Meinertzhagen felt a flood of anger rush through him. He was angry at the fiasco this battle had become, at the generals, at being on the losing side, at the wounded lying in the street and now at this askari who had shot at him. Before the soldier could fire another round, Meinertzhagen strode towards him and, reversing his grip on the truce flag, jabbed its pole into the askari's stomach. The man bent double, and as he did Meinertzhagen wrenched the rifle from his grasp and stabbed him through the ribs with his own bayonet, thinking of the sepoys in the furrow as he did. Leaving the man curled on the dusty ground, clutching at the barrel of his rifle and choking on his own blood, Meinertzhagen went back to pick up his helmet. He examined the bullet hole with his forefinger, put it back on, glanced towards the writhing askari, then carried on down towards the beach and the British transports, swinging his truce flag as he walked.

After the failure at Tanga and the disastrous fighting at Jessin, where again Von Lettow had the pleasure of parading defeated British officers and commending them on their gallantry, the morale of the British forces was badly shaken. Kitchener was furious and advised the British leaders in Nairobi to steer clear of offensive actions and stick to defending their positions. So rather than purging Von Lettow and his troops from German East Africa, Force B had spent the last seven months having to satisfy themselves with just containing them instead. Rather than wiping out the *Schutztruppe* before Christmas, they had merely tolerated and endured its presence. For Meinertzhagen, this was a sorry state of affairs, and one which rubbed raw on his nerves. British naval dominance meant the Germans had no supply access, and no reserve troops to call upon. Every casualty for them was crucial. The British had more troops and were better armed, and yet despite this Von Lettow conducted his guerrilla warfare against the British railway and any other target he could reach. It was like having a gun and no bullet, like hearing your prey on the other side of the wall and being forbidden to go and hunt it.

So far, Meinertzhagen's intelligence work had been his only success of the war; he was particularly proud of the network of African scouts and agents he had nurtured in German East Africa. The jewel of his intelligence work, however, was a practice he called his 'dirty paper method'. Through this he had acquired the signature of every German officer, details of troop movements, private letters, notes and coded material, all brought to him smeared and crumpled in the hands of his African agents who cleaned the German latrines. Meinertzhagen couldn't believe his luck, or how careful the Germans were with their communications and code switching and yet how free they were with their choice of toilet paper.

Rifling in German shit, however successful, still didn't feel much like a war to Meinertzhagen and to date he'd only had one truly satisfying encounter with the enemy. It was last Christmas Day. Meinertzhagen had seen German troops at Christmas time before. He knew they grew sentimental and relaxed during the season, and he took this opportunity to take matters into his own hands and go on a raid across the frontier. He was accompanied by another European, Major Drought, an English farmer from British East Africa who'd raised an irregular unit of wild Masi whom he commanded over like a tribal god. This unit was known around the lake as the Skin Corps, their own skins being the full extent of their uniforms.

Drought brought fifteen of his Skin Corps with him on Meinertzhagen's raid across the frontier that Christmas Day. Padding through the bush next to these lean warriors, stripped of all his gear except a small rucksack, his rifle and ammunition, Meinertzhagen had at last felt he was at war. He revelled in how silently all seventeen of them crept through the grass and the thorn trees, his own breath barely audible in his ear, and he marvelled at the easy control Drought had over these wild Africans. The unsuspecting German outpost they found was unguarded. Open fires smoked between a loose gathering of tents, and Meinertzhagen could see, through the blades of grass that covered him, the Germans' rifles propped together in neat groups of three at the centre of the camp. Close to where the British raiding party lay in the grass a *Schutztruppe* officer crouched over a hole in the ground behind a green canvas screen, his breeches around his ankles and his shirt tucked up under his armpits, showing his white, freckled lower back. Two others were playing cards on an upturned crate outside their tent, while a group of askaris sat around a fire talking and drinking from clay mugs.

Meinertzhagen led the way, moving silently to within a few paces of the card-playing officers, then rushing them with fixed bayonets. Everyone got his man, and Drought excelled himself, stabbing three. Hearing a noise from one of the adjoining tents, Meinertzhagen pulled his bayonet from between the ribs of an officer at the card crate and rushed in through its canvas flaps. A large man was sitting up in a bed beside a table laid with the full trappings of a Christmas dinner. Meinertzhagen covered the officer with his rifle and told him to put up his hands. The German, an older man with greying hair, looked astonished and fumbled with one hand under his blanket. Meinertzhagen fired immediately, the only shot of the raid, and the German dropped back on the bed, a patch of blood spreading above his pyjama pocket like a carnation growing at his breast. On inspection Meinertzhagen found the man had been reaching for his spectacles, not his gun. Hearing the gunshot, Drought joined Meinertzhagen in the tent and the two of them sat down to the Christmas dinner while the Skin Corps outside guarded the nine prisoners and fifteen dead. They were finishing the Christmas pudding as the first flies began to gather on the dead man behind them, multiplying in black over the spreading stain of red like the black seeds of a growing poppy.

That Christmas Day raid had the been the last piece of positive action that Meinertzhagen had seen. Since then the War Office had reiterated its position that the British troops in East Africa must remain on the defensive. And so for seven months the soldiers of Force B had done little more than endure the flies, the heat, the camp food, and collectively lick their wounds while their leaders came to accept that this war was not the game they had thought it might be.

Until tonight. Tonight, Meinertzhagen thought as he strode on down towards the body of the camp, his war was starting again. Kitchener had been persuaded to let them off the leash, and they were heading out for the hunt again. Their prey, the German port town of Bukoba and its wireless tower, lay on the western shore of the lake, just 200 miles away. Tonight they would no longer be defending. Tonight they would attack. Tonight, they would be an army again, and this thought alone lent Meinertzhagen's stride a revived energy that he hadn't felt for months.

As he came into camp Meinertzhagen spotted the chaplain, Father Cripps, walking in from the direction of the Fusilier tents. From this distance he looked like a regular soldier, khaki shorts and a khaki jacket. Only the faint gleam of the bronze crosses on his lapels and his dog collar gave him away for what he was. Seeing him now unsettled Meinertzhagen; he didn't like it when the vultures flapped about on the masts of the steamers, stretching their raw necks, and he didn't like seeing priests before battle for the same reason. Both were too portentous in times of war.

Reaching his tent, Meinertzhagen bowed into its dark interior, sat heavily on his folding canvas stool and shouted out to his askari batman to bring him his dinner. He leaned back and breathed in. Canvas, leather and steel. The smells of war. He felt his battle excitement rising in him, a dipping in his stomach and a tingling sensation running along the nerves of his limbs. Reaching onto his bed he picked up his revolver, black and heavy in his hand. Taking a cloth from a hook in the centre pole he laid it on his knee and began to clean it, rubbing his thumb and forefinger hard through its curves and hollows.

◇

Arthur had been looking for Tendai in the carriers' camp for over an hour. Passing between the shambas, shacks, torn tents and open fires with pots of sadza and pans of tremoring peanuts propped over their flames, he scanned the faces. There were so many his mind had trouble keeping up with his eyes. Women, children, babies swaddled to their mother's backs, Indian coolies, gaunt men and boys of every African tribe. He looked at them all, but recognised none of them as Tendai. A few he had seen before, Christian converts who had been to some of his services, but most were new to him. The ranks of the carrier corps seemed to be filled as quickly as overwork and disease depleted them.

Tendai had been recruited into the carrier corps late in 1914. The British Army did not consider the Mashona one of the 'martial races' suitable for combat so the Enkeldoorn area had been saved the recruiting officers of the KAR. Porters, however, could come from any tribe or creed and Arthur had soon noticed that large numbers of young men were absent from the villages and his church services. And now, with the help of Reverend Liebenberg, Tendai's mother had written to Arthur to say that he too had been recruited and she had not heard from him for several months. She thought he was at the lake but as yet Arthur hadn't found him or heard mention of his name.

Ever since that night when he'd softly translated Gufa's speech to him, Arthur had noticed that Tendai was a child of rare intelligence. Over the years he'd been a regular attendee at his school and although farming his mother's land had taken up much of his time Arthur had fostered real hopes of recommending him to the Bishop for ordination. But then the war came and now it looked as if like himself, Tendai had been drawn into its vacuum.

Reaching the far end of the carriers' camp he looked closely at one more young man struggling back from the shore with a bucket of water. He studied his features but like all the others, he wasn't Tendai, so turning back towards the main camp he began to make his return, aware that he should hold a communion before the steamers were boarded for the journey across the water to Bukoba.

Coming out of the carriers' camp he walked down the long line of open stables where a group of men were dragging another dead mule from its box. Its slack muscles hung off its bones like half-empty sacks of grain and its open eyes stared through a film of green fluid. Another victim of the tsetse fly. Arthur walked on, hearing the intermittent drag and slump of its hooves across the ground as the men heaved it away from the stables. As he got nearer the main camp he passed the orderly tents of the 25th Royal Fusiliers, where he heard a man shouting. He carried on walking, shouting being common enough in these camps. But then, as the shouting continued, he realised the man was shouting at him. He stopped and turned towards the voice.

'Hello there! It's Father, er . . . Father . . . isn't it?'

A short man with balding, greying hair and a salt-and-pepper moustache was striding out towards him from the Fusiliers' tents, his hand outstretched in greeting. Arthur didn't think he recognised him, but there was something in his voice that loosened a memory. The man, who wore the uniform of a Fusiliers officer, reached Arthur where he stood on the edge of the camp. He was red in the face from running to catch up with him. He looked up at Arthur, as if checking for something on his face, and then, apparently at a loss as to what else to do in the absence of his name, he smiled. Arthur smiled back down at him.

'Cripps,' he said. 'Father Cripps.'

'Yes, that's it. Cripps, of course.' He offered his hand again. His face was that of a man who had been larger and fuller than he was now. Thinned by heat or illness, the skin hung from his cheekbones and shook around his jowls and his throat when he spoke. 'Pruen, S. Tristam Pruen, MD. Zanzibar,' he added helpfully. And then Arthur remembered. It was hard to forget an introduction like that. His visit to Frank in Zanzibar. The Cathedral built over the slave cells. The Princess's palace, the open balcony, the warm night beyond the candle's burn. The Governor's love story about Salome and her German. It all felt such a long time ago. And Pruen, sitting at the end of the table offering his African advice. He still had his book somewhere. In his trunk in his rondavel in Mashonaland probably. That too, he thought, felt far away now.

'Yes, sorry,' Arthur said, taking Pruen's offered hand. 'I should have remembered.'

'Nonsense, of course you shouldn't. Must have been over fifteen years ago, and a lot's happened since then.' Pruen cast a glance around the spread military camps, the steamers sitting grey and bleak on the lake, a vivid red and orange sunset firing up the sky behind them. 'But you're still with us nevertheless, eh, Father?'

'Sorry?'

'In Africa. When we met all that time ago you were starting a two-year tour as I remember.' He smiled again, but this time with pride. 'Still got my memory you see. Can't afford to lose that in my game.'

Arthur nodded, not entirely sure what game that was. 'Yes, yes, still here. Somehow that lure of a country parsonage never developed for me.' His attempt at a joke fell weakly on his own ears. 'And two years, well, it didn't seem enough time to, I mean, well, even get started on the work I wanted to do.'

'Still in Southern Rhodesia, though?' Pruen asked, hooking his thumbs into the straps of his Sam Browne.

'Yes, Mashonaland, near Enkeldoorn'

'Oh, I know the land around there.' Pruen looked off up the little hill by the lake and narrowed his eyes, engaging his memory again. Looking back at Arthur with another proud smile, he said, 'Wreningham is the mission station there, am I right?'

'Yes, you are.' Arthur laughed. 'But I'm not there actually, not any more anyway. I have my own mission farm now, near Wreningham.'

'Have you now?' Pruen asked, like a father showing admiration for some feat performed by his son. 'Well done, well done.'

Out of the corner of his eye Arthur became aware of another figure approaching them from the direction of the khaki tents of the Fusiliers' camp. Pruen sensed the figure too and turned to see who was joining them. The man was approaching with a quick, confident stride that belied the age written across his face. He was taller than Pruen, but shared the characteristic bearing of a body that had once been heavier, the same loose skin about his neck and chin. He also, like Pruen, wore the uniform of a Fusiliers officer, but had adapted it to the style of a bush ranger, his sleeves rolled to above the elbow and a beaten soft leather hat instead of the regulation solar helmet. The hat's wide brim was pinned up on one side like a hunter's, beneath which a pair of bushy white eyebrows and a white goatee sat in shocking contrast to the tanned skin of his face. As he got closer Arthur noticed that whatever emaciation had thinned his face and waist had somehow left his arms and chest intact. They were solid and broad, like those of a labouring man.

Pruen greeted the new arrival with the eagerness of a dog meeting his master. 'Ah! Lieutenant Selous! Come here, come here, I want you to meet an old friend of mine.'

Arthur couldn't help smiling at the sudden promotion in intimacy despite the fifteen years since their last meeting.

'Lieutenant Frederick Selous,' he continued, gesturing on either side to the two of them. 'The Reverend Father Cripps. Father Cripps,

Lieutenant Selous – although I suspect the lieutenant needs no introduction?'

Pruen raised the inflexion at the end of the sentence, turning it into a question. And he was right. The Lieutenant did not need any introduction, Arthur had indeed heard of Selous before. It was almost impossible to live in Charter country and not hear of him. His name was something of a legend in Southern Rhodesia. Second only to that of Rhodes himself, his was the most often mentioned in settler circles when the nostalgic fires of frontier memories were being stoked. For the last fifty years he had been the country's foremost big-game hunter and naturalist, famously guiding President Roosevelt on his African safari. He had a reputation as a prolific writer, was a gifted musician and at the age of sixty-four was already a veteran of the Matabele wars of the 1890s. Arthur had, however, first paid attention to his name not because of his talent for action, but rather his fierce opposition to it. He remembered reading some letters Selous had written to the *Salisbury Herald* objecting to the Boer campaign and the treatment of Boer prisoners and their families. The letters made a deep impression on Arthur at the time. He had once overheard a friend of Selous' describe the hunter as 'a moral antiseptic in a country where men are not saints'. It was a welcome surprise to find the same man standing before him now.

The dull clatter of the loading process continued on the lake shore behind them and the flies kept up a dog-fighting buzz around their heads as the two men shook hands.

'Yes, your name goes before you, Lieutenant,' Arthur said. 'It's a pleasure to meet you in person.'

'And if you're the Cripps I think you are, then it's an even greater pleasure to meet you. I've read your work – I admire it. *Bay Tree Country* especially.'

Pruen looked on, beaming, like a chemist who had elicited a satisfying reaction from the introduction of two unknown substances.

'And I'd like to talk further,' Selous continued, 'but I'm afraid I've come to break up your reunion.' He turned to Pruen. 'The men are almost ready, Pruen. Driscoll's getting jumpy. We should have them fall in.'

A seriousness fell like a veil across Pruen's face and Arthur suddenly thought how old he looked. How old they both looked. Too old. Too full of examined life to go and risk it all before the German guns. In Flanders they were sacrificing boys. Here, it was grand-fathers.

Selous turned back to Arthur. 'Will you be blessing us on our way, Father? "Onward Christian Soldiers" and all that?'

'Well, yes, I will, but it needn't end there. I'm coming along as well.'

'You're coming with us? To Bukoba?'

'Yes.'

The two older men raised their eyebrows in unison. Selous nodded slowly and looked at Arthur from under the brim of his hat. 'Are you now? Well, there's a thing. A parson coming along for the ride. Good for you, Father, good for you.'

Maronda Mashanu, Mashonaland,
Southern Rhodesia

——◇——

'Good for you, Baba, good for you.'

Fortune's voice reaches him as if down a long corridor filled with cotton wool. Faint, blurred at the edges. Then he feels the cup again, its tin lip at his own, the taste of the wild apple juice spilling over them, running down his chin.

The war. That had not been an easy decision for him to make, philosophically or practically, and he remembers now how the question of what he should do wore away at him, night after night, when the mud walls of this rondavel were still barely dry. At first, like his friends and his family who wrote to him from England, he'd thought the war would be a military, not a civilian conflict. A breast-beating of the countries' professional armies. But like most of Europe they'd underestimated the strength of its magnetism after so many years of peace. They had not foreseen the efficacy of modern warfare – but then how could they have? Kitchener and his finger, part accusatory, part elective; the million-man army drawn from sons, brothers and fathers. Mons, Ypres, the fingers of the war stretching as far as their homes, the tight black print of the casualty lists, the soft drop of the telegram, the silence in bedrooms in a million houses.

But even then, when war was gathering Europe in its fist, he'd still been surprised when it drew the colonies in too; when the guns fired at the battle of Tanga, sounding the note that war had arrived in Africa despite both the British and German governors' reluctance to enter the arguments of their parent nations. And that was when the recruiting began. The farmers and their sons went eagerly enough. The English and the Dutch around Enkeldoorn, whose countries had so recently been fighting each other, displayed a particularly natural talent for mobilisation, for the transition from civilian to soldier. Gradually, the area became emasculated. Parties of men set off for Nairobi to offer their services to the king. Cullen Gouldsbury, feeling the duty of his youth, had already joined the KAR, and after Tanga most of the other Enkeldoorn officials followed his example.

Unlike so much else in the country, colour was no longer a barrier to entry. The Matabele who lived around some of Arthur's outlying mission stations were soon taken into training, their warrior past qualifying them as a 'martial race' on the clipboard forms held under the arms of the upright recruiting officers. But the war needed men for more than just fighting, and soon the Shona men who Arthur lived and worked among began leaving their homes too, not for the regiments of the KAR but for the carrier corps. They often took their families with them and it was then, when so many Africans were leaving for war, that the decision about what he should do had risen to the forefront of his mind.

Initially, the recruiting of Africans into both the KAR and the carrier corps had simply evoked his now familiar sense of moral exasperation with the colonial government. Since the first days of their presence they had treated the African as a child. A child they could put to work, but still an infant, intellectually and socially. And the analogy was not purely metaphorical; many settlers still accepted the 'medical evidence' that proved an African's brain ceased to develop past the age of fourteen. It was an anthropological perspective he had struggled against throughout his tour in Mashonaland and now it was further distorted by the administration's decision to recruit Africans. Though regarded as a child, the African was suddenly honoured with the responsibility of a man. The right to kill and be killed.

However much this paradox outraged him the fact remained that the war was a reality and it would spill African as well as European blood. Black hands would fight, carry, cook, clean, wash, push and pull. War had spread its shadow across the races of the world as it had across its countries. Native Africans along with the other empire races were caught in its darkness and as long as they were he felt he should be too. He knew how the Africans would exist within the British Army. As they had done under all British administration, multitudinous in body and non-existent in voice. Someone had to speak for them. And so, despite his long-held pacifism, he eventually went to war, and for largely the same reasons he had first come to Africa. To lessen the impact of European affairs on the natives of the country. Another disease had been imported by the settlers and he hoped his presence might provide some protection against its symptoms of Honour, Might and Majesty and its lasting scar of loss.

Fortune has left him, tutting and, he thinks, probably shaking her head because he did not drink as much as she wanted him to. He senses her body, momentarily covering the light of the door, of the day, then passing on through, opening a warm ray of sunlight again.

He reaches his hand in front of his face and finds the beams, imagines the universes of dust orbiting in them. Cupping his hand slightly, he follows the light, as if it were a rail supporting him, until it comes to rest against the stone wall of his hut. Here, he flattens his hand against the surface; feels the pock-marked rock and the smooth, dry mud paste. The ridges and the valleys of the stone.

Having made his decision, he'd found the practical implications of leaving these stones, his mission work in Mashonaland, an equally hard dilemma to bear. Just a year earlier he had established his own mission station here, ten miles north of Enkeldoorn. It stood on one of four farms he'd bought with the aid of a government grant, the royalties from his books and a trust fund his brother William had tried his best to keep him away from.

The mission took its name from that he had given the whole area: Maronda Mashanu, the Saint of the Five Wounds. Although it was eleven years since his arrival in Africa, the purchase of the farms and the establishment of this station felt like a true beginning for him, as if the previous time in the country had been a false start. In moving to his own mission station, on his own land, he felt the potential of his work, the purpose of his living in Africa might finally be reached. Free of Charter government native land law and the restrictions of the Anglican Church, an era of self-sufficiency, both spiritually and materially, was close at hand.

Many families who had lived with him at Wreningham followed him to Maronda Mashanu. Two local headmen, Mashonganyika and Pfumojeni, chose to move their kraals from the Manyeni reserve to his farms and more families came in their wake, persuaded by their headmen's choice and attracted by his vision of free land for Africans. Because there would be no hut tax on his land, no government inspectors, no controls and no rents. Each man would farm and live on his own portion of land as freely as the white farmers tilled theirs.

At night he lay in his hut re-reading his battered copy of Theocritus' *Idylls* by the light of a stuttering candle, and by day he saw the poet's vision reflected in his four African mission farms. He felt his idea of an Africa independent from European influence begin to take shape. Simple, pastoral, prelapsarian. An edaphic, unhindered existence.

The four farms covered a sweep of veld that lay across the path he had walked so often between Wreningham and Enkeldoorn. The land was good, requisitioned by the government for white purchase only and covered a total of 7,800 acres. It was the type of land that he had at first found so monotonous, but which he had, in time, come to love. Expansive, scattered with low contorted bush trees, ancient baobabs with their obese, knotted trunks and the crimson fire blossom of the fever, acacia musasa and mtiti trees. Sculptures of granite outcrops gave way to huge, bare-sided inselbergs, motte and bailey kopjes, swathes of blond grass – a land criss-crossed with dusty paths and vibrant with cicadas. A land capable of awesome stillness or, under the rain, the wind, momentous movement. It was raw and basic and yet for him imbued with a sacrosanct quality he valued as much as any cathedral.

A few weeks after he'd purchased the land he trekked alone across the whole area, looking for a place to establish a church. Late on the second day of his trek he followed a branch of the main river that ebbed and rushed through all four of the farms, a slither in the dry season, a torrent in the wet. The branch stream ran down through a shallow dip in the land, through a band of thorn and bush trees, into a cluster of euphorbia and out into a clearing below a small kopje. Pushing his way through the low branches he walked out and stood at the centre of the clearing. His cotton shirt was heavy with his own sweat and a pair of flies circled him, buzzing at his ear, lighting on his skin and buzzing away again. Tipping his hat back on his head he'd looked up above the ring of green treetops. A single eagle circled in the bare sky above him, its wings and tail forming a dark crucifix against the evening sunlight. He knew he had found the place where he would build his church.

A month later he'd returned to the clearing again and began work with the same Matabele workmen with whom he had built the school at Wreningham. Since his last visit to the clearing he had already built the church many times in his mind, and even as the men first swung their mattocks to break the red topsoil he could already see the finished building in the clearing, its high thatched roof encircled by the trees and the shadow of the kopje falling across its bleached stone walls.

He knew the church before it was built because he had already seen the building he wanted it to look like. Earlier that year he'd trekked down as far as Fort Victoria and camped out in the Zimbabwe ruins. Sitting with his back against the trunk of a mopani tree he had smoked his pipe and watched the setting sun transform the conical tower, the high walls, the crumbled pillars, into a shadow show of silent grandeur. He did not know the history of the place – whether it had been a gold mine, a fortress, a city, a temple – but he knew it was in some way sacred, and made all the more so by its current supplication to nature. Lizards stop-started across the tall tower, slipping between its flat stones; cranes, hornbills, weaver and secretary birds nested in the trees that grew in the shelter of its walls and baboons sat back on their haunches, solemnly chewing on damba fruit at the bases of its fallen pillars.

He'd stayed there, against the mopani tree, until it was pitch dark. And even then he hadn't moved, but stayed sitting there, among the ruins, trying to imagine what they had looked like when they were freshly built, roofed with thatch domes and alive with people.

The next morning, as he prepared his breakfast of chapatti and peanut butter, he'd been joined at the ruins by a carload of tourists. They were led by a businessman from Johannesburg. He'd listened as the businessman explained away the history of the place to his colleagues, attributing the skilled building work to Semite or Phoenician traders. Of course, he could not be sure of their exact origins, but at least he was sure about one thing, that the ruins were certainly not the work of native Africans.

'Ja, believe me,' he'd said as the group strolled between the fallen gateways and through the passage between the tower and the outer wall. 'I know natives, and I know the natives never built these walls. They're always in want of bossing up, isn't it? But as for this display of art – the kaffirs haven't it in them, and never had.'

He hadn't been surprised. The businessman's view was a respected one among many of the country's scholars and historians. And he even understood why it might make sense to them. A denial of the ruins was a denial of African history, and it is easier to yoke a man who has no history than a man whose ancestors built great cities of blue-grey stone.

As he'd worked with the Matabele tribesmen in the clearing at Maronda Mashanu he'd kept the businessman's words in mind and built against them, towards an alternative idea of the Zimbabwe ruins. An African idea. But it was not an easy idea to follow. The local stone did not break as easily as the neat granite flakes of the ruins, and whatever skill lay in the blood of their ancestors had been diluted by time in the veins of the Matabele. The curved walls often fell under their own weight and the red mud plastered between the stones was twice washed away by the rain. But eventually, one bare hot afternoon, as they tied the last bundle of veld grass to the tall thatch roof, they finished. Standing back at the edge of the clearing he'd looked up at his new church. It did not resemble the church he had built in his mind. It was a little crooked, and not as tall as he had hoped it would be, but its ancestry was still unmistakable. Formed in a rough crucifix, its rounded stone and dagga walls were repeated inside by parallel walls and chambers and its five domed, thatched roofs were supported by five tall round stone pillars. It was Zimbabwe, breathing through Mashonaland stone and a Christian church. It was the church he had wanted since he came to Africa, a church for the Black Christ.

On the day they finished work Reverend Liebenberg came out from Enkeldoorn to admire the building and to photograph him in front of his new parish church. Standing him by its open doorway, Liebenberg set up his tripod, told his friend to remain as still as he could, and, shielding his eyes from the glare of the sun, released the shutter.

Like a key turning in the lock of the land the completion of the church opened the borders of his farms, and over the ensuing months a steady stream of African families moved their homes and their stock to Maronda Mashanu. He watched the geometry of their settlement imprint itself on the veld: neat squares of ploughed earth worked over by heavy-shouldered oxen; rows of maize, mealie corn and pumpkin plants; the pattern of the kraals punctuating the plain, each echoing the other with a circle of rondavels around a beaten patch of earth and a *dare* of stones where the men sat and talked. Away from the kraals shifting herds of cattle and goats melted over the banks of the river, shepherded by small boys who carried spears taller than themselves. The fly-flinching heads of the cows set off the bells at their necks, and the peal of these bells became a regular percussion to the ongoing music of the veld – of wind, grass, birdsong and insect call.

Routine entered the land too. Each morning he would see the women slow-striding through the mist with bundles of wood or clay pots of river water carried on their heads. Those not yet baptised were naked but for scraps of limbo around their waists and bead necklaces falling across their long, flat breasts. A child was nearly always swaddled to their backs, asleep, its face massaged against its mother's shoulder blades. With an easy raised hand they would call to him as they passed, '*Magwanani Baba*,' and he would call back, '*Magwanani*.'

He developed his own routine too. Doctoring, preparing sermons, writing, corresponding, trekking, baptisms, births, marriages, deaths. Increasingly his time was taken up as a mediator between husbands and wives, working energetically to overcome their differences and keep marriages together. And he was still something of the in-between man in Enkeldoorn too. He knew he would never master the small talk that seemed so essential to communicate in the town. He had always been awkward in speech, the spoken word coming to him harder than the written. And yet, at the same time, most of the farmers found him too rarefied, too intellectual to welcome him completely into their circle. He had, though, over the years come to some sort of an unspoken accommodation with the Europeans in the area. They respected his physical endurance, feared his fierce defence of the natives and accepted his eccentricities. He had been living in the area for long enough now for only new in-comers to find anything strange in the sight of his tall, rangy figure striding across the veld, shabbily dressed in an old golf jacket, his pockets stuffed with ink pots and pens and a battered satchel over his shoulder overflowing with letters, books, tobacco and tinned food. He was, though, still most content when removed from European society. Leading the singing under the open-topped thatch of his church, the starlings darting in and out of its poles. Or alone on the veld, settling down under his red blanket by a camp fire after a long day's trekking, the four bright points of the Southern Cross developing in the dark blue sky above him.

His wider society of friends had suffered the usual expansions and contractions of time. Through his work with the Aboriginal Protection Society he had made close ties with the Methodist John White and the Anglican Edgar Lloyd, with whom he maintained a regular correspondence. He also wrote to friends in England: Maynard Smith, James Adderly, Laurence Binyon, and weekly to his sister Edith, who kept him supplied with literary journals and books of poetry.

Closer to home there were a few families and individuals with whom he had reached a deeper understanding. The Nashes often fed him and provided him with a bed when he trekked over to Umvuma, and the Tullys, farmers outside Enkeldoorn, had even asked him to be godfather to their son, William. When he had been at Wreningham he had campaigned for women missionaries to join the station, and eventually his requests had been granted in the shape of Mary Prior and Agnes Saunders. The women were fiercely independent and he and Agnes in particular did not always agree on methods of pastoral care. He knew she found him awkward to deal with, stubborn, but a shared bias towards the African provided the foundation for a mutual respect. He'd frequently found Agnes asleep in a rondavel, the brown legs and arms of several sleeping children wrapped around her neck and her body.

But he had also lost friends. The drain of recurring malaria and the TB he had recognised finally defeated Bishop Gaul. He stood down from his position and sailed from Beira Bay for England in 1907, embarking at the same dock where he had stood waiting for Arthur seven years earlier. Then in 1913 his mother died. He received the news from his brother William, reading the letter in his rondavel at Maronda Mashanu, sitting on his bed beneath the only picture in the bare hut: a portrait of his mother, Charlotte Cripps. Early in 1914 he returned to England on furlough to conduct a memorial service for her and to settle his affairs in the wake of her going. He'd stayed with his brother at The Lawn in Tunbridge Wells, but England and her countryside which he had missed so much when in Africa now felt alien to him, as did his brother's way of life. William went shooting in Chase Woods, clouds of pheasants beaten into his line of sight, made regular trips up to the Spread Eagle pub and worked long hours in his study that looked out over a manicured lawn to the town below. Like the country itself, his life seemed crowded, rich, its destiny long settled, so unlike the sense of new beginning he felt with each morning he woke in Mashonaland.

He did not visit Ada. He dreamed about her, as if just being nearer her unlocked his memories, and he often woke early in the morning, listening to the racket of the rooks outside his window, imagining how seeing her again might be. But he did not see her. He could not bear to make the journey, take the risk. And it was not just for him. Theresa would be seventeen now. No longer a child. The same age Ada was when he'd met her. So he did not see either of them, and it was on that voyage back to Africa that he'd recognised how his mother's death had cut his last tie with England. Standing on the deck of the ship, listening to the sea part and gather behind it, he'd watched the lights of Southampton slip beneath the water, and known he was not leaving, but returning to his home.

Lake Victoria, German East Africa

◇

Arthur sat against the handrail of the foredeck, one arm hooked through it, looking down the steep side of the steamer, listening to the sound of the water parting about the hull. It was a clear night, star-dusted, lit by a luminous full moon. He watched the water catch the white light, peeling away from the prow in a frill of foam-headed wavelets as the boat ploughed steadily through the mercury surface of the lake. Minutes before, word had passed up the ship, whispered from officer to officer, that they had crossed the border with German East Africa. Arthur studied the water below him again. He had seen no border interrupt its continuity. He had seen nothing but the moon-light, mineral across its supple surface. He thought to himself how ridiculous it was to take a ruler and a pencil and dash a border through a lake. Like portioning the sky or claiming the stars. And how childlike to label one side of the lake German and the other British. Childlike and futile. The imbricated obsession to own, to possess. And yet that ruler and pencil laid over the lake was enough to send two thousand of them across her waters tonight, weighed down with ammunition and intent. Two thousand of them, steaming towards the land on the other side, the land labelled German. It was all they need-ed to consider killing and being killed. Words on a map.

In his heart, after his fourteen years in Africa, he was increasingly sure that the futility of those words was not just in their idea, but in their conclusiveness too. They looked so final, stencilled in black against the pink and yellow of the map. But they may as well have been written in dust. The land they covered with their capital letters could not be labelled. It did not belong to anyone, it could not belong to anyone. Even the African who farmed the soil his ancestors farmed was no more than a tenant. As Bishop Gaul had pointed out to him all those years before when he first looked out over the plains of blond grass, even the name Africa was futile, manufactured, unrecognised by millions who lived on her. In time that label would slip too, as words will, until it has travelled so far from meaning that it is no longer a word at all. Once again only the land it had tried to describe will remain. Un-named, un-owned and the only victor of all the bitter battles fought across her soil.

He looked back down the steamer across the huddled mass of men crowded on her deck. Their dark shadows were bulky and strangely inhuman, made awkward by the webbing, packs and weapons strapped about their bodies. The unhindered moon caught the gun-metal of the boat, softening edges, lighting the top of the handrail in a clean white strip; magnesium on the point of ignition. It illuminated details of the men too. The flash of a watch face tilted into the light, the tightly wrapped turbans of the 28th Mountain Battery, the still expression of an askari's face looking out across the water. It lit the tools they had brought with them as well: the corrugated barrel of the Vickers machine-gun; the flat blade of a shovel protruding from a rucksack; the sharper blade of a bayonet, light running down its blood channel like a single drop of iridescent liquid. The moon's impassive luminosity clothed them all, a benison of light despite their dreadful purpose.

The familiar smell of old and new sweat infused in cotton and serge reached him on a gust of wind, and he thought how little the labels of countries applied to these men too. This was not Britain going to war with Germany. Nor was it Indians, Africans, Rhodesians, boys from Lancashire fighting against Rhinelanders, Bavarians, Masi, Zulus and East Africans. It was men that went to war, not countries. Men that went to war and brought other men with them, as if it were a force that pulled at a peculiarly masculine substance, a rare ore woven in the marrow of the sex. A force that attracted them like flies to a flame, again and again into its terrible vacuum.

Arthur's drifting thoughts were disturbed by a movement behind him. The deck of the ship had been quiet for the last hour, the men either asleep or lost in anxious thought about what lay ahead. Looking up he saw the Company's intelligence officer, Captain Meinertzhagen, picking his way through the prone bodies and the piles of cargo. He was heading towards the foredeck where a Vickers machine-gun perched on its tripod like an insect among the banks of sandbags. As he passed Arthur the Captain looked down and acknowledged him with a curt nod of his head and a quiet 'Father'. Arthur watched him as he went on, past the machine-gun nest, right up to the prow of the steamer. He stopped, put one foot up on the rail and leant forward, staring unblinking into the night, as if he was trying to catch a scent on the warm wind, the faintest aroma of the enemy.

Arthur was unsure what to make of the Captain. Their paths had only crossed in the most cursory of ways at Lake Command. He knew he was respected by the men, both askaris and Europeans. And when Arthur had trekked back with the walking wounded from the capture of Mwanza he'd greeted them all into the camp like a perfect host. But there was another side to him too. Before they'd embarked tonight Arthur had held a brief Communion on an altar of oil drums and ammunition cases. The congregation was small, a scattering of European privates and officers and a few askaris, most of the Sudanese, Swahili and Somali soldiers being either Muslim or pagan in their beliefs. He'd preached hopefully on the text of loving your enemies, doing well to those that do spitefully to you. When he had finished, the Captain had stood up and thanked him, then sent out two runners to gather together a larger group around the congregation. Once these men had arrived, he'd given his own brief sermon. His subject was the bayonet. He reminded the men they were there to be used, of the technique of upward thrust and twist, and of the most effective method of removing a lodged blade. Place a foot on the enemy's chest and discharge a round while pulling back on the stock of the rifle. It was, he informed them, a method that also guaranteed a kill.

Watching him now, standing at the steamer's prow like a macabre figurehead, Arthur contemplated this man who could be so genial, and yet kill so easily. He took out his notebook and pencil from the top pocket of his khaki tunic and began to make some notes towards a poem. The war may have disrupted everything else in his life, but it had not stopped him writing. He had been writing poems throughout his time on the lake and now, as they steamed towards the German shore, he wrote again by the light of the moon, trying to sketch a portrait of the man standing before him, staring into the night as if daring it to break its silence.

The Watcher on Our Theshold
(Intelligence Department)

As in a bad dream I may see you now
Lank, flusht, chin-tufted, eyes as black as coal
Kindling like live coals, in that mood you well
Might pose for him who mortgage held of old
On Faustus damn'd – calling his mortgage in.
Those iron lips will no refusals own,

Forbidden witch-smoke curls in rings of blue
About your head, and your hand sinister
Fondles a swarthy lash of hippo-hide.
Upon your shoulder-straps, beneath your stars
Brass letters spell your errand –
                                        OUT FOR BLOOD

Bukoba, Lake Victoria, German East Africa

◇

When Meinertzhagen burst the lock on the door to the communications room beneath the wireless tower, it was the flies that hit him first. A manic buzzing and swelling as the rush of air from the opened door disturbed them. Black clouds filling the room as if the day was transforming into particles of night. Thousands of them, coming at him in their stream towards the light, tapping against his face, catching in his beard and in his lips. After the flies, the smell. With the force of heat from an opened oven door the stink fumed into his nostrils and down into his throat, making him gag and bring his hand to his face as a mask.

Looking over his fingers around the room at the desks, files, telegraph and radio equipment the thought flashed across his mind that the Germans had discovered his 'dirty paper method' and that this was their ironic revenge. A couple of askaris from the 3rd KAR and a North Lancs sapper sergeant came through the door behind him. He heard them all gag and choke and then the sergeant's Lancashire accent, 'Fuckin' hell, Sir! Oh, Christ, fuckin' hell!' Then their retreating footsteps as they ran back out of the door. Meinertzhagen followed them, equally appalled by the sight of that room.

Every surface, every document, every piece of equipment was covered, daubed and dripping in brown and mustard-coloured human excrement. The room had been the scene of a bizarre act of mass defecation, and leaning against a tree outside Meinertzhagen knew why. They must have known they were outnumbered, that the town would fall sooner or later and this was how they would keep the equipment and documents from falling into enemy hands. Judging by the flies they must have defiled the room at least twenty-four hours earlier. Meinertzhagen tried to imagine it. The British field guns battering the town, the patter of small arms fire in the distance and in here a *Schutztruppe* officer in his white, braided uniform calling out the command to a company of askaris who stood, waiting, the belts of their breeches undone in anticipation.

He turned to the team of sappers waiting behind him. The Sergeant still looked pale from his brief glimpse of the room. 'Go ahead,' he said. 'We won't get anything out of there.'

The team gathered their equipment, long coils of copper wire, tight bundles of dynamite, and began to climb onto the roof of the communications room to set their charges on the concrete base of the 200-foot wireless tower. Beneath them the burst door still swung open, its gap in the wall filled with the low, menacing hum of the flies.

◇

Arthur looked up from the eight shallow graves the porters were trying to dig from the hard earth. Below him thin columns of smoke still drifted up from the white-washed houses of the town and a scattering of huts had been reduced to charred embers. In the town itself, he could just make out a group of men clambering onto the lower struts of the wireless tower.

The scrape and slump of the spadework brought him back to his own job and he looked back down at the eight bodies before him, each covered with a grey standard-issue blanket. Over the last hour he'd knelt beside each one, carefully noting each man's identity in his notebook, their names forming a list after the last line of the poem he had written on the steamer two nights ago: OUT FOR BLOOD. He would write to the families himself, and he had taken the liberty to remove what he could from the bodies to send along with his letters: photographs of wives and children, wedding rings, even a bitten pencil with the dead man's tooth marks imprinted in its wood. Then he'd performed the last rites over each man individually, and now it was just the graves that were left. He sat back on a rock, feeling the weight of the dead men's possessions in his pocket, the watches, the glasses, the half-written letters, and watched as the eight holes grew deeper with every shovel and swing, the deposits of earth and dust mounting up at their sides.

The battle that led to these deaths had begun two days ago, when, at one o'clock on the morning of the 22nd, the four steamers had reached their landing positions. The boats bobbed in the shallow water off a gently sloping beach three miles south of Bukoba as the men waited for Stewart's torch signal from the leading steamer. But instead of a torch flash, another light lit up the sky and Arthur had watched as a burning white point with a long tail described an arc above them, then levelled off and exploded like a giant thunderflash. Two more rockets followed its trajectory. He heard Captain Meinertzhagen curse to himself as he pushed through the men to get to the side of the boat where he could get a clean signal to Stewart. As the second rocket lit up the sky Arthur had looked down the deck and seen that the steamers were completely illuminated in the flare's light: the staring faces of the men looking up, the field guns, even the details of the bridge were all cast in a white brightness that threw shadows in all the wrong places, like a photographic negative. The Germans had seen them and the element of surprise was lost. He thought of Tanga and waited for the guns to start harassing them where they were, but nothing happened. The last flare fizzled out on the night's black, then silence. Eventually Stewart's signal came: withdraw, it said, and steam further north.

Five hours later they disembarked three miles north of the town at the base of a cliff that rose almost vertically three hundred feet above the beach to a scrappy line of thorn trees at the top. A steep path ran diagonally up the cliff face, broken in places by landslides and the roots of plants. Arthur had watched from the shore as the strike force of the North Lancs and the Fusiliers began to tackle the climb, roping up machine-guns and field guns and even managing to coax up a heavily laden mule, its hooves scrabbling and slipping on the fragile path. He saw Pruen among the Fusiliers, directing equipment up the cliff, checking knots and bindings, emitting an energy that belied his age. The Fusiliers were much older and less well trained than the other regiments. An eclectic mix of adventurers, drifters and old soldiers, they had given themselves the moniker 'The Frontiersmen', although around the lake they were more commonly known as the 'Old and the Bold'. Some had seen action before, in the Boer War, the '86 uprising or further afield in their home territories, and as Arthur joined them on the path up the cliff he heard the medals of past campaigns clinking against the buttons of their tunics. Most of them, however, had never fired a gun in anger and Arthur watched as a succession of exiled Russians, a troop of ex-circus clowns and acrobats, a bartender, a lighthouse-keeper, an opera singer, a Buckingham Palace footman and a Texas cowboy all scrambled up onto the lip of the cliff behind him, their rifles strapped to their backs and sweat already gathering at their temples.

The skirmishing had begun as the force marched over a lip at the top of the cliff and down towards a hill that overlooked the town. It was scrappy fighting and hard going. They were covering open ground of bush and swamp while the Germans fired at them from the higher cover of thick banana plantations, rocks, inselbergs and clumps of thorn trees. Arthur had advanced with a company of Fusiliers. Puffs of smoke drifting up from behind tree trunks and boulders was all he could see of the enemy and he'd spent much of his time on the ground as fusillades of bullets spat up flurries of dust around them. He'd been under fire before, on the decks of steamers patrolling the lake and at the attack on Mwanza, but he'd never experienced anything as intense as what they met that day. Lying there, his cheek pressed against the earth, he experienced the same sensation he'd felt all those years ago lying on the deck of the *Hertzog* on the morning of his arrival in Africa. A desire for the firing to stop, for the fingers to freeze on the triggers, and beneath that desire a deeper fault-line of frustration and pity, fracturing him to the core.

They were half-way across a swamp when the German 75s started throwing down shells, and Arthur had had to submerge himself almost completely in a deep stagnant pool to escape the shrapnel that whizzed around him, fizzling and spitting as it hit the water. But then the field guns of their own 28th Mountain Battery had answered, and as the shells landed on the slope before them, throwing up brief flowerings of rock, earth and tree, the Fusilier company had taken the opportunity to advance at speed. Arthur jogged forward with them, bent double alongside the Fusiliers' Sergeant-Major Bottomly. Bottomly was an older man and Arthur could hear the effort of his grunting pant with each step he took. A sudden spray of machine-gun fire sent them both sprawling to the ground again, but as soon as it had passed Arthur got to his feet and carried on, only realising after a few yards that Bottomly was no longer with him. He'd turned to see the Sergeant-Major still kneeling behind him, staring back at him, a wild expression on his face. As Arthur went back to him Bottomly opened his mouth to speak, but he got no further than a rasping gasp before the blood frothed up on his lips and ran down his chin, matting in his beard. It was then that Arthur saw the bullet holes, three of them in neat diagonal formation across his chest, like buttons across his tunic. Another burst of machine-gun fire erupted behind him and Arthur had thrown himself down again, shutting his eyes tightly against the spraying dirt. He opened them to find his face inches from where Bottomly had been kneeling and he noticed briefly how the imprint of the man's cord breeches had made a corrugated pattern in the dust, like a fingerprint pressed in the earth. Then he'd raised his head further and seen Bottomly himself, on his back now, his left eye and cheek missing.

Bottomly was a father. His family were back in West London now, and just days before he'd told Arthur how he felt they'd be safer there, 'back home'. As he'd lain in the dirt, listening to the whizz and whine of the bullets and shells finding their invisible courses through the air, Arthur had imagined the resonance of the death he had just witnessed. The arrival of the telegram on the doormat. His wife reading the official sympathies, and then reading them again. Then his own letter, with the photographs and mementos. The silence after the crying. Her attempts to explain to the children. The erosion of grief over the years and the never-changing strangeness of that name: Bukoba, where their father had left them, staring at the sky through his one remaining eye.

By nightfall the Germans had retreated from their positions on the hill, but they'd still managed to hold the British a mile off from the town itself. With the failing light the firing died down to the odd nervous shot ringing off a boulder, and then nothing, just the dusk chorus of insects and hyenas meeting the moon. The men were exhausted. They had fought all day and for many it was the first action they'd ever experienced. As the adrenalin subsided, tiredness had overwhelmed them. Rations were scheduled to arrive from the shore, but they never came, so both the Fusiliers and the North Lancs had bivouacked down for the night with whatever rations had survived the day. Sharing a biscuit and a lump of cheese with one of the ex-circus clowns from the Fusiliers, Arthur watched the deepening blue of the sky above the hill turn the thorn trees into sharp silhouettes hung with stars.

Not far from where they camped they'd found the shattered remains of one of the German 75s, flanked by her two gunners, an askari and a *Schutztruppe* officer, arranged on either side, their limbs at impossible angles. Captain Meinertzhagen had looked through the officer's pockets before Arthur performed the last rites over the dead men: a chain watch with a smashed face, the fine hands buckled; a silver cigarette case; a soiled handkerchief, and in the top pocket of his shirt a crude hand-drawn map of Africa. The continent had been dotted across with an upside-down T and the three portions labelled: German South Africa, Austrian Africa, Turkish Africa. Perhaps he had been explaining to the askari how the country would look after the war, or maybe it was a personal proposal he planned to show the Kaiser one day. Whatever, it didn't mean much to him any more and now he would never own any part of Africa. But she would own him, if not with her soil, then with her hyenas, her rats, her flies and, come that morning, her vultures.

The night was freezing. After the heat of the day the cold had been a shock and sleep seemed out of the question. Captain Meinertzhagen and Lieutenant Selous had retired to the shelter of an inselberg, where they swapped hunting stories and naturalist notes while a group of the North Lancs had set fire to a couple of grass huts and dried their uniforms by the flames. It was by the light of this fire that Arthur prepared a simple communion service. He was as exhausted as the rest of the men and as he'd lain a piece of cloth over a flat rock and placed a chalice and a paten on it, he'd felt every movement as an effort of will. After he'd taken off his jacket and covered his khaki shirt with a preaching stole, a couple of askaris and a handful of Europeans had emerged from the darkness and knelt on the ground before his makeshift altar, bowing their heads as if in tiredness or shame.

With the morning, they'd advanced again, down the hill overlooking the scattered town of Bukoba. The wireless mast, their main target, stood to the south, a mini-Eiffel Tower rising above the simple whitewashed brick buildings. The shells of the Mountain Battery's 75s landed in puffs of grey-white smoke among these buildings, the sound of their explosions strangely delayed across the bowl of land in which the town sat. A single German sniper, positioned waist-deep in a swamp, had them pinned down outside the town for most of the morning. A machine-gun on the hill kept up a steady rattle as it tried to hit him, but its bullets failed to find anything other than the twigs and branches of the swamp plants. After two men had been killed by his sharpshooting, Captain Meinertzhagen had lost patience with the delay and waded into the swamp himself, shirtless, carrying his rifle above his head. Arthur had watched him disappear into the dark tangle of branches, and as his white back slipped out of sight, the eye of his imagination had taken over instead. The Captain, circling around a thick clump of mangroves, seeing the sniper standing in the water with his back to him. A *Schutztruppe* officer, young, fair-skinned, with a red, sun-burnt neck showing over his collar. His ammunition case tied up to a branch at his side from which he picks out a bullet to slide into the chamber of his rifle. Meinertzhagen respecting his bravery and think-ing how in another situation he may have taken him prisoner, let him live. But then the heat of the day, the thought of his two dead col-leagues, the stink of the swamp. Aiming at the sun-burnt neck, he fires, and the officer's head jerks backwards, then slumps forward as he slides down beneath the surface of the swamp. His rifle follows him until there is nothing where he had stood. Just some slow-popping bubbles on the water's surface, and the ammunition case, swinging on the branch.

That was all just this morning, the swamp, the final push on the town, but already it feels like a lifetime away. And now it is over and the porters have finished their work. The graves, a young private tells him, are ready. Arthur stands up and thanks the soldier, then reaches for his Bible in his jacket pocket and makes his way over to the holes in the ground: deep, root-fringed and waiting for the eight men lying beside them to fill them again.

But then from down the hill, in the town, an echoing roll of thun-der. Arthur looks up and sees a plume of black-grey smoke about the foot of the wireless tower, then watches as it leans, wavers, then suc-cumbs to the arc of its fall, like a giant giving into sleep after years of silent vigil.

<>

The whirring sound of uncoiling wire signalled the arrival of the sap-per sergeant, buttocks first, to where Meinertzhagen sat behind a thick stone wall. Meinertzhagen handed him the plunger, which he con-nected to the two copper wires, then placed his hands over his ears and his head down on his knees, eyes tightly shut. He heard the brief travel of the plunger as the sergeant pressed it down. Then nothing. Then everything. The sound of the explosions rang down the street, followed by a billowing wave of dust and debris flecked with excre-ment. Then the metallic creaking and rush of air as the tower began its collapse. Meinertzhagen heard it come crashing to the ground behind him, then a faint cheer go up from lower in the town. He opened his eyes to see the sergeant signalling to another sapper on the other side of the street. Again a plunger was compressed, and again there was a brief silence, an expectant second when everything was paused. Then the second explosion. But this time it was deeper, sharper, a fissure in the air followed by more detonations and cracks as the German arsenal went up in a cloud of thick black and orange smoke.

It was as Meinertzhagen was walking back into the town from examining the remains of the tower that he realised something was wrong. The men had broken ranks. He could see them further down the hill, running into buildings, breaking down doors. As he passed a house on his right he heard the smash of broken glass and the moving of heavy furniture. The door to the house swung drunkenly off one hinge and looking in he saw a group of soldiers turning the place over. They were men of all ages, European and African, but they all looked like children, smiles on their faces as they ransacked drawers, swept trophies into kitbags and rifled through cupboards and desks. A loud report came from an inner room and Meinertzhagen reached for the revolver at his side, but then a Fusilier, one of the circus troop, entered with a foaming bottle of champagne in each hand and a ceremonial pickelhaube on his head. The other men cheered and rushed the room from where the Fusilier had entered, in search of more champagne, while a young North Lancs lad, still smeared from the day's fighting approached Meinertzhagen with a large photo album held out before him. He looked genuinely disgusted.

'Look, sir, filthy Boche perverts,' he said as he handed Meinertzhagen the opened album. It was bound in leather, with a brass spine and clasp, heavy in the hand. Meinertzhagen took the book from the young soldier and flicked back the transparent paper to look at the photograph beneath. It was a large black-and-white portrait of the town's German commandant standing beside his wife. He was in full dress uniform, crisp white, a parade of medals at his chest, a thick braid looping from his shoulder and a decorated picklehaube under his arm. His wife sat at his elbow, completely naked, her hair undone across her white shoulders and her hands neatly crossed in her lap. Meinertzhagen could just make out where the wicker chair had imprinted its pattern in the flesh of her thighs.

The young soldier was still standing by Meinertzhagen, looking seriously at him as if he had handed him an important piece of intelligence. 'Turn over, sir, there's more.' Meinertzhagen turned the stiff page to reveal an almost identical photograph. The positions and the expressions of the commandant and his wife were exactly the same. He staring from over his thick moustache into the camera's lens, and she looking just past it, into the distance. Except in this version it was she who wore the formal dress, a long evening gown melting over the chair to the floor, and he who stood naked. It was a strange effect. His stern, angular face giving way to a surprisingly pale, flaccid body, a thinly haired chest and the fold of a paunch above thin legs, his penis a stub of white in the black of his pubic hair as he stood there, staring out of the photograph, his picklehaube under his arm and the world under his eye.

Meinertzhagen handed back the album without a word, looked about at the ruined room, the soldiers swigging champagne from the bottle, then turned away and left the house to go and find out what was going on.

The street was bright after the dim interior, the afternoon sun reflecting off the whitewash of the houses, and Meinertzhagen had to stop for a moment to let his eyes adjust. When they did he still wasn't sure he was seeing properly. Further down the hill a group of African porters were strutting about the street dressed in women's underwear, a group of askari and European soldiers cheering and encouraging them in their pantomime. Meinertzhagen broke into a jog. As he got nearer he saw that the porters were drunk. Fat Henry Clay cigars wagged at their mouths as they paraded in front of the soldiers, their hips swaying extravagantly in imitation of a woman's. The lingerie they wore over their own greasy scraps of clothing shone out among the dull khaki of the uniforms. Camisoles and knickers in pastel blues and pinks, an emerald slip, white corsets and a black basque with deep red lace and stitching, the straps hanging loose down a pair of thin dark thighs.

Meinertzhagen pushed past the group. A soldier called out to him, 'Don't fancy the local produce, sir?' But he didn't stop. He was looking for General Stewart and for a reason why this was happening.

He was almost at the quayside when he heard the woman's scream. He stopped. The sounds of the looting soldiers up the hill travelled down to him. A dim rumble of shouting and cheering. The clatter of stones thrown against a portrait of the Kaiser. Then a scream again: wild, terrified, suddenly cut short.

When he reached the house he couldn't see the woman, just a

chaotic bundle of men. But as he stood on the lip of the doorway, looking down at them, the grim order of the situation revealed itself. She was lying on the floor, two askaris holding her arms. One of these also held her head, his clenched knuckles showing pale through the black of her hair. Another pair held a leg each, gripped by the ankle and pulled wide apart. The line between the black skin of her foot and the pale skin of her soles was so neat it looked as though she had dipped both feet in a fine chalk dust. The broad back of a white soldier heaved and dropped between her legs with hard, rhythmical thrusts. He was still wearing his jacket and Meinertzhagen could make out the officer pips on the cuff of his sleeve. He caught glimpses of the woman's face too, between the rise and fall of the man's shoulders. A young black girl. Her mouth was open but she was not screaming anymore. Her lower jaw was tensed and her eyes screwed shut, as if she might squeeze herself back into the darkness behind her eyelids. With each thrust from the officer a tremor passed through her small breasts to her head which rocked back, gave, then rocked back, again and again. One of her eyes was swollen and bruised, like an overripe damson resting on the curve of her cheek.

Meinertzhagen found General Stewart down at the dock, standing next to the four grey steamers, overseeing the boarding of the wounded. He strode towards him, trying to swallow the anger in his voice.

'General Stewart, sir.'

Stewart turned to Meinertzhagen. 'Ah, Captain. Everything all right with the tower? Turn up anything useful?'

'No, sir.'

'Ah, well, never mind. We're just . . .'

'Sir, why are the men looting the town?'

Stewart looked shocked at Meinertzhagen's directness. As was his manner he cleared his throat and began blinking rapidly. 'Well, Colonel Driscoll of the Fusiliers requested the action. And I, er, granted it.' He paused. 'To the victors the spoils, and all that?'

Meinertzhagen looked him in the eye. The man was out of his depth, he could see that now. Lost.

'With all respect, sir,' he said, careful to winnow any trace of it from his tone, 'if you go into the town now you will find no victory there.'

Feeling the flush of anger rise up his throat into his cheeks he didn't wait for an answer, but turned on his heel and strode away from the blinking general.

And then he saw the priest. He was returning from burying the eight British dead where they had been gathered at the edge of the town. A group of porters stood behind him, their shovels over their shoulders. His dog collar was smeared with dirt and Meinertzhagen noticed he had lost one of the brass crosses on his lapels. Their eyes met for a moment, but then a crowd appearing at the end of the street distracted them both. It was the drunk porters, still wearing the lingerie. Reeling behind them came a group of European soldiers and askaris, laden down with candlesticks, ceremonial swords and other trophies from the town. One of them dropped a silver tankard which clattered down the dusty slope. Meinertzhagen made to go and pick it up, but as he did, above the noise of their excited chatter, the short sharp soprano of a woman's scream travelled across the bay, followed by a single shot. Meinertzhagen looked in the direction of the echoing report, then out across the lake. He heard the priest walk behind him, but he did not turn around. He knew he couldn't meet his eyes again.

24 JUNE 1915

British Lake Force Camp, Kisumu,
British East Africa

———◇———

Private Smith of the Loyal North Lancs lay on his field bed in the hospital tent by the lake. It was early in the morning and the camp was quiet. He had heard the steamers come back from Bukoba late the night before; an hour of endless clatter and movement as the force disembarked, then silence. Now though, with the coming of the sun, there was movement again. The shuffle of feet outside. The stirring of the other wounded around him, the sun's growing heat distracting them from their sleep. And now Mrs Cole, moving between the beds with her bucket of cold water and supply of fresh flannels. He knew it was Mrs Cole and not the doctor or another nurse because he could make out the red of her dress through a crack in the bandages over his face. A flash of crimson as she passed through his line of sight. And then, as she got nearer, her perfume. Sweet and feminine, rising like a promise from the stale smells of disease, sweat and rotten skin that usually filled the hospital tent.

The young boy with the burnt face seemed to be stirring. She could not tell if he was asleep or awake as the bandages covered his eyes, but she went to him anyway. Dipping a fresh flannel in the water she wrung it out, but not too much, so it was still heavy and wet, then folded it into a long strip and placed it across his forehead.

'There you go, darling, you'll need that. I think it's going to be a hot one.'

She leant over him and adjusted his pillow. He tried to thank her, but his lips were crisp and the bandages tight against his skin. She patted his arm and carried on up the tent between the rows of prone white patients. Further up, after a partition of screens, the faces changed colour: first the pale brown of the sick Indian sepoys, then the black heads of African askaris looked out from over the sheets and blankets. The illnesses and wounds remained the same.

She called all her patients 'darling' for the same reason she wore her old red evening dress and sprayed her neck with perfume. Because she wanted to bring something from the world of women into the lives of these men. Something from life outside the war. A reminder of what else did and will exist. The dress also helped her to remember these things herself. To remember herself. She had forgotten herself once, and she didn't want to again. But the dress was not just a psychological prop. It was, in its way, practical too. It was red, a good colour for the hospital tent. Blood didn't show so starkly against it as it did against khaki or white.

She was on her way out to refill her bucket with fresh water when she saw the chaplain. He was at the African end of the tent, sitting on the edge of a patient's bed. It was the first time she had seen him. She'd come up on the railway to Lake Command from Nairobi the day after the steamers left for Bukoba, in preparation for their return. She had been told to expect heavy casualties.

The chaplain stood up and she caught a glimpse of his face that stopped her mid-stride. It was thinner, more gaunt than that night fourteen years ago. All traces of the young man had gone; his hair had thinned and greyed, his eyes sunk a little deeper under his brow, but it was still unmistakably the face of Father Cripps. She had forgotten many things over the years, but never that night. She watched him move to another bed, bend and speak to the soldier there. The movement confirmed it was him. The same tall, angular body. The strange mix of physical possession and awkwardness.

Remembering that night she felt a rush of affection towards him. But then, close on its heels, a sudden anger which surprised her in its ferocity. The last time they had met he had listened to her. Well, this time she wanted him to talk. Last time she had spoken freely, answering his questions, but now she had questions of her own, and she wanted his answers.

She waited for him to finish speaking with the patient before she approached him.

'Father Cripps? It is Father Cripps, isn't it?'

He turned at the sound of his name, but his face showed no sign of recognition at seeing her. She helped him along.

'Mrs Cole. We met once in Salisbury. You came to dinner.'

A moment of thought, then she saw the memory engage.

'Yes, yes, of course. With Bishop Gaul? Of course. Well, how good of you to remember, I mean, after all this time.'

'It isn't often I entertain a poet and a Bishop at my table, Father.

You were something of a special occasion for me back then.'

'Well, I'm glad you thought so. How good to see you again. But have you been at the lake long? I mean, I don't think I've . . .'

'No, I came up yesterday. Posted here for the push on Bukoba.'

'Oh . . . yes. We got back from that last night.'

'You were at Bukoba?'

'Yes.'

'Well, congratulations. I hear it was a success.'

'Yes, I suppose it was in a way, but . . .' He looked away for a moment and she saw he was uncomfortable talking about the attack. Turning back to her, forcing a smile, he changed the subject. 'It's strange, I met someone else here just a few days ago. Someone else I hadn't seen for a long time. It seems as if we're all being washed up on this lake.'

Arthur thought of Pruen. He was one of the eight who had not returned on the steamers. Shot through the throat as he stood to rally his men. One of the eight he had buried in the earth of Bukoba, marking their graves with wooden crosses and their rifles, stuck in the ground.

'Well, you shouldn't be so surprised,' she replied. 'There aren't many of us to go around in this war, we're bound to bump into each other from time to time.'

She had not aged in the same way Pruen had. He remembered her clearly now from that night in Salisbury. When he was so new to the country, to its heat and its people. Her face had kept its shape. Age had not obscured the younger woman, but somehow enhanced her. She seemed larger here, not just physically, but in her character. More confident. He couldn't be sure but he thought she was wearing exactly the same red dress she wore that night fourteen years ago. Dulled and thin at the elbows, but the same dress. She wore her hair in a loose bun, the brown stitched with grey, and she had developed the white African's characteristic crow's feet about her eyes, the mark of years spent squinting in the sun.

'I was just going outside, will you join me?' she said, picking up her bucket. She walked towards the end of the tent and he followed her, surprised by the scent of perfume as she passed.

Outside, Mrs Cole sat on an upturned crate facing out towards the lake. Arthur joined her. She lit a cigarette from a silver case and he lit his pipe. Together they smoked and looked out over the water, the morning mist still hanging at its centre, and at the distant crowds of flamingos gathered further along the shore. They brought each other up to date with their lives. He told her of his move to Maronda Mashanu, his decision to stay on in Africa, about his schools and his church in the south. She in turn explained why she was there, at the lake. How she had felt she had to do something, had to be involved in the war in some way. Salisbury, like most of the colonies, was apathetic towards the war. Many of the white settlers felt that it was not theirs to fight, that the British army was more an army of invasion than an army of protection. But her daughter Anne was still in England, and her letters made her feel closer to the conflict, to the struggle and the loss of it. When Anne wrote describing a daylight air raid on London, of coming out from the shelter of a department store to see a mother and child impaled on the railings, she knew she could no longer stay at home in Salisbury. She had to be involved. So she travelled to Nairobi and presented herself at the army HQ. She didn't leave until they gave her a post as a nurse.

'And Mr Cole? Was he happy with your decision?'

She smiled and blew out a long plume of thin smoke. 'You never met him, did you? He wasn't at the dinner as I remember?'

'No, he was away. At the war in the south.'

'Yes, well, as you can imagine, he was pretty keen for this one too. The day after the news came through he was off to volunteer. Doing his duty. Not that he ever did much else.'

She stopped, took another pull on her cigarette. 'He was killed at Tanga. That first attack. Apparently he was covered in bee stings. Head to toe. But he'd been shot too, in the legs. They don't know which killed him.'

'I'm sorry to hear that. Very sorry. God rest his soul.'

'Oh, if he's anywhere near God there won't be much resting, believe me – he'll be sorting through his ledgers and making plans to expand heaven's territory or something!'

Mrs Cole laughed, but Arthur was wrong-footed by her joking about her husband's death.

She turned to him and smiled again, 'Don't be mistaken, I do miss him, Father. It's just, well . . . we were hardly ever together. He lived on a larger scale than me. He organised countries, I had trouble with my pantry.'

'Of course,' Arthur said. 'I understand . . . and you must miss your daughter too?' A patch of flamingos took flight from the shore. A flurry of water and wings. Arthur watched them, their pink legs held straight out behind them, their slow wing-flap.

'Anne? Yes, I do, though I've not seen her for three years now.'

Her voice petered out, and for a moment just the sound of the flamingos filled the silence between them. Eventually she turned to face Arthur again, but her expression had changed. Her eyes were serious, grave.

'She's twenty-six now. Has a young man back in England, Jack. They're engaged,' she explained, 'and would be married now, were it not for the war.' She paused, took out another cigarette and lit it. Taking a deep breath she drew the smoke into her lungs and exhaled it with a sigh, as if she were breathing out more than just smoke.

'Three months after war was announced he volunteered. And do you know who persuaded him to volunteer, Father?' She looked back at Arthur and her eyes were hard, as if she were reproaching him. 'A priest. The local church gave a recruitment sermon. All the boys went and listened. The vicar preached about a Christian war, about fighting the good fight. And they followed his words. Jack joined up with three of his friends after that sermon. Well, Anne had told me he'd always been keen on machines, good with his hands, and he was lucky, in a way: he joined the flying corps. His friends weren't so lucky. They went to the line. I don't know what's happened to them. But Jack, well, he went to fly above those lines in his plane, spotting and recording. Three months ago he wrote to Anne and told her about a strange flight he'd had, an early patrol on a fine day, so he could fly high and still see clearly. There had been heavy fighting all week, he said. No-man's-land looked as if it had been squashed under a giant's foot. He was high enough to see both sides of the line, and as he said, they were only a few hundred feet apart anyway, when he noticed two identical formations on either side. A large group of men were fanned out around a point in the German communication trenches, and another group in the same formation were spread out opposite them on the British side. He flew lower to get a better look. First over the Germans, and then over the British. And then he realised. It was Sunday. The groups were communion services. They were praying, Father. He flew higher and looked down at them again, and there they were. Two church services worshipping the same God, spread out like a pair of butterfly wings either side of no-man's-land.'

She held Arthur's eye, then looked away, taking another draw on her cigarette.

Arthur was about to say something when she turned back and spoke again.

'I was treating a young lad in Nairobi last month. He'd been badly wounded at Jessin. One morning as I was changing his dressing he took out two belts from under his bed and said to me, "Look at this, Sister, he's got to be fibbing one lot of us, don't you reckon?" One belt was his. It had *Dieu et mon droit* written on its buckle. The other was a German soldier's. It also had a motto on its buckle: *Gott Mit Uns*.'

This time she did not look away but kept her eyes on his. But they were not the same eyes. They had lost their hardness and they were no longer challenging, but questioning him, willing him for an answer.

She continued, speaking more softly, 'The thing is, Father, I don't see God anywhere in this war. With them or with us. And if he isn't here, where I'd say we need him most, then I want to know where he is.'

Her face softened even more and Arthur saw she was holding back tears. He laid his hand on hers. He felt exhausted, drained by the attack and its aftermath.

'I'm not sure I have the answers you're looking for,' he said. 'I mean, I don't know if I have them myself. But I understand your confusion, and you're right, in a way. This isn't God's war, it's man's. But I do believe that God is here. If not in what happens, then maybe in what doesn't. If that makes any sense. When a gun jams or misfires. When a bullet misses. I believe he is here then.'

Mrs Cole looked up into his face and he could see she wasn't convinced. He looked out towards the flamingos, at their question mark necks lengthening to meet their reflections in the water.

'Do you pray before a battle?' Her voice was still quiet, careful.

'Yes, I do.'

'What do you pray for?'

'Well, not for what I'm meant to, I'm sure. Not for victory.' He paused. 'In fact I don't even pray to St George. I pray to St Michael instead. I ask him to cover our heads in battle.' He looked out across the lake. 'And I'm sure that over there, there is a German padre praying to St George to cover his soldiers' heads.' He turned to look at her. 'Because I think that is the only way to pray before battle, Mrs Cole. For its failure, I mean. To pray any other way isn't a prayer at all, but a petition for murder.'

She sat back and looked at him, then down at her feet, shaking her head, as if she was still unsure. As if she couldn't be sure of anything any more. Eventually she looked up again, towards the tent. 'I should get back. They'll be waking soon.'

Withdrawing her hand from under his, she stood and picked up her bucket. Arthur noticed the seam of her evening dress had split. As she bent down it gaped, an opening eye, showing a blink of pale flesh beneath.

'I'm glad we met again, Father,' she said.

'Well, I'm certainly glad you're here,' he replied. 'If St Michael doesn't hear me, then at least I know I'll be in good hands.'

Arthur watched her walk back towards the hospital tent. Another flock of flamingos took flight from the shore. He turned to follow them, feeling tiredness wash through his body, and thought about what Mrs Cole had said. Had God been there at Bukoba? He thought about the fresh graves outside the town, the body of the girl, the whine of the shells, the eyes of the Captain, burning, and then of Jack, flying high in his plane looking down over no-man's-land. The butterfly wings of men spreading out from their shared body of mud.

24 JUNE 1915

Longido, German East Africa

———◇———

Tendai was trying to keep still: as still as a stone in moving grass, as a lizard paused on a rock in the sun. But as the sun rose higher flies began landing on his face and his neck, making him twitch. He kept his eyes closed and willed himself to ignore the tickling hair-touch of their legs, around his lips, over his eyelids. The sound of their wings buzzing loud in his ear.

He had been lying in the tall grass since late last night, hiding from the German *ruga-ruga* who were still pursuing him. They'd spotted him the day before when he approached a bush settlement in search of food. Tendai had thought he was still in British East Africa. He hadn't known the collection of rondavels and one square brick hut was a *Schutztruppe* outpost. An African was hoeing a patch of ground behind the brick hut, and Tendai had called out to him in English. But as soon as he spoke he knew something was wrong. The man looked up at him with wide eyes, then turned away and called out in Swahili. An askari came out of the closest rondavel. The man pointed towards Tendai and the soldier levelled his rifle at him, shouting at him in German. Then a *Schutztruppe* officer rushed out of another rondavel and put his hand on the askari's arm. He also shouted to Tendai, but in English, 'Halt, stay there!' But Tendai had heard what happened to prisoners caught by the Germans. So he ran. He heard the askari fire and waited for the bullet to hit him, but it whined past over his head, cracking through the branches of a tree. He ran on as the askari fired again, pushing his way into a thicket of bush as the bullet hit the ground. He kept running, wildly smashing through the foliage, his arms over his face. But he knew it was too late and he could already hear the deep chest grunting of the *ruga-ruga* streaming out of the camp, making chase behind him.

That had been yesterday evening. Since then they had chased and tracked him through the night, deep into the veld, down the valley of a shrunken river to a lower plain, dotted with kopjes. His body ached and hurt from the night-long pursuit. He had cut his foot on a piece of wire, his limbs were weak with hunger and his head was full of questions. He didn't understand how he had wandered into German territory or why the Germans were so anxious to capture him. He wasn't wearing uniform and wasn't armed. He couldn't have posed a threat to them or the people of the area. But what Tendai didn't know was that the *Schutztruppe* had recently broken a network of British spies, Africans working for British Intelligence. Von Lettow was said to be furious and the order had come down from the General himself as a matter of urgency: all suspects were to be caught and interrogated or killed. The porters who cleaned the officers' latrines were already dead.

The *ruga-ruga* were Masi warriors recruited as German irregulars. Tendai knew they could track and hunt any animal on the veld. He'd caught a glimpse of one of them the day before as he hid behind a rock by the river. A tall, lean man, about his own age. His hair was shaved into a tuft at the front of his head, a water gourd was slung across his chest and he wore a simple limbo cloth and a blanket, also tied across his chest. He carried an old German musket. As the man had stopped to drink from his gourd, Tendai saw that the stories were true: both his lower and upper teeth had been sharpened. Another porter at the lake once told him the Masi ate the flesh of their enemies. Tendai hadn't believed him, but now, lying in the tall grass, listening to the *ruga-ruga* work their way nearer and nearer to his hiding place, he couldn't help but remember both the porter's tale and that flash of sharpened teeth.

More flies were gathering on his back, drawn to the unhealed scars that criss-crossed his spine; long wheals of thickened skin like stout white string. His shirt was thin and torn, and the blood seeped through the cotton in long, dark patches. Worried the flies would attract the attention of the *ruga-ruga*, he carefully rolled from his side onto his back. Every rustle of the grass against his skin seemed loud in his ears. His breath felt clumsy and his heartbeat so strong he was sure its echo through the ground would be enough for the Masi to find him.

The scars on his back were from a *niboko*, a hippo-hide whip. He had left the lake camp shortly after receiving them but his troubles had begun long before that whipping. Lying in the grass, his eyes tightly shut, his body aching and his throat dust-dry, he knew exactly the moment all his pain could be traced back to: one minute on a trek several months before. The minute when they killed the rhino.

They had been coming back from a patrol. Tendai was with a party of porters bearing for a company of the 3rd KAR. He was used to the assumed superiority of white men. He had grown up expecting the Europeans in and around Enkeldoorn to treat him and his mother as if they were hardly there. To shout orders at them, to hoot their cars to clear them off the road. It was the way of things. But bearing for askaris, other Africans, was something he had been finding hard to understand, to adjust to. They treated him like the white men did, as if their uniforms changed the colour of their skin.

He remembered that trek as one of the worst, not just because of the askaris, but also because several porters had died, leaving the remaining carriers loaded with more than their usual baggage. And of course because of what happened later. As they marched two abreast in a long line through the veld, his arms ached as if they would fall off his body, and his legs felt as if they were rooted in the earth. Every step was an effort, a tearing of these roots from the dry soil. But then perhaps that is why the rhino had come then. Because he was so unhappy, and the rhino knew he was, because the rhino was his animal.

When he was very young Tendai's father told him the rhino was his totem. He had whispered it to him, very quietly, as if it were a great secret, an important message to be remembered. He even gave him a totem name, *Chipembere*. Rhino. Tendai listened carefully, wide-eyed, to his father as he told him he must never kill or eat his totem animal. If he did, it would bring very bad luck.

The next day Tendai proudly told his mother that his totem was the rhino: the strong, brave, rhino with a hide like iron. She had picked him up, laughed and said, 'So, little man, is that your father talking again?' The next week the white men came and killed his father. Tendai was sure the telling of his secret had brought bad luck. That it had brought the white men and his father's death.

The rhino's first charge smashed through the line ahead of him. No one had seen it behind the trees. The marching soldiers must have surprised it; perhaps it had been asleep. Tendai heard its pounding hooves, a scatter of screams from the askaris, and then it was through them, trampling the men like blades of grass. The line broke in every direction as the rhino slowed and heaved its body around to face the fleeing soldiers and carriers. Tendai stood, frozen. Perhaps he would have some power over the animal because it was his totem. He stared at it, watching its blinking short-sighted eyes, willing it to leave. But it lowered its head, pawed the ground and began a second charge, smashing through a Scotch cart, splintering the wood and throwing boxes and sacks of supplies into the air. Again it slowed in a cloud of dust on the other side of the line and turned. Gathering its shoulders underneath itself, it leant forward and began a third charge. But then the machine-gun fired. A cracking rattle of bullets from a juddering Vickers gun mounted on a rock. Tendai saw the shake and stutter of its ammunition belt, the vibrating arms of the askari firing it, the shouting face of the white officer behind him, screaming 'Fire! Fire! Fire!'

The rhino was charging straight at the gun. The bullets splintered and shattered its horn, sprayed its face, exploded an eye, raked across its body, breaking its hide. But still it charged, straight into the rain of lead, slowing against the bullets as a person might slow against an oncoming wind. Its gallop faltered to a trot, then to a stumbling walk, then, as the gun kept up its relentless firing, finally it collapsed. The gun stopped, its last report ringing out over the veld, the panicked rattle of its firing replaced by silence, then by squawks and screams of frightened birds. The rhino lay before it, shattered and broken, bleeding into the dusty ground. Its armoured body shook with a last grunting breath and then was still. Everyone stared at its broken bulk while the officer behind the machine-gun walked forward and nudged at its neck with his foot. Satisfied it was dead, he took off his helmet and wiped his pale face with the back of his sleeve.

Slowly, the line re-formed. Men emerged from behind rocks and bushes, gathered their rifles, their baggage and arranged themselves into marching order. The wounded askaris were placed on stretchers. An officer blew a whistle, and they trekked on, back towards the camp. As he walked behind the marching soldiers Tendai was certain that now he would have bad luck. His totem had been killed before his eyes. He had not tried to save it and now it would have its revenge.

So Tendai was not surprised when disease swept through the carriers' camp, leaving hundreds of porters dead in a month. And he was not even surprised when he was arrested and wrongly accused by the pay master of stealing a tin of ghee from the supply store. He attributed everything to the death of his totem animal. But the punishment for the theft of the ghee had been too much for him, and it was after this that he decided to leave the camp and return to Maronda Mashanu. Four askaris had held him down, one at each limb, with a fifth sitting astride his shoulders. His shirt was pulled up to his neck, and his shorts down over his buttocks, exposing the skin between. A sixth askari stood over him and Tendai could smell the scent of the coconut oil rubbed in the *niboko* as he flexed the whip in his hands.

After the fifteenth lash Tendai managed to escape the grip of the askaris and begged the officer in charge to stop. But Captain Meinertzhagen had insisted the full punishment be carried out, and they had pinned him down once more for the remaining five lashes.

He was in the hospital tent for a week after that, but as soon as he could move his back again he left, slipping out of the camp in the middle of the night. He knew if he stayed there he would die, and he knew he could not die yet. He had no children to prepare his burial, to perform the necessary rituals. His spirit would be lost, left to wander for ever. So he left. To save himself and to save his spirit. He would, somehow, make his way back to Maronda Mashanu. There, he would care for his mother and farm the land. He would grow maize and pumpkins and sell enough of his crops to buy cattle. With cattle he would be able to marry and then, when he had a wife and a farm, if Baba Cripps taught him to, perhaps he would teach the children in the school. He would never leave Maronda Mashanu and he would never carry or work for another man again.

Tendai had his eyes shut, so he did not see the *ruga-ruga* part the long grass with the blade of his bayonet. He did not see the filed points of his sharpened teeth, the raising of his rifle, or the fine dark tattoos etched on the cheeks of his face. He just heard the grunt of effort as the man brought the bayonet down. Felt a sudden cold on the right side of his groin, a rasping scrape as the blade caught the edge of his pelvis, the tug on his body, as if he were a puppet, as it was pulled out again, the cold turn to heat, spreading up his stomach. Then the heat punctured with more cold, as the man stabbed and stabbed again. He did not see anything, but kept his eyes shut, and as the bayonet pierced his throat, he was already dreaming of rhinos charging through the veld, of his mother and his father, standing at the top of the kopje, welcoming him home.

Maronda Mashanu, Mashonaland, Southern Rhodesia

—◇—

Fortune is kneeling at his side, holding a tin bowl in front of him and guiding his hand into its contents. He feels the soft, warm sadza there. Like mashed potato, but thicker in the grain. Pinching a little between his finger and thumb, as if he were testing cotton, he brings it to his mouth. Her hand is resting on his knee and his is on her shoulder. This is how he eats now. Holding on. Slowly, like a child.

Outside he can hear children. The delicate peal of a goat's bell. The rising of life in the veld. After he has eaten he will sit outside and wait for Noel Brettell to come and read to him. And as he waits, he will smoke his pipe. The doctor who visits him says he should not smoke his pipe. Fortune says he should not smoke his pipe. But he will still smoke his pipe. He will feel the heat of it linger in his mouth, the smoke work its way over his palate and smell its thick scent in his nostrils. He will live in sensation, in now and not in the past, where the memories crowd at the edge of his mind. The tobacco will help him forget, and it will help him remember; reminding him, in his dark, half-deaf, rise-and-fall world, that he is alive.

Alive. He did not expect to return from the war alive. He preached a Christianity of witness and the war had been no exception. He went out on every patrol, on every attack, on every slow gunboat across the sheet-metal water. And every time he expected to die. He was not afraid, but he expected to die, the way he had seen so many others die. But he did not. St Michael kept the bullets flying past him, gave him shelter when the shells fell and jammed the rifles aimed at him. When he returned he built another mission church to celebrate his survival. It was another echo of Zimbabwe and he called it Zuwa Rabuda: Rising Sun.

He remembers his return from the war clearly. But not for the relief it brought. And not even for the unsettling sensation of being back in Maronda Mashanu where so little had changed. Where, despite all that had happened, the goats still grazed and the women still walked from the river with firewood and water on their heads, making it seem impossible they had lived through the same period of time. That the same dates had passed over them. That is not why he remembers his return. He remembers it because for eighteen months at the lake he witnessed the insult of war. The injury of it, man to man, black and white, and he thought his return would mean an end to such witness. But he was wrong. On his arrival back in Mashonaland he found the insult continued. Not in the way of the war: carriers withering under neglect, askaris cut down under machine-gun fire, men dying in a war that was not theirs to fight. But in a quieter fashion. Delivered in the language of the law. Devised by ministers and commissioners not generals and captains. Slower, less immediate in nature, but still fuelled by the same idea. But then, as he came to realise, in Southern Rhodesia it was always the same idea. There had only ever been one idea in the country, one idea that dominated all others. The idea that shaped the country and fuelled its forming. The idea of Land. It was the only idea that mattered. Land had brought the settlers, the missionaries, the war. Land held the stones, the iron, the gold. Land held the Africans' ancestors, their spirits and their myths. Land held the past of the country, locked in its earth, and, as he realised on his return from the war, its future too.

The insult came in the form of an Imperial Commission report on the native reserves. The author, Government Surveyor Atherstone, recommended a reduction of one million acres in this land set aside for native use. In the Sabi Reserve, in Arthur's own district, the land taken by the government would be used to build a railway. The reserve would be cleared of native villages for six miles on each side of the line, and the land there assigned for white settlement only.

Arthur knew the reserves were already too small for the growing population that lived there. That water supplies were short, and much of the earth infertile. And he also knew the BSA Company didn't want the Africans to be able to farm their own land, so they would take the best land from the reserves. They wanted workers, not farmers. He also knew the Company had millions of acres of unassigned land it could draw upon elsewhere. But that unassigned land would be left and kept for when more white settlements would be built, and now, after a war where thousands of Africans had died, land would be taken from the reserves instead.

He was exhausted by his experience of war. His soul felt shredded.

But he recognised that without land the natives would become strangers in their own country. The reserves were not the answer, but as he wrote to his friend John White at the Aboriginal Protection Society, they were the 'best makeshift harbour of refuge'. So he chose to fight again and began writing a pamphlet, *A Million Acres*, in protest. Looking back it seemed inevitable, but there must have been a choice. He could have allowed the report to go unchallenged. Returned to just his local mission work. Perhaps even returned to England. But really, there had been no choice. He had to fight the Commission's report. He had always fought. He had only ever chosen not to fight once in his life and he'd never stopped regretting that choice. Even now, years later, pinching sadza to his slow mouth, holding Fortune's soft shoulder, her hand on his knee, the thought of that choice, that walking away, still haunted him. Like a recurring dream that he will never wake up from, that he will only forget when he never wakes up again.

◇

Annual Meeting of the B.S.A. Company, 1917
Address by Company Chairman, Dr Starr Jameson

Now gentlemen, besides the record of progress, in various directions, measures have been taken to clear up ambiguities and uncertainties, to consolidate our position, and so make our property more valuable. Our native areas have always been in rather a fluid state. A commission was appointed by the Imperial Government to inquire into the necessary areas to be set aside for natives . . . The needs of the natives, both now and in the future – after careful examination by this Commission – which travelled all over the country, accompanied by the surveyor general – have been amply provided for, and the net result is that more than 1,000,000 acres of land have been added to the land which may be leased for white settlement. That means really that you people get another million acres odd of what is called unalienated land in the country. That is very satisfactory . . .

◇

13th March, 1918
Waddilove Methodist Mission
Mashonaland

Dear Arthur,

When this Commission was investigating I was asked to give
evidence and refused. I thought that the composition of it was so
palpably one-sided that the British Government would take no
notice of its findings. Had things been normal, I am sure they
would not have done so. This war has meant the passing of many
things that would have been more fully investigated and probably
turned down. The fact that such a large number of Natives in the
whole of this country are living on private farms and paying in
many cases big rents, proves conclusively that the land set apart
for them is either unsuitable or very insufficient.

It seems to me a shameful thing that when quite a number of
Africans are assisting the Empire in this gigantic struggle against
tyranny that this time should be selected to rob them of their
heritage.

With kindest regards,
Yours affectionately,
John White

October 30th, 1918
Private Secretary to the B.S.A.
Company's Resident Administrator
Salisbury

Dear Rev. A. S. Cripps,

I am directed by the Administrator to acknowledge receipt of
your pamphlet entitled 'A Million Acres'. His Honour regrets that
your zeal for the natives should lead you to make such an un-
deserved and offensive attack upon those responsible for the
administration of this territory . . . the unfairness of your action
seems to His Honour to be quite inexcusable.

I think you will be well advised to accept without further
protest the Commission's decision and you will find, I feel certain,
that in the result of putting the decision into effect, the natives
will suffer no hardship.

◇

From *The Sabi Reserve* by Arthur Shearly Cripps,
Missionary to Mashonaland

Tour in the Sabi Reserve, Oct. 1919

From map 2 (appended) some idea of the lie of the land in the Sabi
Reserve may be obtained. The route A marked upon it represents
what is by far the more probable railway route. Route B – the Government Cattle Road (used in moving cattle towards Odzi for East
African Campaign supplies), generally speaking, represents a possible alternative – a route much less likely I should think. The map
shows approximately the defined areas of several native clans. The
commission's recommendation of reduction applied to Route B
would wipe out much of perhaps the loveliest stretch of natives'
open country in all the Reserve – that ruled by paramount Chief
Marara. On the other hand applied to route A, which is much the
more probable railway route, as I believe, the recommendation, liter-
ally carried out, would wipe out most of the fine, if hilly block of
Chief Magaya's country, and slice deep into the adjacent territories of
Chiefs Kwenda and Tshitsungi.

Moreover, I suppose that Chief Mambo would be mulcted of
some land, possibly not worth much to him, in the neighbourhood
of the Sabi river-crossing. For practical politics, it seems fair to
assume that route A is the railway route we have to reckon with.

It occurred to me that it would be well if one would make effective representations against the proposed tampering with the
Reserve, to make certain investigations of sorts on the spot myself.
So I set myself a route through some of its reputed dry bush-veld
country last October, and followed it out without much deviation. It
was the end of the dry season proper then; I make that admission for
what it is worth, with the qualification that a quite unusually early
September rainfall had demonstrably made itself felt in some of the
parched country I passed through. Indeed, in a patch I visited,
munga (native bulrush-like millet) seemed to have made real head-
way already. I left the Assistant Native Commissioner's Camp at
Buhera's behind me and travelled on by Matindera Ruins and Mutshutshu's Ruins, through some desolate country, towards Betera's.
Afterwards I crossed the Mirihari river not far from its junction with
the Sabi, and passed on amid interesting big-game and (reputed)

lion country. I went thence into Mambo's tract, that seems to have been much depopulated (owing to the pressure of droughts in recent years, time and time again). Then at last I came into fine native hilly country (I was in Tshitsungi's realm then), and on to the beautiful river Rwenje, up whose right bank (going upwards) route A runs. I was to see something for myself of an already well-populated country, that promises soon (under pressures of evictions from private lands) to be quite thickly populated as Mashonaland goes, a country that is threatened by the Reserves Commission's verdict, a country that our big but partially barren Sabi Reserve can ill afford to lose.

I went through bad country that the Commission has proposed to leave our natives undisturbed in their possession of, a real bad class of country, comparatively speaking. I pursued my travels on this Reserve in a countryside of some very fair country (on the whole) that the Commission has seriously menaced with a loss of over a quarter of a million acres. I give some extracts from my revised notes such as they are:

Saturday, October 11th
I saw no water for some while after that on the ground we travelled. The water bottle that had been lent me was to do me splendid service . . . Not far beyond was the site of the old Camp, which is reported to have been abandoned owing to shortness of water supply . . .

Sunday, October 12th
After service and breakfast we came through some very dry country indeed . . . The country we had got amongst seemed of a different class to that around Enkeldoorn, generally speaking. Shown a plant with purplish pink flower that is used to burn salt. Saw a comparatively small number of human inhabitants and cattle. We struck paramount Chief Nyashano's wagon road some way from Matindera Ruins . . . Great baobabs stood up fantastically with but small show of earth to nourish them . . . We saw water on rock near, a small rain-fed pool in appearance; it was screened with turfs . . .

Monday, October 13th
We travelled on to Mutshutshu's where there seems to be a fairly well-watered sort of oasis in a very dry countryside . . . We decided not to go on till morning; the road ahead was said not to be very well watered. We slept outside near the little town of grain-bins beside

the kraal. Smallness of grain-bins was, it appeared to me, rather a feature of this countryside.

Tuesday, October 14th
There seemed to be cultivation and inhabitants about, for some way, then the country became wild. Bush grew very thick in one strip . . .

Wednesday, October 15th
I heard how people had migrated from Mambo's drought-stricken country – making for Magaya's and Tshitsungi's countries. We came on to paramount Chief Mambo's tiny village . . . country very desolate apparently. We came on . . . into Tshitsungi's country. We had got into better-looking country now, at least country more of the sort one knew nearer home, not that water-short bush-country of Nyashano's realm. We had crossed a small flowing stream (it was my first sight of such a thing for full five days, I believe) . . . We descended by a great descent to the River Rwenje – a beautiful and ample stream where we crossed it. We were now in the country menaced by that decision of the Reserves Commission, which claims as reversion not only a fifty-yard strip, but a six-mile belt on each side of the proposed railway.

Friday, October 17th
There seemed to be fine open ground about in that valley, as well as rough ground . . . I had just been directed towards my journey's goal by a native iron-worker. I found him hammering with a stone at a hoe-head, his anvil being a rock. The goatskin bellows blew while he left his job to help me. We came on . . . sighting various villages, some rough ground and some open ground. I noticed some promising-looking red soil, and also some swamp-ground. We came on largely by a sledge-way, to Kwenda's mission farm . . . Let us hear one conclusion on this whole matter! – *There is some poor land apparently very ill-suited in its present state to carry a large population of folk or cattle in the Sabi Reserve. Therefore the Sabi Reserve can ill-afford to lose fine native ground.*

Saturday, October 18th (St Luke's Day)
I saw some more threatened land that can be ill-spared, but before many miles were travelled I was doubtless in the Wiltshire Estate. It is not of course proposed to ask from the European Co.'s Wiltshire Estate more than a fifty-yard strip to feed the promised railway.

The Native African Sabi Reserve it is that stands to lose a twelve-mile belt to the railway, involving a loss of 291,800 acres, much of it good land surely, while large tracts in other parts of the Reserve are bad. God help us!!!

BSA Company's Resident Administrator's Office, Salisbury, Southern Rhodesia

———◇———

'Do you know what the local police call that place of his? Sherwood Forest. That's what. There are that many thieving piccaninnies and shirkers hiding out down there.'

Atherstone's face was strained, taut across his temples, the veins in his neck standing proud above his collar. He turned on his heel and paced back to the far end of the Administrator's office.

The Company's Resident Administrator, Sir Donald Chaplain, did not want to be in his office. It was a fine evening and he would rather be in his garden. There were some petunias that needed tending. And a clematis to be tied back. But instead he was in his office at the end of a long day and although the window was open, the room was stifling. And now Atherstone had started shouting again.

He gestured towards a wicker chair in the corner of the room, but Atherstone ignored his offer and kept pacing up and down. Sir Donald sighed and looked across at the Chief Native Commissioner, who sat in a reading chair staring at a point on the floor, Atherstone's shadow flicking across his face with each pass of the open window.

'How about you, Herbert? You've spent some time down there. Have you been to Cripps' place?'

The Chief Native Commissioner adjusted his position in the chair. He too would rather have been elsewhere. His wife was cooking a dinner party tonight and he wanted some peace at home before the guests started arriving.

'Well, his running of things down there is somewhat unconventional. It certainly contributes to the difficulties faced by the Native Department, I mean in our efforts to maintain the prestige of the European community, not to mention discipline amongst the natives.'

'And do you know why the veld fires never touch his farms?' Atherstone was still caught up in his own round of rhetorical questions. 'Not because he's blessed, which is what the kaffirs think of course.

No, the only reason those fires never touch his place is because there's no bloody grass left there to burn. He's got so many of them farming there that the ground is bare, dust!'

'Yes, I know. You've told us already.' Sir Donald turned back to the Native Commissioner. 'Well that would seem to support what Hadfield had to say about him.' He reached forward from his chair and shuffled through some papers on his desk. 'Yes, here it is. ". . . . an absence of order and restraint which revealed an attitude of mind in that great and honourable man not in itself commendable when detached from his good qualities".'

'I'll tell you what it's like,' Atherstone continued, finally pausing from his pacing at the far end of the room. 'It's like those weaver birds, the ones that build their nests by the hornet's so when you try to shake the buggers down you get a face full of hornets instead. That's what it's like. The kaffirs are the bloody weaver birds and he's the bloody hornet, buzzing his way up here to sting us.'

'Oh, please sit down!' Sir Donald raised his voice for the first time that afternoon. Atherstone took a seat in the wicker chair, sullen as a scolded schoolboy.

'I don't think it's as bad as all that,' Sir Donald continued more calmly. 'He may be an irritation and I know from my own experience that the man's certainly a very difficult person to deal with. But he's harmless enough. Herbert?'

The Native Commissioner shifted his position in the reading chair again. Nodding his head and frowning he opened his mouth to speak, but Atherstone interrupted before he could get any further.

'Look, with respect, Your Honour, it's all very well him tramping up here from the bush, ranting about injustice done to some piccaninny, but this is a different matter. I don't think you realise. We need that railway, and we need that land for that railway. And he's not just complaining to us, you know. Those pamphlets went all over the place. He's had questions asked in the House, letters in *The Times* and the *Manchester Guardian*. And now the Archbishop of Canterbury wants to see him about the "Native Reserve Affair".'

'Believe me, Atherstone, I've made it perfectly clear to him that I don't like what he's doing. Inexcusable, really.'

'Bloody treasonable,' Atherstone agreed.

'Well, yes . . .' Sir Donald didn't like the way this was going, but the Surveyor did have a point. The missionary was certainly causing a stir in Britain, and as the British government still had an Imperial veto on all native affairs, he had good reason for concern.

He turned to the Native Commissioner again. 'What do you think of this?'

This time the Native Commissioner spoke quickly, pre-empting any attempt at interruption from the Surveyor. 'Well, I don't think he'll stop until he's got his way. He's more native than European, you see, defends them like his own because he thinks he is one of them. And they love him for it.' He cast a glance at the Chief Surveyor, 'Try to budge him and you might find it's him who's the weaver bird and they who are the hornets.'

The sun had edged a little further into the window, dipping under the frame on its descent towards the horizon. Its rays shone into Sir Donald's face, igniting orange stars in his eyes and playing across his desk, sparking to light the nib of a pen, a silver letter knife, a marble paperweight. He wanted to be in his garden while the sun was still up, to watch its deepening glow across the petals of his flowers and the leaves of his plants.

'Yes, well, leave this with me, Atherstone. I'll have a word with the Bishop, see what he has to say. He sails for London soon, maybe he can put things right there.'

Atherstone rose from his wicker chair and crossed to the open window. He stood with his back to the room, his arms on the frame, blocking out the sun from Sir Donald's face.

'The Company needs that land, it's as simple as that. I mean, who came here and found it in the first place?' He turned back into the room. 'Some bloody sky-pilot can't stop us getting it.'

Sir Donald leant forward, put his elbows on the desk and pulled his hand down his face, feeling the heavy cool of his wedding ring pass over his skin. As his fingers passed his eyes, he exchanged a glance with the Chief Native Commissioner, who was still sitting in the reading chair, nodding towards the Surveyor's back, his eyebrows raised and tapping the face of his watch with his forefinger. Sir Donald knew what he meant. Time was getting on. It was time to go.

The Times, 11 June 1920

SOUTHERN RHODESIA
to the Editor of *The Times*

Sir – During the past four months, while in England on furlough, I have noticed with surprise and great regret the attempts recently made in the Press and on public platforms to create a feeling that grave abuses exist in the administration of the natives in my diocese of Southern Rhodesia, and that they are subjected to oppression at the hands of the British South Africa Company, or the European settlers, or both. From my intimate knowledge of that territory, and considerable experience for 17 years of the manner in which the native problems have been dealt with, I can unhesitatingly endorse the recent high tribute of our High Commissioner (Lord Buxton) to the sympathetic treatment which our natives receive at the hands of the administrative officials and of the white population. The remarkable progress which they have made in numbers, wealth and education during the last 20 years is in itself a sufficient testimony to the prudent, just, and benevolent methods adopted by the Company, with the whole-hearted support of the white community, in handling this, one of the most difficult branches of Colonial administration. It is not my intention to enter into any controversy on this subject, but I feel it my duty to say what I know and believe to be true.

Fredric Southern Rhodesia

12, St John's Street, Chichester

14 July 1920
Maronda Mashanu,
Mashonaland,
Southern Rhodesia

To John Harris,
Anti-slavery and Aboriginal Protection Society,
London

Dear John Harris,

Many thanks for sending me the Bishop's letter. I suppose he means well and is in his own way conscientious. Personally, I quite sympathise as to the picture your vivid words conjure up of the disciples of the Black Christ forsaking him and fleeing. There is some stern work ahead of us (D.V.) assuredly. Well God bless your society!!!

Yours ever,

A. S. Cripps

P.S. I have just read a report from the West Sussex Gazette of another of Bishop Beaven's speeches. The Bishop emphatically denies that there was oppression of the native races, who, he declared, 'were dealt with in the spirit of even-handed justice for which the flag of Britain stands'. God forgive him if he really said that. Would it possibly help the Native Cause if I challenged him to disown or withdraw this statement, or if he would do neither, to take three months' notice from me?

1 January 1921
Maronda Mashanu,
Mashonaland

To John Harris,
Aboriginal Protection Society,
London

Dear John,

. . . This unawakened race does not perceive yet the injury that has been done it. But one day it will arouse itself, become articulate . . . and then . . .? But this is for the next act in this sombre drama.

Yours
A.S.C.

PART FOUR

Our souls are love and a continual farewell.
W. B. Yeats, *Ephemera*

Marondera, Zimbabwe

◇

Another Blue Arrow morning. The touch of the bus's air condition-
ing, its taste of dry ice after the heat outside. The shake of its awaken-
ing and the stop-start weave and roll, out of the thinning town and
into the scrubland of the veld.

This time I am on the Harare–Mutare service. On the road that
winds south-east out of the capital, rising towards the highlands and
the scent of pine amid the eucalyptus. But I am not going all the way
today. Seventy-two kilometres and an hour after we left Harare I step
down from the coach into a sun-blast of heat and go to wait outside
the pink plasterwork of the Marondera Hotel.

I have come to Marondera to meet another person who knew you.
Canon Richard Holderness is ninety years old; sixty years ago he
drove 100 miles from his own mission station to visit you at Maronda
Mashanu, because, as he told me later that day, he 'wanted to find out
what made you tick'. Well, I am still trying to find out myself, so I've
come to Marondera to ask Canon Holderness what answer you gave
him. I have read your letters, seen your photographs, heard your stories, read your poems and knelt at your grave, but the elemental nature
of you still eludes me. And there are unresolved questions: the shadow
granddaughter, the name in your will, and why you left Britain in the
first place.

After camping at Great Zimbabwe I returned to Harare. There was a
book in the National Archives I wanted to read there. One of your
books that Leonard had mentioned, called *An Africa for Africans*.
Leonard described it as your statement on land in Africa, your thesis
on why the Africans should be allowed to buy and own their own
land. He told me a story about a visit from Paramount Chief Mutshutshu. One night, in the middle of a great storm, the chief's house
was struck by lightning. It was burnt to the ground, a sparking, fizzing
bonfire lighting up the rain-filled night. He lost everything, including
his copy of *An Africa for Africans*. Leonard remembers the chief walk-

ing to Maronda Mashanu to request another copy from you. That was all he wanted. Not shelter or help or blessing. Just your book and the possibility of a different future.

At the archives I have to talk my way in. I am told I have already had all the time I'm allowed in there without a permit from the Ministry of Information. But the porter at the front desk is sympathetic when I tell him why I am here. He nods his head earnestly, as if he understands the importance of what I am doing.

'It is good that you have come here to learn about your uncle,' he says. 'He is your *Vadzimu*, your ancestral spirit.'

Then his serious face breaks into a smile and he laughs, hits his desk and wags his finger at me. 'So you had better go in and read his book, otherwise he will be angry, and then you will be very, very sick.'

So I am allowed an extra day in the archives, and as instructed by the porter I spend it with you and your book.

In Harare the papers, the coffee shops and the taxi drivers are all busy with the same conversation. The talk is of the land situation, the redistribution of the white farmlands to the rural blacks. A group calling themselves the War Veterans, led by a Zanu PF MP, Dr Hunzvi, are threatening land invasions and forced occupancy. Sitting at the dark wood desks of the National Archives, the librarians and archivists moving silently about me, this contemporary conversation gives your eighty-year-old words an added weight. I realise you saw this coming. This cycle of taking. The land question. The idea of land, tied like a Gordian knot at the centre of the country, tightening over the years until now, when it seems that nothing will undo it; nothing but the fall of the sword.

From *An Africa for Africans* (1927)

Self-determination and self-development are surely required by our Natives, and how are they to attain to a proper measure of either – conditions and feeling in South Africa being what one has found them to be by long experience? Self-development and self-determination need to be stressed in my opinion if we are to seek any really hopeful settlement of the Native question in our Colony . . .

'But to hold all natives down in a position of permanent inferiority will ultimately beget a deep and bitter race hatred which will aim, not at the autonomy of the black but at the extermination of the white. If once such a huge war of extermination between white and black broke out in South Africa, it is idle to argue that the white would win. He would, of course, with his machine-guns and aeroplanes and other "civilised" devices, but it would be a Pyrrhic victory.' (Professor Brooks)

'Survivors,' as Tacitus puts it, 'not only of the others but of themselves.'

Let us remember that in considering the interests of Southern Rhodesia's Natives we are considering the interests of eight hundred and thirteen thousands of our fellow British subjects. Let us remember, in reckoning out the due proportion of the land proposed to be devoted to them and their children, the proportion of their numbers to the number of the settlers, also what a mighty proportion of the whole Southern Rhodesian revenue they pay.

The position of our Natives encouraged to plunge into the new go-ahead life of the Southern Rhodesia Colony, but denied a place in the sun as regards that self-development on the soil which really appeals to them, while the arts of cajolery are used to induce more and more Europeans to acquire vested rights on easy terms in that soil appeals to me as pathetic and ominous of tragedy. Oh the pity of it! . . .

Before I make an end here I want to avow my hopefulness as to a Territorial Segregation Policy proving a welcome remedy for our sick sub-continent's racial bitterness, but I am hopeful as to such a Policy, only if it be coupled with a REALLY liberal settlement of our Native Land Question. In a report to the Government of the South African Union (Blue Book U.G. 41–1918) the late M. Evans, CMG, summarised the condition on which a Territorial Separation must depend, if it were to have any real hope of working prosperity. He wrote to this effect:

'The native population is rapidly increasing. By contact and example we are altering their outlook on life. The present generation is not like their fathers, and the next will differ more widely. For a better adjustment in the interests of both races we propose to take away the present right of the native to acquire land where he will, and to strictly limit his opportunities within certain recommended areas. If the scope within such areas is not such as to enable him to reasonably develop with the general progress of the country, then I fear that our attempt will not result in that racial peace and satisfaction which we are attempting to secure.'

Granted that saving clause – I avow myself a fervent segregationist at this present critical time in Southern Rhodesia's history. I see the splendid hope of Freedom for the Self-Development of Native Africa, which a Segregation Policy provides at this present juncture when indigenous Native Life is being so hard pressed in our Mixed Areas.

This last passage is something of a shock to me: to see you declare yourself a 'fervent segregationist'. I understand your motives, and that you were writing in a climate that nurtured serious arguments of opposition on the grounds that European diseases in the Mixed Areas effectively 'culled' the natives living there. But still, with my knowledge of the history of apartheid I find yours a hard conclusion to follow. Reading it again, however, I realise that you were already aware of the weakness in the theory, those capital letters seeming to spell out your desperation for a solution against another instinct: that given the opportunity humanity would choose advantage over equality – 'a REALLY liberal settlement . . .'

Turning the page I find a loose piece of paper, and I remember something else Leonard told me. Before you died you instructed him to insert a typewritten statement into each of the last six copies of the book. I pick out the paper now and read the date: 11 July 1950.

Note on Segregation by A. S. Cripps: When I wrote this book, which was published in 1927, I was willing to approve of Segregation for Africans and Europeans – if Africans should be given a fair share of the land in the Colony. But afterwards I did not consider that Africans, in my opinion were given a fair share in the S. Rhodesian scheme of Land apportionment, and lost my faith in Segregation for S. Rhodesia.

I am thankful for Segregation as planned by the Morris-Carter Commission for opening the way for Africans to purchase plots of land but I do not believe that Segregation is a righteous policy for a British Colony. Can it be a right policy for Christian people? Certainly not! A. S. Cripps.

While in Harare I spend some time with white Zimbabweans, testing your name against their memories just as I had against the memories of black Zimbabweans in Chivhu and Maronda Mashanu. Jeremy left me a list of names and numbers in his house, of people I should contact if I wanted to go out, if I wanted company. I hire a mobile phone and call Stassi and Alice Callinicos. Stassi lectures in Classics at the University of Zimbabwe and Alice is a teacher who used to scout for film locations. They weren't expecting my call, but in the laid-back Zimbabwean manner Alice tells me, 'Sure, why don't you come round? We're going to a party tonight, come along.'

The party is at a house on a hill, its lower fields ranked with parked cars, guided into place by a young black man in a waistcoat and a reflector belt. Flares line each side of the long drive up to the house, a flickering, primitive runway leading to the glow of a room filled with people, talking, drinking, smoking. There is an open veranda, and an undercurrent of music. Another black man in a waistcoat serves me from behind a bar. I don't remember any black faces among the guests, but the people at the party are not the 'Rhodies' I have met elsewhere, the residue of Ian Smith's regime, the white hardliners who have stayed in the country under majority rule, still holding their minority rule views close to their chests, like a deck of forbidden cards. These, at the party, are another breed of white Zimbabwean. They are the ones who stayed after the War of Independence and who welcomed Mugabe and his policy of reconciliation, his promise of a multi-racial success story. They are the liberal whites who still have black cooks, nannies, gardeners, not because they feel it is right, but just because that is the way of things. I meet teachers, university lecturers, documentary film makers, rose farmers. All have the easy-going nature that is naturally inherited in this country, the calm acquaintance with fate. They are people to whom history seems to have happened, not passed by. It is there in their talk of 'before', in their grandfathers who came here in ox-carts, and is palpable in the recent changes in their lives. The changes in the country have effected changes on them. History is alive and real in their memories in a way I have rarely encountered with their peers in Britain.

John is like this. A carpenter in his late thirties, he still seems to be blinking into the light of his new country, a little unsure of how it all happened, but perfectly pleased to be here now that it has. I ask him if he has heard of you. He says he has one of the Shearly Cripps recipe diaries at home. Then he thinks for a moment, a smudged champagne glass in one hand, a smouldering cigarette in the other. He takes a draw, looks out above the flares into the dark night beyond.

'There were a bunch of graves with the name Cripps near my school,' he said. 'In the highlands.'

He looks back at me.

'Ja, there was a funny story attached to them too. They were in the garden of a house abandoned early in the war. But you know what? The servants there cleaned it every day. Polished the silver and everything – and nothing was ever stolen, how is that? That fella's name was Cripps – he your guy, is it?'

No, I say, not him. Just the name game again.

Someone who does know you is Pelline, who I was introduced to by Alice and Stassi. Pelline lives on a tobacco farm near Mvuri, eighty miles north of Harare. I went to visit her because I wanted to see a white farm. And I wanted to get into the country again. Harare was already feeling too concrete, too tall.

Pelline tells me what she knows about you as she sits knitting beneath the shade of a spathodia tree. It is the familiar story. Your love of the African, your belief in a black Christ. Your walking and your poetry. Your life fitting the narratives of a story moulded by its telling as a stream is shaped by its running. As a Catholic she particularly identifies with your witness to Francis of Assisi.

Pelline is in her sixties. She speaks in a clear English accent. She lives on the farm with her husband Laci (pronounced Lot-see), who came to Zimbabwe as a Hungarian refugee after the war. Their house is cool inside, bare and simple. Walking its empty, whitewashed corridors to my room with its single bed, mosquito-mesh window and bedside table, I am made to think of a convent or an isolated boarding school.

In the evening we eat crisp corn on the cob at the large wooden dining-room table. Then Laci settles down with the BBC World Service news, smoking his pipe and Pelline takes out her knitting. Outside the cicadas chirp and are answered by the intermittent crackle of the farm's CB radio, the outside world breaking on us here as distant as waves falling on a faraway shore.

In the morning Laci gives me a tour of the farm. I sit on the back of his dusty red Honda scooter, my arms around his waist as we bounce along the pock-marked tracks and paths. He is older than Pelline, but lean and tanned. The skin on the back of his hands is loose, like the skin of a tree monitor, but the legs that echo mine on each side of the scooter are sinewy and strong.

He takes me into the dark of a large corrugated warehouse and pulls out a rack of drying tobacco leaves, sliding it out like a file from a cabinet. They hang in tight rows like bats asleep, graduated in colour, fading along the line from green to yellow to brown. He tears off a corner of a leaf, rubs it between his finger and thumb and holding it out, tells me to smell, as proud as a chef asking a customer to taste. The scent is rich, edaphic, filled with the sun. It is dim in the warehouse but I can make out Laci's white grin, appearing rare and bright in his tanned face.

In the fields they are picking fresh tobacco beneath the huge steel sprinklers of the irrigation system. We bump and totter along the track through high-sided alleyways of deep green tobacco. I can feel Laci's ribs under my arms. A lorry is parked at the end of the track, its open back piled high with picked leaves. Workers walk towards it from all directions, bundles of tobacco fanning over their heads like extravagant head-dresses. *From Burnham wood to Dunsinane . . .*

Laci talks in Shona to the overseer, a middle-aged man in blue overalls and black Wellingtons, then we continue on the tour of the farm. He shows me the school he has built, and the medical centre and the village of workers' rondavels. And I begin to see the problem. This is not just a farm. It is a community, an infrastructure. Take away the farm and you take away the medical centre, the school, the workers' homes. It shouldn't be like this, but it is, and I realise once again how tightly the land knot is tied, and how hard it will be to undo.

Over the last few days Hunzvi's War Veterans have been pressing further for forced occupation of white-owned land. Fuelled by political motives against the MDC, the only opposition party, Mugabe's rhetoric seems to be moving their way, despite the possible consequences of economic ruin and, as I recognise touring the farm on the back of Laci's scooter, the mass disruption to thousands of black Zimbabweans. But then Mugabe understands land in the same way you did. He understands its potential, how it can be used, to favour and punish. How it is easier to keep hold of power in a country of subsistence farmers than a country of economically independent people.

The next day I visit Laci and Pelline's son, Miki, on his own nearby farm. Like most men his age Miki was conscripted to fight in the War of Independence. There is a framed photo of him in his parents' house, in uniform, his blond hair curling from under a beret, leaning against the armoured plate of a Humvi. Now though, he is a farmer like his father, and a keen polo player and race horse owner. He shows me a video of his winning mare, a 15.2 bay, galloping from the pack in the last furlong to cross the line, ridden by his favourite piccaninny jockey. Taking me outside into the garden he points out features of his house in relation to races won. The pool – the Gold Cup; the extension – the Jockey Club steeplechase; the new stables – the season's opening meet at Borrodale. He is amiable, popular with his workers and possessed of the easy physical sturdiness of many white Zimbabwean men. A sense of Africa in the blood, of an outdoor life. A heritage of being obeyed and making your own world from what you find in front of you. After a game of tennis (Miki wins, playing like a farmer, bare-chested, holding the racket like an axe and chopping at the ball) I ask him about the land disputes. He nods his head. He has already told me that in principle yes, some of the land should be redistributed, but it is a matter of how and to whom. He also points out that three quarters of the whites' farms were bought after independence, and that no one complained then.

'It's a problem,' he says. 'The last lot went straight to Mugabe's cronies, and then they did nothing with them. The farms are still there, just wasting, isn't it? And those bloody war veterans. I'm telling you, most of them weren't even born when that war happened. But there has been no serious trouble yet.' He pauses, watching his kids splashing in the pool. 'Some guy was badly beaten a few farms away, but I think he was British Intelligence. No one has tried anything here.'

Like his father, who came to Zimbabwe with nothing, I feel Miki would not take kindly to anyone who did try something. Both, I sense, would defend their farms to the end, and if necessary, with their lives. As I drive Miki's old pick-up back down the shaky road to his parents' farm, it is this that worries me. This potential for violence, seeded under the soil, planted in the very land that gives this country both its strength and its identity.

I drive through the farm's boundary fence, its wire sitting neatly along a straight line; lush green lawn on this side, African dust veld on the other. As I do, I pass from Miki's world of swimming pools, stables and sprinklers into the world of the workers' rondavels: goats tethered to poles, chickens shaking themselves into the earth. Children wave from the side of the road, laughing at the strange white man driving their fathers' boss's car.

The Marondera Hotel is waking to business: green-boiler-suited gardeners watering the pot plants, receptionists and waiters arriving in commuter taxis that unload their passengers, turn on full lock and sputter off back into town, trailing clouds of dust in their wake. Canon Holderness told me down the crackling line of my hired mobile that he would meet me here at 9.30 a.m. He arrives exactly on time, pulling up in front of the hotel in a long beige 1960s Chevrolet Coupé and looking small behind its large, thin steering wheel. I pick up my bag and walk towards the car as he opens the driver's door to get out and greet me. He is old, but looks much younger than his ninety years. A half-crown of white hair about his bald, freckled head, a straight nose, full cheeks and lively eyes. He wears a pair of sky blue shorts and a matching safari shirt. The shorts fall to just above the knee but his legs are barely exposed. A pair of thick white woollen socks are pulled up his shins, folded neatly at the top, leaving just his knee caps on show, like the tops of two bald heads.

He extends his hand, 'Owen Sheers? Hello, Richard Holderness. Please, get in. We'll go to my place. Do you like Coke?'

◇

'Oh, he was too much for most of the white Rhodesians, for the average church-goer. They didn't understand him. But I thought I must find out the secret of this chap, because the influence he had on the people on the mission was so profound. They were the best genuine Christians I had ever met. So I think I wrote to him and said may I come and visit you, and he said you're very welcome. So, I went alone, I left my wife at the mission and drove across to Enkeldoorn. When I got there he was living in a hut, sleeping on a mattress on the floor. Well, when I arrived he pulled his mattress out and put it under a tree for me to sleep on and he slept on the floor. I stayed there several days and I like sleeping under a tree so we enjoyed that. He used to walk into Enkeldoorn to get his post, which was about an eight-mile walk, and I would walk with him. And blow me, trying to keep up with him walking was something!'

I am sitting in Richard Holderness's front room, drinking a glass of Coke while he talks about his memories of you. His voice is steady but high, cracked at the edges by age. The room is filled with books, boxes of papers and photographs of his family. There is one of his grandson, recently killed by a crocodile while on a canoeing trip.

Like Betty Finn a few weeks before, Richard has also been telling me about his own life in the country. Also like Betty, he too fell in love with a poet, falling in love with her poem before he had even met her. It was published in the Rhodes University student magazine when she was twenty. Knowing it by heart, he recites it to me;

> How narrow is my faith if I should dream
> of easy virtue and the world's esteem
> of flights of joy without the vales of sorrow
> thinking no trial will test my faith tomorrow.
> In such a soft, rewarded life as that
> where would we build the men we marvel at?
> Wherein would virtue lie? What be our goal?
> How would love prove itself or lift the soul?

When he did meet the poet who wrote the poem, a young girl called Lockie, he married her, his twenty-year-old college sweetheart, and they lived at missions together throughout the country ever since. From the day they were married they were hardly ever apart he tells me. When they retired they built a retreat in the mountains at Bonda and lived there together, in the clear air, among the mountain streams. And then, some years ago now, she died and Richard came here, to the Borrodale Trust: a community of bungalows, neat lawns, high walls and an automatic barrier at the exit and the entrance.

At first, when he talks about his wife, he is excited, often saying 'we' when he means 'I', as if with her he, alone, no longer existed. But then, as he talks of the later years his voice slows and he grows thoughtful. Like Betty Finn he assures me that love, a true love, does not fade, but grows. He stands up from his armchair and leads me into his bedroom where he takes down a book from the bookshelf. It is a copy of C. S. Lewis's poetry. Without saying anything he opens the book, which falls apart at an often-opened page. He reads the poem there, aloud:

Oh doe not die, says Donne, *for I shall hate*
All women so. How false the sentence rings.
Women? But in a life made desolate
It is the joys once shared that have the stings.

To take the old walks alone, or not at all,
To order one pint where I ordered two,
To think of, and then not to make, the small
Time-honoured joke (senseless to all but you);

To laugh (oh, one'll laugh), to talk upon
Themes that we talked upon when you were there,
To make some poor pretence of going on,
Be kind to one's old friends, and seem to care,

While no one (O God) through the years will say
The simplest, common word in just your way.

When he has finished reading Richard remains standing by the bookshelf looking at the poem, as if expecting another line to emerge from the blank page under the text. An alternative thought to turn the poem around, another last line to answer that which closes it now. He holds the book before him, open across his joined hands like a prayer book. I look at his face and I see his lively eyes have dimmed, rimmed with red and filmed with tears.

After lunch in his little dining room we go back into the front room. Richard sits in his armchair. The day is at full heat outside, the window a white square of pure light behind a thin curtain. I want to know what else Richard knows about you, what he knows about your life before Africa.

'Well,' he says, his English accent laced with traces of South African flat vowels, 'I've always been interested in people and when I was with him I thought, well, did I dare ask him about, you know, how he became a Christian and all that? And no trouble at all, he told me his kind of spiritual story.' Richard leans forward, his elbows on his bare, bald knees. 'Well, he said, it goes back to one moonlight evening. He was reading Keats' poetry – he was living in someone's house, his uncle's house I think he said, but I don't know now – and he said, "I was overwhelmed with beauty and I walked out into the moonlight garden and all the cadences of Keats' poetry were surging through my mind and I fell in love with beauty. But I didn't know that was God at the time.'"

Richard sits back in his chair, a playful smile on his face and his eyes sparking up again. Resting his hands on his stomach, he continues with the story, speaking Cripps' words as if from a well-rehearsed script,

'Then he came across a book called *Trooper Peter Halket* by Olive Schreiner. In this book Trooper Halket is horrified when he kills an African, and as he looks at the body lying there he sees the figure of Christ, a black Christ, hanging on a cross. A black Christ. This impressed Cripps very much and he wanted to learn more about the cross and Christ, so the next thing he came across was the Life of Francis of Assisi. Now, he put all those things together you see: beauty, Keats' poetry and God, Christ in people, black or white, and the life of poverty and simplicity of Francis of Assisi.'

Richard begins to cough and takes a drink of water from a glass on the table. So far this is all a story I know. Your story again, in yet another person's words. The same story, different words.

'Well, he decided he wanted to become a priest. He did his training and as a young priest or a deacon he was sent to a church, now I've forgotten the name of it, but there, well, something happened, so that although . . .' He trails off, suddenly less sure of the well-trodden path of this tale. His manner changes and his voice falters, gets quieter. 'You see, I only learnt what happened much later . . . Now this is the strangest thing – I don't know whether to jump the gun and tell you. I only learnt this years, years later you see. It was when I took early retirement, when I was about sixty-two or sixty-five, and my wife and I moved to the retreat, back in Bonda. While we were there we got a letter from a girl called Mazzy, Mazzy Shine, saying could she come and visit us because, like you, she wanted to find out about Arthur Shearly Cripps.'

He shakes his head, smiling again, 'It was the strangest thing really. She was a nurse in London and she shared a flat with my brother's daughter, Grizelda Holderness. So they were living in London, and she read, I think the life of Bishop Paget, which has a number of quotations from me, especially about Arthur Shearly Cripps. So she said to Grizelda, "Who's this Richard Holderness, because I want to get in touch." Anyway, she came to stay with us at Bonda, and when we were all there she told us the most startling, strange story. She said, "You know I am Arthur Shearly Cripps' granddaughter?" And I said, "But he never married," and then she said, "But no, that's the story.'"

Icklesham, Sussex, England

◇

The piano stands in the middle of the hall where the delivery men left it, each of its four carved feet set on thick swabs of cloth, raising it off the floor's scarred flagstones. Ada sits in a chair opposite, her apron untied, a dishcloth and a letter in her lap, looking at it, trying to stop a sob that is gathering like a cloud in her chest from rising into her throat and her eyes.

The letter came with the piano, folded in an envelope slid into the back of the polished lid over the keyboard. It is from Arthur. It is short and to the point, written in his sloping handwriting, dark across the page. It says he is leaving England. That he is going to Africa. A place called Mashonaland in Southern Rhodesia. It says that the piano is a present. Something to remember him by. It says now she will always be able to sing and play. It says he loves her and he loves Theresa, but it is best for all of them if he leaves. And as always, on another sheet, there is a poem.

Ada reads the letter again. So that is why he came last week. Out of the blue, the first time she'd seen him for over four years. He'd said he was visiting Reverend Churton and wanted to call on them while he was here. He'd said he was sorry he hadn't warned her he was coming, but he was worried that she would say he could not come. He did not say he had come to say goodbye. He did not say he had come to see his daughter for the first and maybe the last time. He had said nothing about this. Until now. Ada looks up from the letter to the piano again. The front door is still partly open and a slab of winter light falls across it, catching the carvings on its legs and its lid. A dark wooden upright, carved all over with leaves as if it were overrun with dark ivy. Delicate and ornate, it looks out of place in the bare hall. From another world, its clawed feet fantastical above the stone floor.

Ada stands and goes to it. She lifts the lid of the keyboard. Still holding the letter and the cloth in her other hand, she presses her finger against the middle C. The action of the hammer is smooth and effortless, releasing a single note through the body of the piano into the still air of the hall.

As it fades she hears the kitchen door open behind her. She turns and sees Theresa standing there, looking at her. Then she looks at the piano. She walks towards Ada, frowning at the instrument.

'What's that?' she says, pointing at its carved legs.

'It's a piano, sweetheart.'

'Is it yours, mama?'

Ada sits back on her chair and draws Theresa to her, stroking the hair from her face. 'No, love. It's ours.'

Ada knew she was pregnant long before she began to show. It was the summer of 1896. A hot summer full with scents and tastes which became more vivid to her overnight. Some just stronger, others repulsive. The honeysuckle in the lane, the turned hay, the pig food, the fermenting hops. The smells she had grown up with all her life, startling and pungent in a way they had never been before. And tastes too. She remembers crushing a raspberry against her tongue and its sweetness seeming almost unbearable in her mouth. As if she were feeling for two. And when she didn't bleed for the second following month, she knew her instincts were right. She was carrying Arthur's baby, and it was already alive in her, feeding her sensations as she was feeding its growth.

When she was sure, she told Arthur. He held her and reassured her, told her everything would be all right. He loved her and he wanted her to be his wife. But then they had to tell her father. And Arthur's brother. She had been so unprepared, she sees that now. She had not expected her world to be taken out of her hands like that. As if her life were not hers after all; as if any sense of it being so had been nothing more than an illusion. She remembers feeling like one of her father's prize sows, an item of stock to be traded on, passed into another farmer's hands. She had always hoped one day her father would give her away, but never like that.

And Arthur. Where was he then to tell her everything would be all right? He had always seemed so worldly compared to the other men in Icklesham. Educated, assured. But in the face of her raging father . . . that had been a terrible thing to see. She had witnessed her father's anger before – when some chore was left undone, when he thought he'd been swindled at market. But never like this. An anger so complete that at first he was silent. Arthur and her standing before him, and him saying nothing. Just the throbbing vein at his temple and her mother going to stand behind him, placing her hand on his shoulder. Then his shrug when she did, flinching her hand away with a jerk of his arm as if the touch of any woman would have scalded him then.

And then his anger found its voice. Ada had collapsed and cried to see him so: his face, filled with blood, the skin tight across his jaw and phlegm spitting from his mouth as he threw Arthur out of the house. And the words he said. She had never heard her father talk like that before. And to hear him she couldn't help but think that he was right and that she, his daughter was the worst sinner on this earth. 'You've brought shame on us, you hear me Ada Sargent, shame!' 'Think you can have your way with us, do you? Well, damn you, Mr Cripps!' And Arthur, with his learning and his poetry and his university, Arthur the man whom she loved, became a boy before her father's rage. Age slipped off him like water and when she last saw his face, through the closing door, over her father's shoulder, it was the face of a young man who was lost in a world he had thought he knew so well.

She never saw him again until that day last week. He wrote, but soon her father found the letters and forbade them in the house. And then it was all so quick. His brother William came. One night, a week after that day of rage and tears. She didn't see him, just heard the low bass of two men's voices in the parlour below her bedroom. She couldn't make out their talk, but she recognised their tone. She had heard it a hundred times before. At the market, in the village shop. They were bargaining.

And then her father made up his mind.

'Tom Neeves,' he told her, 'is a good man. He's always liked you, you know that. His farm yields well, and as I say, he's a good man. So, there it is Ada. You'll marry Tom Neeves and I won't hear a word said against it.'

Her mother said it was chopping the onions that made her eyes so red, but Ada knew that wasn't true.

And it was so quick. All her life before then seemed as leisure, and now it was running downhill. Reverend Churton announced the marriage banns. At the same service he told the congregation that Father Cripps, now he was ordained, had left Icklesham to take up a Trinity living at Ford End, Essex. He married her and Tom a month after that service. She was beginning to show and although folk would recognise the baby was early, her father reckoned he'd rather they thought Tom Neeves had been too eager than his daughter had birthed a bastard child.

So no one knew that Theresa was not Tom's child. Except, of course, for Tom himself. He alone had that knowledge and the knowing of it rubbed sore at him like a stone in a shoe. Soon, too soon after Theresa was born, he made sure Ada was carrying his own baby. But Theresa was there now. A reminder to him every day of Ada's romance with Arthur. 'His flesh and blood in my house,' he would say when they'd argued. Then, turning to the child herself, he'd bend down low and face her, though still speaking to Ada, saying in a low voice through a tight mouth, 'Not one of us, this one.'

And Arthur made it worse for her. He sent letters with money and books. He was trying to help, but if there was one thing sure to fire Tom up, it was finding a letter from Arthur with those notes neatly folded inside the envelope.

And now he had sent this. Ada looks over the carved piano again. What will Tom say about this? She knows he will not let her keep it, not if he knows it is from Arthur. And now Arthur has gone. Sailed to Africa. For a moment when she had seen him standing there last week, nervous, tall, his blue eyes unsure, his hat in his hand, she had thought he had come to take her back. But he had not. He had come to say goodbye, she sees that now. But at least he had seen Theresa, and, from where she stood half-hidden behind her mother's skirt, Theresa had seen him. This strange man who spoke so softly to her mother and who looked down at her long and hard, like he was seeing right through her.

The latch on the back door clicks. The door opens and slams shut. Ada hears Tom stamping the dirt from his boots in the porch. She looks into the kitchen, his lunch half-done on the table. Standing, she puts the palm of her hand against Theresa's back.

'You go and play now dear,' she says. 'Your father's home, he'll be wanting his lunch.'

She opens the door to the parlour and Theresa goes through. Ada pushes it to and knots her apron. She slips Arthur's letter into the pocket of her skirt and stands in the hall against the piano, the light from the open door falling across her shoulder, waiting.

Maronda Mashanu, Mashonaland,
Southern Rhodesia

——◇——

Noel Brettell lets the bike free-wheel down the slope towards the wooden bridge over the stream, feeling the rough surface of the road shake and jolt in his legs and his arms. It is after midday. The sun is high, and as he rattles over the planks of the bridge a pair of black-collared barbets strike up a duet from the branches of a jacaranda tree overhanging the bank. On the other side he begins to pedal up the slope. At the top of the hill he disturbs a yellow-billed kite pulling on the carcass of a rodent at the side of the road. The bird hops and flaps away as he passes. Looking back over his shoulder he watches it strut back to the carrion, its bright beak dipped with red.

He is cycling out to see Baba Cripps again, the cloth bag slung across his back heavy with books of poetry. Heavy with the words of poets which he is bringing out here, into the bushveld, to read for the blind old priest. How long has he been doing this, every Thursday afternoon, cycling out to read for Cripps? Six, maybe seven years? He remembers that first visit well. Arriving at the clearing, the old man waiting for him beside his pole and dagga rondaval, his spread of peanut-butter sandwiches on the makeshift table. And then, when he was seated beside him, the strange welcoming ceremony performed by children from the missionary's 'dame school'. A long file of them, all heights, all ages, parading before him under the eye of their African school mistress. Shuffling, clapping, twisting, knees bent, arms akimbo, repeating a shrill chant, over and over.

'What are they saying?' he had asked, leaning in close to the priest's ear.

'They are saying,' Cripps had replied, a faint smile on his lips, 'we are glad you have come to be a friend to our father.'

Noel remembered turning back to the crocodile line of children and looking at them again, their earnest faces, their singing mouths. An idiot boy was weaving in and out of them, performing his own dance, eyes aslant, his face throwing grimaces, his bare limbs grey with dust. And then he had looked back at Cripps, watching them, or rather not watching them with his blind eyes, tapping his carved walking stick against the ground in time to their chant. He had reminded him of a chief he'd once seen, watching a parade of his warriors, or of a grandfather listening to the songs of his grandchildren.

Back then, all those years ago, Noel offered to read for the old priest out of sympathy for the isolation of his blindness and his peculiar form of self-exile. And that was still partly true. Cripps' life had become increasingly eremitic: he was retreating into the bush like an old lion or an ancient elephant, rooting himself in its silence and its wilderness. But over the years of Thursday afternoons Noel had carried on with the readings, not just out of sympathy, but also because of his interest in Cripps as a poet. He became fascinated by his primitive writer's eye, isolated as it was from the modern world of cars, cold storage and literary coteries. He knew Cripps' poetry had suffered as a consequence of this isolation: unexposed to the onward movement of form and language, he had remained committed to the outworn style he had grown up with. A diction suffocated under anachronistic mannerisms, learning his craft as he had between the Pre-Raphaelites and the Georgians. And yet, when he wanted to, Cripps could capture Africa. His use of the Anglo-Saxon term 'wold' to describe the gaunt lines of stony hills he trekked across was as strangely apposite as it was archaic. And when he let his anger subside from a poem, when he looked with his eye that had lived under the African sun for so long, then he made moments of bush life live:

> So, when the sun is almost down,
> Bright in the slanting light we come,
> Bearing our rustling grass-sheaves high
> Against the splendour of the sky,
> To thatch for Christ a home –

It was no surprise to Noel that on that first visit Cripps had wanted to hear the poets he knew in his youth. Tennyson, Murray, Vaughan. He remembered reading Vaughan, his voice loud in the quiet glow of a bushveld evening: 'I saw eternity the other night –'

When he finished the poem Cripps was silent, looking away towards the Manesi hills. When he did speak, he didn't turn to Noel, but just carried on staring towards the horizon through his one blind and one failing eye. 'Thank you,' he'd said quietly. 'I never thought I should hear that again.'

On that first visit Cripps had decided what to read, but now he largely left the choice to Noel (although today he had sent a note written in Leonard's handwriting with the faint scrawl of his own signature at the bottom: 'Please bring your Keats and your Tennyson. A.S.C.'). Noel enjoyed the freedom of his choice. He enjoyed bringing newer poets out into the bush and testing them against its grand indifference and Cripps' timeless ear. Edward Thomas had worn well, Eliot intrigued him, but Auden had not survived the austere nature of that sequestered place. He could tell Cripps was not impressed, and he had to agree. He liked Auden, reading him in his chair in his house, but here it was not the same, the verse skidding off the backdrop of Maronda Mashanu like a chisel off a granite boulder.

It was as a poet that Noel knew Cripps and as a poet he approached him. He had managed over the years to evade the other areas of his life, his religious and social ideas which had so alienated him from much of the local white population. Most of the English farmers of Charter District regarded him with exasperation and contempt and the Afrikaners were equally thrown by his work, loathing any 'kaffir' who had dealings with him. Even so, Noel had met some who were willing to admit a grudging respect for his way of life. 'He's a bloody fool of a rooinek predikant,' one Afrikaan farmer had said to him, 'but, man, he's a real Christian. I've seen him walking along the Umvuma road carrying a black baby on his back. Any white man who can do that, man, he must be like Jesus Christ.'

For himself, Noel had recently been reconsidering many of Cripps' opinions that had once seemed so extreme. In the light of the past few years they had gained something of a prophetic quality, and the thought had crossed his mind that perhaps the old man had been right all along. That it was not he who was the extremist, but they, the rest of the whites, who had been complacent and indolent in their attitudes. He was, however, still unsure about some of Cripps' more stringent tendencies. He had recently heard that Cripps refused government agricultural experts onto his farms, and that he had even been imposing fines for 'immoral behaviour' on the Africans living there. He also knew that Cripps held an unenthusiastic view towards the Africans' desire for education. He provided for it, but he was sure the old man would rather they left such Western ideas alone.

When Noel visited on a Thursday afternoon, though, they did not speak of such matters. They did not even enter into serious literary discussion. Cripps was content to smoke his pipe and listen, and Noel in turn, was happy to sit in that clearing, the strange crumbling African church at his back, and read aloud from the poets of the past and the present.

Coming to the bottom of another slope in the road, Noel slows his bike and dismounts by the trunk of a marula tree that marks the mouth of the narrow foot track into Maronda Mashanu. He pushes his bike along the track in front of him, through the mopane and the acacia, the fever tree and the rain tree, its branches dripping with water from the froghopper nymphs, over the river and up through the low thorn bushes and out into the clearing. To his left the old VD clinic that Cripps built and administered to is disintegrating into rubble. Further up, nearer the church, two young children play around a smoking fire at the centre of some huts. An old man sits beside them on a stone, bent over and intent on his basket-weaving. And there, nearer the church again, sitting outside his rondavel, is Cripps, waiting.

Noel lays down his bike on the grass and reaches around into his bag to pull out his camera. Cripps has not heard him. He walks quietly and softly towards him. He is already quite close when Fortune emerges from behind the church, carrying a tray of sandwiches. When she sees him he puts his finger to his lips, and she understands, beaming a big smile at the joke and waving her hand down at him in one playful swipe.

Cripps is sitting on an old wooden box, wearing a threadbare pale jacket and a battered panama, his long legs crossed and his elbow on his knee, smoking his pipe. His pockets are full with notepaper, books, a handkerchief. A clean white dog collar hangs loose from his neck, where once, Noel supposes, it was held firm by the fuller flesh of his youth. He is almost completely still. Noel cannot see his eyes, which are obscured behind a pair of large round medical sunglasses with thick, dark lenses. Perched there on his stool, his features sharp with age, he makes Noel think of a hawk, motionless above its prey: an old, frail hawk, who is still hunting, though he can no longer see or hear.

Noel bends to one knee and takes the camera out of the case. All these years and he has no photo of Cripps. For some reason the old man didn't like cameras any more. He brings the camera to his eye and frames him there. Although the smell of the pipe is strong, he can smell Cripps himself under its odour. The smell of illness, of death. Old skin, tired breath.

He presses the release button and takes the photograph, then waits, expecting Cripps to turn on hearing the click of the shutter. But he doesn't move. He heard nothing, and Noel knows that today will be a loud day. Today he will have to declaim the poetry as if on a stage if the old man is to hear the words at all.

'I said I have brought the Tennyson and the Keats, Father, as you asked!'

Noel leans over from his chair and speaks loudly into the old man's ear, a half-eaten peanut-butter sandwich in his hand.

Arthur nods. 'Ah, yes, thank you, Mr Brettell, that's very kind of you, I'm glad Thomas got the note to you.'

Noel picks the two books out of his bag. They are from the same series, faded leather and peeling gold leaf on the edges of the pages. 'What would you like me to read for you? I mean, which poems?' he asks.

A cowbell is hesitant in the distance, and somewhere, not too far away, someone is plucking the metallic harpings of a marimba. Arthur looks down for a moment, or at least moves his head in the manner of a man looking down, the darkness swilling in his eyes.

'I would like to hear "The Eve of St Agnes".' He speaks quietly, not like a deaf man. Quietly and deliberately.

Noel smiles to himself. 'Yes, Father, but which one? They both wrote poems with that title.'

And now it is Arthur's turn to smile. He turns to face Noel. 'I know. I should like to hear both of them please, both poems.'

Noel takes up the Keats and thumbs through it, looking for 'The Eve of St Agnes', but Arthur has not finished, and he stops turning the pages as the old man continues speaking.

'I knew them both by heart once. Especially Keats'. I thought on it a good deal and even thought, once, that it might come true for me. But that was not to be. So I have tried to live by Tennyson's version instead. I think his, at least, has come true, in some way.'

It was the most the priest had ever offered of himself, but Noel didn't think he was inviting comment or conversation. He felt he was only addressing him as a bystander, that he had really been speaking to himself.

A couple of crowned plovers land in the clearing and begin picking their way through the patches of dust and scrub grass. Noel watches them for a moment, their halos of white feathers about their heads, their earth-coloured plumage and their bright red legs. Then he lifts the Keats, clears his throat and begins to read the first verse, the Tennyson ready and open across his knee.

PART FIVE

Sudden in a shaft of sunlight
Even while the dust moves
There rises the hidden laughter
Of children in the foliage
  T. S. Eliot, 'Burnt Norton'

Chimanimani, Eastern Highlands, Zimbabwe

———◇———

'Ja, they gave us these Land Rovers isn't it? Converted to carry two AK47s on either side. If you were ambushed, you hit the red button' – he makes a stabbing gesture with his forefinger – 'and they'd start shooting. Really effective, I'm telling you, and better than what we were doing at the start of the bloody war – just getting out and running at the terrs yelling our bloody heads off and firing.' Jonathan laughs, shaking his head. He is a white Zimbabwean, in his forties, with large, farming hands and a heavy body, muscle turned to fat. His jowls shake when he laughs, but then, as if remembering a grave matter, he stops and says, 'You must fire low with those AKs, y'know? Because of the kick, isn't it?' He holds an imaginary rifle before him, his forefinger hooked on an imaginary trigger, and demonstrates the kick of an AK47, his right arm vibrating as the imaginary bullets spit from the barrel. The action makes his jowls wobble again, but this time he looks deadly serious.

I am at Heaven Lodge in Chimanimani in the foothills of the Eastern Highlands, waiting to be taken up into the mountains themselves. It is early in the morning and their peaks are still clearing of mist in the distance. Jonathan is staying here too while he oversees the building of his own backpacker lodge down the road. He's going to call it Paradise.

'It'll be a tough choice for you lot, hey?' he jokes. 'Between Heaven and Paradise.' Then he drops his voice to a whisper. 'But I'm telling you, Paradise will be better.'

For the last half hour he's been telling me and a group of Americans on an overland tour about the last time he was in this area. It was during the war, when the guerrillas of ZANLA were heavily active throughout the eastern region.

'They'd come over the border, lay some mines, piggy-back some of them too, the bastards, maybe take out a farm, then bugger off back into Mozambique.'

Jonathan has been telling us he was a member of the Rhodesian SAS, fighting back against the 'terrs', but I'm not sure if I believe him.

His stories sound true enough but he retells them with too much eagerness for a man who has really lived through them.

I have come to the Eastern Highlands because this is the area you used to trek to, once a year, for an annual week's camping with your friend Edgar Lloyd. I read a letter in Rhodes House Library in Oxford in which you referred to that week's camping as your time to 'meditate'. In another letter Edgar Lloyd describes how you would arrive for a week in the hills with little more than your blanket, your tin mug and a tin of mealie meal.

I suppose, like you, I have come here to meditate: to think over the story that Canon Holderness told me two days ago, about you, Ada and your child. And that is why I am going up to the Highlands on my own this morning. Some other travellers I've met will join me tomorrow, but I want one day up there alone. With you and your story. One day to think it through, to work it out.

Unlike you, however, I am not going into the Highlands so sparsely equipped, even though I'll be in the hills for just three days. I spent all of yesterday afternoon buying supplies: a paraffin stove and a saucepan, packets of noodles, bread, cheese, some apples, cutlery, a waterproof and a sleeping mat. I also took the opportunity of being in the town to have my hair cut at a barber's, although the hairdresser there didn't know how to use scissors on my hair. She said she'd only ever cut African hair, and for that she used clippers. She tried the scissors but we could both tell it wasn't going to work, so I had my hair cut with the clippers instead.

The Chimanimani range of the Eastern Highlands is a ridge of mountains peaking at over 2,000 metres, running north to south over a distance of 35 kilometres, with a plateau and a flat-bottomed valley in the middle of them. The climb up onto the plateau is steep – a scramble over rocks up a slope thickly covered with yellowwood trees, protea bushes and ferns. The path is unclear in places and more than once I find myself retracing my steps to find where I have gone off course. My rucksack is heavy with my supplies and I have soon emptied my water bottle. When I reach the top, an hour and a half after I was dropped off at the base camp by the driver from Heaven Lodge, my shirt is drenched and the sweat is stinging in my eyes.

The ground begins to level off. Flat slabs of rock are layered on either side of me, embedded in the slope at the same obtuse angle like the body of a great stone ship, sinking into the mountain. I pick up a path, a narrow red earth track that meanders through acres of bright green, sharp-bladed grass and sparsely spread bushes punctuated with the domes of brown-red termite mounds. I walk through this landscape for about half an hour, the peaks of the mountains on the Mozambique border steep-sided in the distance, sharp-edged against a brilliant blue sky.

Then, coming through a gap between two huge boulders that lean and touch above me as if they are kissing, I am in a sculpture park. The path carries on meandering before me but the bright grass and the bushes have been replaced by a field of granite standing stones, contorted and sculpted by erosion into individual pieces of natural art, standing apart from each other on the sandy, scrub-grass soil. The larger ones look like half-finished Henry Moores (I think of the sculptures on the streets of Harare), while the clusters of smaller ones remind me of the ranked armies of miniature clay soldiers buried with the ancient Chinese emperors. I walk on through these rocks alone, feeling as if I am trespassing, a child in the giant's garden.

Eventually the alien landscape of stone gives to a more familiar view. For the first time all morning the ground begins to fall away again, and I find myself emerging into the side of a long green valley, flanked with rolling hills that could be in the Brecon Beacons back home. The floor of the valley, though, is African. Blond savannah grass cut through by a thin river, flecked white over patches of rapids. Above the low hills on the other side, the earth gives to stone again; a ragged line of high peaks, cradling the blue sky between them, marking the border with Mozambique.

I stop to make and eat a sandwich at a ranger's hut a little further down the valley's side. The ranger is there, a wiry Zimbabwean in the dark green uniform of the national park: safari shirt with sleeves rolled to above his elbows, shorts, walking boots, a bush hat and a rectangular plastic name badge on his chest, with his name, MOSES, printed on it in clear white capitals.

Moses tells me the rangers live up here for up to a month at a time, alone, except for the walkers who come and stay in the park. I ask him how many walkers are in the park today. He says there is an overland tour group due to arrive soon, but they'll be going back down later.

'You will be the only person in the park tonight,' he tells me matter-of-factly.

I ask him if there is anything I should watch out for.

'Not really,' he says, whittling at a stick with his sheath knife. 'Just be careful for the gaboon viper, they are sometimes here, and if they bite you, that is very bad news.'

He is smiling, but I can tell he is serious. I ask him what to do if I do get bitten. He shrugs his shoulders. 'Wait for me to find you. Do not try and walk, that will just spread the venom around your body more quickly. Stay still, and wait for me to find you.' He doesn't say if he means find me alive or just find me.

Voices behind us signal the arrival of the overland group. Moses stands and looks up at them through his binoculars and I go to fill up my water bottle at a tap inside the hut. When I come out Moses still has the binoculars held up to his face. I ask him if he is counting them. 'No,' he replies. 'I am looking for the pretty girls.' He brings the binoculars down and turns to face me, a broad smile opening over his white teeth, shaking his head. 'But no luck, there are none in this group today.'

I shoulder my rucksack and set off before the group arrive. As I have said, I want to be alone today. I haven't brought a tent so I head off looking for a suitable cave in which to set up camp and spend the night. Moses pointed one out to me at the northern end of the flat plain in the middle of the valley. He said it was called the Red Cave, and looking through his binoculars I could just make out its dark fissure in the rock, like a blinded eye looking out from the grey stone beneath a mat of grassy hair.

The walk through the valley floor to the cave is an easy one. The heat of the sun is already softening, the tall grass that stretches away on either side of the path is alive with insects and the sky is clear above me. I reach the end of the valley where the ground begins to rise and the grass gives way to rocks again, strewn and tumbled at first, then solid cliff faces, a waterfall gushing from a narrow gap in their granite wall.

The Red Cave has obviously seen recent habitation. There is still dried grass matting the floor, the charred pock-mark of an old fire surrounded by some stones, and even stubs of candles melted onto the rocks against the back wall. But it hasn't been just people who have been here before me. I notice what look like leopard prints in the dust around the old fire, a concentric pattern of them, closing in on its scorched patch as if its flames have been hunted, not extinguished.

I lay out my sleeping mat, hang up some damp clothes, leave my rucksack in the back of the cave and go out to gather some firewood. By the time I return the light is already draining from the sky. I build a fire over the ashes of the old one and set a match to the dry grass at its centre. The wood takes easily, crackling into flame. Using the fire to cook some noodles, I sit by its heat, watching the sky bleach, then darken to evening, then night. I am sat back from the lip of the cave which is set in a shelf of rock about three metres off the ground. There is an overhang above the mouth and the cliff closes in on it to the right, leaving a jagged portal a few metres across and several metres high through which I watch the view: rocky outcrops against a backdrop of the bare valley wall. Eventually, when the sky is deepening to an indigo blue, a few stars come out, low and bright above the black silhouettes of the hills. There is a steady dripping at the back of the cave, and just once the dark spark of a bat signs itself off through the space of air in front of me. The silence is heavy, thick and black.

I sit there, in the live light of the fire and think of the story Canon Holderness told me, wondering if it is a product of the mirror-man again. Betty Finn, stranded in her house, saw you through your loneliness. Ray Brown, the literature academic, saw you through your poetry, and Canon Holderness, who lives with the love of a woman at the centre of his life, has placed such a love at the centre of yours. All three of them reflecting your story through the prisms of their own experiences. But increasingly, as I sit there at the cave mouth, testing what I know of your life against this new element, it does seem to make sense.

There are several poems which backlit by this love affair gain a new resonance. 'Eurydice', based on the myth of Orpheus and Eurydice, is one. In the last verse the myth's heroine addresses her lover:

> Can you ever lose me out of your song?
> Can I ever lose you out of my love?
> Must we put our passion back to school?
> Must we two to lock hands wear the body's glove?
> For my sake turn from this world beneath!
> For you I turn from that world above!

Eurydice and Orpheus. The mythic touchstone of parted lovers, turning away from each other because of the presence, not the absence, of love.

Another poem, 'Found', also sounds a new note in the light of Holderness' story. It appears early in the book of poetry you published just before you left for Africa, and now I can't help but see the characters of you and Ada imbricated in its lines:

> Yes, I have found thee, and no longer now
> Seems song a mirage, or romance a dream;
> And I will sing, altho' I am not he
> Whom thou hast deemed best worthy of thy grace –
> Heart of thy heart and all in all to thee.
> Thanks be to God that I have seen thy face!
> A goal of bliss before my song is set,
> Altho' its consummation comes not yet!

And of course there is your will in the archives: 'I the Reverend Arthur Shearly Cripps, do hereby give and bequeath to <u>Mrs Ada Neeves</u> of <u>Icklesham, Rye, Sussex</u>'. There, it would seem is the final proof of the veracity of Holderness' story. Your last testament.

And already, sitting in the Red Cave, the impulse to explain, to remember in story, is overtaking me. Already I am colonising your life with my imagination, re-casting you as another of the remittance men of Rhodesia: in Africa not because of what didn't exist for you at home, but because of what did. Is that how this love affair informs your life? When you left Ada and Theresa you were obeying the majority's moral code, bending to society's will. And then, in Mashonaland, you lived by the knowledge formed in the crucible of that loss and for the rest of your life you never followed society or the word of authority again. And you never left anyone again. Is that how the story goes? Is that how it all fits in place? Perhaps. Perhaps not.

The truth is that I do not know, cannot know exactly what happened or why. I can have the facts – your letters, photographs, people's memories, the Last Will and Testament – and from these I can know the punctuation points of your life. But between those punctuation points is everything I do not know, everything that does not last, and it is only that which will ever really tell me what happened between you and Ada Sargent. Why you left her and her daughter. Why she married another man. Why you never returned and why you only wrote her name in your will years later, when you were blind and dying in your hut at Maronda Mashanu. It is these intimate diaries of our lives that tell the true history. The emotions that pass in a moment like light passing over skin, the seams of thought layered deep in our minds at every instant, the impulses, observations, nuances. The daily epiphanies, the tone and timbre of a voice, the fleeting expression of a face, the few breaths alone, head craned back studying the stars in a black sky. But these diaries of our lives are written in dust; they are not what remain. History scatters them and leaves only the stories, the writing, the punctuation points and the narratives imagined by those in our future as they try to understand their past, as they try to fill the gaps left by the dust diaries of our intimate selves.

The Enkeldoorn to Umvuma road, Charter District, Southern Rhodesia

—◇—

The back wheel of the Royal Enfield Model C motorbike is still spinning, but slowing down, the silences between each swishing brush of its tyre against the buckled mudguard getting longer. Shuw . . . shuw . . . shuw . . . shuw. With each pass of the guard a little dust falls from the rubber tread to the road beneath. It lands in the dark pool of oil bleeding from the bike's engine, the pipes and heavy carburettor hanging from its frame like the powerful chest of a cheetah. The pool of oil spreads, seeping into the dirt and moving over itself with slow, liquid determination. Eventually its dark edge touches and gathers around the tip of the metal hand-brake on the left handlebar, marooning its steel in a lake of oil. A file of ants crossing the road to the dust-grain volcano of their nest's entrance are caught in its thick slide. One of them struggles in its darkness, another is already dead, carried along on its flow, slow-turning like a log on water, or a body, passed along the hands of mourners at a funeral.

The oil continues to spread, beneath the bike and around the distorted front wheel, its spokes snapped and bent, until an arm of its flow touches the pale swirls of hair on the gazelle's underside. The animal lies in front of the prone motorbike, its spine broken and its hind legs splayed awkwardly behind it. The onward flow of oil gathers at its body, then disperses to either side along the line of its belly. The gazelle's shallow, rapid breathing is the only sound other than the turning rear wheel, and the rise and fall of its black-striped ribcage the only other movement. If you were close enough to its face you would be able to see a reflection of this scene in the convex surface of its open eye. The broken bike, the long, straight road narrowing into the distance and by the side of the road, an umbrella tree with a gathering of vultures waiting patiently in its branches, shifting their positions and stretching their wings as they watch the scene on the road like theatre-goers watching the final act of a play.

The man who is also lying in the road would not appear in this dark reflection, because he is behind the gazelle, ten or twelve feet closer to

Enkeldoorn, which is where he was travelling to when the buck leapt out of the bush and into the path of his motorbike. He is lying face down in the red dust, his arms by his sides and his knees drawn up towards his stomach. Although he is too far away to be touched by the oil there is another dark pool spreading from under his head, matting in his greying hair and his ginger moustache. Unlike the gazelle he is not breathing, and over the next week many people, black and white, will hold Arthur Cripps responsible for his death.

The man is Jack Beardsley, one-time British East Africa merchant turned Southern Rhodesian farm manager. Jack came to Africa at the end of 1900 with his fiancée, Charlotte. He was thirty, she was nineteen. Charlotte's father had forbidden their marriage on the grounds of Jack's character, so Jack had taken the man's daughter without his permission. They set up in Mombasa and Jack began his own import and export business. For a while their new life looked promising, although Charlotte missed England terribly and often woke Jack with her early-morning crying. Eventually, one morning three years after they had come to Africa, he woke not because of her crying, but because of her silence. He could not even hear his young wife breathing and when he turned on his side he found a note on the pillow where her head should have been. Her father had sent her money for passage back to England. She had left him.

Charlotte's departure left Jack bitter with the world, and his bitterness spread through him the way the oil is spreading now around the body of the gazelle, which is still breathing, fast and shallow, blinking the flies from its eyes. Like the spark that starts the fire, the bitterness spread to the rest of his life and especially into his luck. His business began to fail. He married again, the daughter of a colonial office clerk who died giving birth to their first child. The child, a son, was taken away by his parents-in-law, back to England, where Charlotte had gone too. Jack thought it was as if the country was taking back everything he valued, punishing him for taking Charlotte away all those years before. But then, not content with taking his life away, England came to him, bringing with her a war which brought the end of his business, and in 1918, when it was all over, he found himself old, bankrupt and with a set of rotting teeth that seemed the manifestation of the pain festering inside him. But he would not return to England. That, for Jack, would have been to admit his failure. So he moved further south instead, to the Charter District of Mashonaland, where he secured a position managing a large cattle and tobacco farm outside the dead-end town of Enkeldoorn. But the farm was not a good environment for him and he became sullen and even more lonely than he had been in the crowded streets of Mombasa, with too many hours to consider the mistakes and regrets of his life.

Cyprian Tambo came to Enkeldoorn in the same month as Jack Beardsley, but they did not meet for another three years after their arrival and exactly one week before this morning with the vultures waiting in the tree and the flies gathering in a halo about Jack's bleeding head. Like Jack, Cyprian also came looking for work, walking for three days from his home in Chipinga in the Eastern Highlands, staying with his brothers who worked in towns and villages along the way. He wore just his new khaki shorts and shirt with no shoes or a hat and carried his blanket and belongings in a bundle tied over his shoulder.

Cyprian had first arrived in Umvuma, bearing his 'book' before him, a greasy notebook of character references and payment dates from his previous employers written in faint grey pencil over the rough pages. But however much he proffered his book to maids, wives and managers, there had been no work available. Most had simply shaken their heads and waved him away, but some people had taken the time to speak to him. They told him he should go and talk to 'Baba Cripps', a white priest who lived on the road over to Enkeldoorn.

When Cyprian arrived in Maronda Mashanu the schoolmaster told him the priest was away, but he should wait for him to return. Cyprian waited for two days and eventually the priest arrived, completing a one-hundred-mile walk from Salisbury. He did not look as Cyprian had expected he would. He was tall and thin, a gaunt look about his face. His pale suit was dirtier than Cyprian's own shorts and shirt, and his boots so cracked and broken that he may as well have been walking bare-footed as Cyprian had. He asked Cyprian to join him for a cup of tea and listened to his story. When he had finished Baba Cripps spoke to him in Shona, but he did not say the words Cyprian was hoping for. He said instead that he had no money to pay him, and although he could see he wanted to learn, there was no room for him in the mission school. He would have to leave and go back to his home in the Eastern Highlands. Cyprian said he understood and prepared to leave, but then the priest asked him to take a letter into Enkeldoorn for him, which Cyprian did, running as fast as he could. The letter was to a Reverend Liebenberg who wrote a quick reply and asked Cyprian to return with it to Baba Cripps. When he returned to Maronda Mashanu it was nearly dark again and Baba Cripps told him he should stay until the morning, when he could begin his journey home. But in the morning Baba Cripps had another letter for him to take over to Wreningham and a parcel to Altona. Cyprian stayed another night at Maronda Mashanu and in the morning Baba Cripps thanked him, '*Ntatenda kwazwo mukuru wangu*', 'Many thanks my brother.' He made no mention of Cyprian starting his journey home.

For the next three years Cyprian worked as Baba Cripps' messenger and helper, accompanying the priest on his treks across the Charter country. At the end of the third year Cyprian said he wanted to train to be a priest like Baba Cripps and Cripps, satisfied that the boy was serious, arranged for him to go and study under his friend John White at Waddilove. Before he went he asked Cyprian to carry one last message for him, and it was then, one week ago, that Cyprian met Jack Beardsley, who had been waiting for him behind the trunk of an acacia tree long enough to scatter the ground at his feet with a confetti throw of cigarette butts and ash.

Jack was waiting behind the acacia tree because however much he fenced this patch of land the piccaninnies and women from the missionary's farms persisted in using a foot track that ran across it. Signs and wire were no use, so he had taken to waiting and catching the perpetrators in person. At first he merely gave the native a beating or chased them back down the track past the fence, but recently he had become more inventive with his punishments. Last month he made a boy climb the trunk of the acacia tree while he stood beneath prodding him on with the barrel of his shotgun, and the week before he'd made a girl knock down a hornets' nest that hung in the same tree with her bare hands. He just wanted to make it clear this land was no longer theirs, that the path could no longer be used, and if it was, they would be punished for their trespassing.

With Cyprian Jack was in playful mood, the morning's whisky having not yet sunk so far as to drag him down with its cooling plumb-line weight, and so he made the boy dance. Leaning against the tree with a handful of pebbles and his stick under his arm, he threw the stones at the boy's feet, and shouted at him: 'Dance, kaffir! Maybe we'll have a little rain if you do, hey? Dance for more rain!' He even clapped out a rhythm, clapping faster and faster and never stopping until Cyprian's eyes began to roll from exhaustion and his whole body was shining with sweat.

Cyprian told Baba Cripps what had happened, and the next day Cripps walked out on the track himself. He told Cyprian not to follow him, but he did, keeping at a distance and crouching behind a bush when Baba Cripps confronted the farm manager. He could not hear what they said to each other but he could tell the two men were arguing. The manager was waving his arms around and at one point he picked up his gun, and Cyprian wondered whether he should run out and knock the man down. When Baba Cripps finally walked back down the track Cyprian saw the priest's face was flushed and that one vein was standing proud, running across his forehead and scalp into the greying hair above his ear, like the snakes Cyprian had seen, disappearing into the grass when disturbed.

Cyprian told his friends about Baba Cripps and the farm manager and when Jack went into Enkeldoorn that night he complained loudly in the bar of Vic's Tavern about 'that bloody priest sticking his nose in'. The other drinkers who had lived in Enkeldoorn for longer than Jack were familiar with Cripps' behaviour and though they nodded sagely in agreement, they couldn't help smiling to each other at his outbursts. Still, they told him, slapping his shoulder, it was nothing to worry about, leave the mad old priest to his ways. They bought him drinks to ease his temper and before too long both Jack and the others had forgotten about the troublesome Baba Cripps.

But when Jack is found this morning lying dead in the middle of the Enkeldoorn to Umvuma road, it will not take long for those same men to remember his confrontation with Cripps, and as his body is lifted into the back of William Tully's new Ford truck they will already be whispering about the priest's involvement in the accident:

'Bucks don't just jump out like that, they just don't, not when there's a bike on the road.'

'I'm telling you, that priest, man, he's dealing with more than just our God now. He's been learning that black magic shit from the kaffirs, I tell you.' And in Maronda Mashanu too, people will speak in hushed tones about the miracle of the gazelle buck and the farm manager. Old men sitting at the *dare* of their homesteads will nod their heads slowly when they are told, as if the story of the gazelle buck merely confirmed what they could have told the teller many months before. Small boys will begin trying to command the birds that hop between their parents' huts and as they fry a pan of peanuts over the fire, mothers will tell stories to their children about Baba Cripps and his power over the animal spirits of the veld.

The rear wheel of the bike stops spinning. The oil has stopped flowing and the gazelle's breathing has slowed to nothing, like water settling to stillness after a pebble has broken its calm. A couple of the vultures flap down to the road from the umbrella tree. They are joined by a stork and a pair of crows, strutting in the dust. The crows are the first to the body of the gazelle. Hopping onto its muzzle with quizzical heads, they begin pecking at the dark reflection of the broken bike, the flat canopy of the umbrella tree and the road, disappearing into the centre of the animal's eye.

Maronda Mashanu, Mashonaland, Southern Rhodesia

—◇—

When the Society of the Divine Compassion withdrew from Wreningham at the beginning of 1933 the newly appointed Bishop Paget was forced to find a suitable substitute to run both the church and the mission school. Although Wreningham was close to Maronda Mashanu and Cripps had started his career in Southern Rhodesia at the mission, approaching Father Cripps was out of the question. Paget didn't doubt that even at the age of sixty-three the old priest had the energy for such a task, but over the years he had applied that energy in such a way as to rule himself out of any candidature. A refusal to accept government subsidies for his schools had led to a split between Cripps and the Anglican Church and it was a fissure that Bishop Paget feared too deep to breach. Cripps had even gone so far as to leave Southern Rhodesia, although in the end he came back, four years later, as the Bishop had suspected he would. The old man was more African than European now and Paget couldn't imagine him settling into an English country parish with anything other than difficulty.

Although Cripps returned to the country, he did not return to the Church. Refusing a licence from the Bishop he gave himself the title 'Independent Missionary to Mashonaland' and when necessary followed his name simply with 'Clerk of Holy Orders'. Again Paget could not pretend to be surprised. At the last Synod before he left for England Cripps had sat, eaten and slept with the African clergy rather than the European. Even his presence was dependent on there being some pressing case in defence of the native and he would rarely attend for any other matter. His world had become black and white and his vision, just black. A black Christ in a black country, in which they, the white settlers, were merely tenants, obstacles to harmony and a presence to be endured.

Many in Salisbury were surprised the Bishop let Cripps carry on his work in his diocese – a rogue missionary operating without official licence.

'Isn't he more trouble than he's worth?' the Company's Administrator had asked him at the Governor's lawn party, hoping, Paget suspected, that he might rid himself of Cripps' endless petitions via the authority of the Church. The Bishop pointed out, as he did to all such enquires, that Cripps' land was his own and that he still accepted Cripps' candidates for ordination, and yes, he would continue to do so until given good reason not to. 'And besides,' he had added, wanting to leave no doubt in the Administrator's mind of where he stood on the matter, 'I think I know a saint when I see one. I just let him well alone.'

The Reverend Smith of Nyasaland, arriving as an interim appointment at Wreningham in early 1933, did not share the Bishop's liberal views. He had been forewarned about the presence of Cripps in his parish and he established himself in his new post with a series of announcements designed to bring some order to the chaos that he found around him. Within his first week Smith insisted that individual church payments for each African mission station be paid in full. Those behind in their dues, he refused Communion, and those stations which remained delinquent in their payments would be disestablished as places of worship altogether. Which is why, on this May morning at the end of the rainy season the Reverend is travelling across the rough dirt roads of the district, a match box rattling in the glove compartment of his car and a steel can of petrol swilling and sloshing in its boot.

Since his arrival in Mashonaland Cripps had built over thirty native mission stations. They were primitive structures, no more than pole and dagga shepherd shelters, built in the style of his church, with crude wooden crosses and altars of piled stones. Cripps stayed in them himself on his long treks through the area, and performed marriages, christenings and funerals in them for the Africans who lived too far from the mission centres of the district. Reverend Smith had counted thirty-seven such stations on his books when he arrived at Wreningham. This morning though, as he drives on through the veld sitting beside Peter, his African driver, peering through the wiper arc in the dust on the windscreen, there are just thirty-three. The remaining four no longer exist other than as patches of darkened earth and blackened stone, carpeted with a soft floor of ash blown in the morning breeze.

Although failure of church dues was his public reason for the burning of these shelters, the Reverend Smith also had personal motives founded more on ideas of aesthetics and theology than administration. The buildings were clearly unsafe, and they were dirty and untidy and their architecture, though no doubt authentically African, was in no way a suitable reflection of the glory of God. There was, he felt, a purifying quality in the flames that gathered at the fringes of the thatch before rushing hungrily up to the apex of the stations' roofs. A holy judgement and an eradication of chaos where he would build order.

Encouraged by his morning's efforts Reverend Smith was now making his way over to Cripps' own church. The man had no licence from the Anglican Church, refused to pay his dues and taught his African parishioners an obstinacy and wilfulness that could only encourage instability. He had clearly lost his way and the local clergy, cowed by long acquaintance with his bullying tactics, had lost their nerve. He, however, had not, and he drove towards Maronda Mashanu filled with the satisfying inner warmth known only to those of holy righteousness and decisive intent.

Patrick is tending his father's herd of goats, following their gradual flow all morning as they move across the river bank, their heads down, tearing and chewing at the grass. He is only ten years old but he knows how important his job is. As he told his friend Denys yesterday, his grandfather is Chief Wadsango, one of the two headmen who first came to live on Baba Cripps' farms. As such, his grandfather is one of the most important men in the area and as his youngest grandson, Patrick is one of the most important sons. When Denys asked him why he is so important Patrick simply answered, with the certainty of one possessed of great knowledge, because his father had told him so. No other proof was required.

At first Patrick does not see Reverend Smith's car, just the dust it disturbs behind it, a pale plume dispersing as it rises, hazing the clear morning air. Still, he knows it is the sign of a car, so he stands from where he has been crouching against a tree and moves the goats further from the side of the road. Holding out his stick he shoos them on with short barks from the back of his throat, the bells at their necks sounding a tremulous percussion to their movement. The goats settle at their new patch and it is when they are grazing again, the sound of their bells trickling out to the odd hesitant ring, that Patrick hears the other noise. At first he thinks it is the car, then maybe one of the new planes the farmers use to spray their crops, their fabric double wings fragile against the sun. But it is too low, too near to be a plane. A droning hum gathering in volume, a ball of sound rolling down a hill.

Suddenly the sound hits the trees and becomes physical, a thousand tiny thwacks and clips as it streams through the leaves and branches of the bush. Patrick looks about him, trying to see what he can hear. At first there is nothing, just the same still morning, gathering heat, the tall trees at his back, a clear sky. But as he looks up at it the clear sky develops dots of darkness which grow like cells dividing. And then Patrick sees the swarm. A tower of bees, rising out of the foliage from the direction of Baba Cripps' church. A dark plume mirroring the plume of dust behind the Reverend's car, that also disperses as it builds, but then tightens again, a black lung of air, swelling and contracting above the treetops – waiting.

Patrick doesn't move. His father has told him stories about Baba Cripps and the bees. How, like the most powerful *n'angas*, Baba Cripps can control their flight, move them about the air as easily as he moves his goats across the river bank. When he wants to be alone, or if there is a storm at night and the rain is slanting into his hut, then the bees come and gather at his doorframe, covering it right across, a moving, buzzing curtain to keep Baba Cripps warm and undisturbed. Patrick is sure these are the same bees and as he stares at their gathering mass he tries to think what he might have done wrong. But then he sees the Reverend's car coming around the corner of the road, hears the rattle of its engine under the bonnet, and he realises that the bees may not have come for him after all.

Reverend Smith cannot hear the sound of the bees above the car's engine and the clatter and bumping of its chassis as they drive over the pock-marked road. He is staring so intently through the clouds of dust rising past his window that he does not see them either, and the first time he is aware of their presence is when he feels the sun pass away from his lap, as if a large cloud had blocked out its light. He glances up at the sky through his side window, confused. It is clear, as it has been all morning, with not a cloud to be seen.

Suddenly the car stops, jerking the Reverend forward so he hits his head against the edge of the window frame. Rubbing his temple he turns to reprimand Peter, but stops, his mouth open, half-way through the first word. Peter is staring, white-eyed, through the windscreen with both his hands on the steering wheel and his chauffeur's cap tipped to the back of his head. And it is then, as the Reverend follows Peter's locked gaze, that he sees the bees: a broad swarm of them, hanging in the air above and just in front of the car, blocking out the sun, rising and falling as if on the currents of the sea.

'Please, sah, your window!' Peter is looking at the Reverend now, winding his hand in rapid motion in an impression of the window's mechanism. But the Reverend cannot take his eyes off the bees. A thick dark stream of them is still rising out of the trees, flowing into the swarm, bulking it out by the second. Peter reaches across him and winds the window himself, then, shifting the car into gear with a grating noise that is hidden under the white noise of the swarm, he accelerates forwards, the car's tyres skidding and sliding on the dusty, pebble-strewn road.

From where he is crouched with his goats under the red and gold leaves of a seringa tree Patrick watches the sleek black car jerk forward and begin its charge towards the swarm. As if they share a symbiotic relationship with the machine, the bees move at exactly the same moment, contracting their mass into a darker, tighter ball, before dropping to the level of the car and streaming towards it. The swarm and the car meet with the sound of pepper shot fired through iron, the bees enveloping the bonnet in their darkness, driving through the shiny steel grille of the radiator, flowing up into its undercarriage. The car continues accelerating, but then slows again, faltering against the onward avalanche of the swarm. The engine chokes and coughs, vibrating with the bees in its system, clamming its pistons, drowning in its oil, until suddenly the vehicle comes to an abrupt, jolting halt.

The car does not move, as if stung into stillness, beached on the dusty road like a boat on a sandbank. Its engine, though, is still running, battling for its life, shaking under the chassis as the bees swarm into it through the silver grille until Patrick is sure he can see the hinged black bonnet move and shake with the pressure of them, clouding under its steel. Then with one last grinding, metallic screech the engine dies. Seconds later, as if they had known the exact mass with which to clog its workings, the last of the bees flies into the body of the car.

And suddenly there are none left. Where moments before a multitude had hung in the air, buzzing, droning, there is nothing, just the sudden silence of their disappearance. The day is still again. Almost.

Shuffling forward until he is crouched at the edge of the road Patrick can hear the tick, tap and drone of the few insects still alive under the bonnet of the car. He can see the faces of its passengers too: one white, one black, ghosted and faint behind the dun-dusted windscreen. He stares at the car, waiting for the bees to re-emerge, but they do not. Behind him, his goats carry on grazing, unperturbed, tearing at the grass with rhythmic efficiency, tinkling the bells at their necks. Patrick, meanwhile, who still cannot believe his eyes, puts his hands over his mouth and laughs into his fingers at the wonder of what he has seen.

The Reverend Smith did not reach Maronda Mashanu that day, and he did not get the opportunity to try again. When Bishop Paget heard about his activities in the area he immediately dismissed him from his post and travelled down to Maronda Mashanu to apologise to Cripps himself. In a symbolic gesture which he knew would not be lost on the priest or his African parishioners he offered to accompany Cripps on a preaching tour of the burnt mission stations. Cripps accepted and for the next week Paget and Cripps visited the charred remains left in the wake of Reverend Smith's passing, the Bishop standing by as Cripps preached from the blackened altar stones, his old boots dusted grey with the ash of burnt thatch and wood. The African congregations gathered around the old priest, intent on his sermons and singing out the Shona hymns with an energy that Paget had never witnessed in his own services in Salisbury. He watched Cripps preach and could not help but feel that these shattered mission stations, open to the veld, were perhaps the most suitable churches of all for this maverick priest. Here, there was no partition between the church and the land, no entrances, no windows, the birds flew above them and the wind moved through them. And, Paget noticed more than once, the crucified Christs behind the altars, having passed through Smith's flames, were coloured a deep, charred black.

Maronda Mashanu, Mashonaland,
Southern Rhodesia

———◇———

Noel has left him. He made his farewells and Arthur listened to the whirr of his bicycle's wheels through the grass and his cheery '*Masikati*' over his shoulder. It wasn't addressed to him, he had already said goodbye to him, but to someone else. Fortune perhaps. And then he was gone, taking the words of the poets with him.

And then Fortune's hands, gently pressing through the threadbare cotton of his jacket. He is so thin now he feels her fingers cupping the ball joints of his shoulders, as if she were holding the bone itself. She is talking to him, easing him up and moving him back under the shade of the rondavel's roof.

The day is already older. He can feel the changing quality of the light in his eyes. He cannot see it, but he can feel it, a warm darkness cooling in the crucibles of his sockets. The sunglasses are heavy on the bridge of his nose. He hears the single cry of a bird, a young hawk perhaps, trying its wings for the first time.

And now Noel has left him. But then, they all leave eventually. Like the neglected thatch that falls from the hut's pole, like his flesh fallen from the bone. This is how they have left him. His mother, his sisters Edith and Emily, William, Frank Weston, John White, Edgar Lloyd, falling away like sheaves of grass, leaving him like the lonely pole, dry and trickling with ants. The letters would slow, ebb and then finally stop. For a fortnight or so he could pretend the mail had got stuck somewhere, a broken Scotch cart wheel, a forgetful boy, but then notice would reach him. Another letter, written in a strange hand: a sister, a wife, a colleague or a nurse. But more often now, the direct speech of the telegram: 'PASSED AWAY STOP'.

He would write in reply, he always did, making carbon copies in blue ink on skin-thin paper and sending them out – his elegies and tributes, a final wreath of words following them to their graves. It had happened like this so many times, why should it ever stop? The leaving, the word so suitably cutting both ways: those that leave us and that which they leave us.

Legacies, memories, a resonance of their selves living on in the thoughts of those they have loved.

He had once left himself. In both senses, in 1926, but it had not worked out. He remembered steaming away from the African shore and thinking it would be the last time he would ever look on her trees, her purple hills, her towering skies. But of course it was not. In Africa he had missed the countryside of Essex, the England of his youth, but once there, back in his Ford End living, he had missed Africa even more. Missed her with the violence of another loved one died. He was the in-between man again and within four years he was back. England had moved on in a way that he did not understand, and in a way that meant she no longer understood him. There had been unease and then mild outrage in the town when he gave over his vicarage as a shelter for the vagrants and moved into a one-room lodging for himself. And the skies, the heavy skies seemed to weigh down on him with their low, dense clouds. Cars were everywhere.

And of course, there was Ada and Theresa. They were there too. Again, he did not go and see them, for the whole four years. He wrote to them both, but he did not visit. He suspected that they too would have moved on and so he lived instead with just his memories of Ada and the one memory he had of Theresa. She was four years old when he last saw her, the only time he saw her. Blonde hair and blue eyes like her mother, peering up at him from behind the folds of Ada's skirt as he stood there, saying goodbye to them without words.

And what of Ada? Had she left him yet? No, he didn't think so. She was younger than him and he cannot even imagine her old, let alone dying. And anyway, he feels sure that she could not leave without him knowing. Not by way of a letter or a telegram but by another kind of communication. She could not pass away without the current of her going somehow touching him. He was sure of that.

It was like the baobab tree. The ancient two-thousand-year-old baobab with its massive gnarled trunk, its branches like roots and its flower, so transient, so delicate that it opens just once in the evening and is dead by nightfall the following day. But however brief the flower's passing, the animals still know it is there, the bats and the bush babies all drawn to the scent it releases in the one day and night of its existence.

Sitting here now, under the shade of the rondavel's overhang with the light dying in his blind eyes, he sees his eighty-three-year-old life as the great trunk and branches of the baobab. Rough, long-lived, enduring. And the years he shared with Ada are the tree's brief flower, opening and closing in a day. And like that flower, she can not pass him, her life can not open and close without him knowing. Her death will release a scent that he will feel, even here, in Africa after so many years. It had to be so. Two people could not share like they had shared and not feel each other's passing. He would not believe it to be any other way. She is still here, still alive. She has not left him.

Now Fortune is telling him that he must leave. The doctor has sent his orders and he has been encouraged by his friends in Enkeldoorn and by his friends in Maronda Mashanu to listen to them. They are all telling him he must leave, that he must go to the hospital. They are saying he can come back when he is well, but he knows he will not. He knows he is leaving.

Thomas, who helps Fortune look after him, is here to guide him into town, and Leonard has returned from teaching at the school. He heard the rattle of his bike as he arrived, and then, later, the chatter of the children coming home. Leonard has come to take care of his letters, to pack up his unanswered correspondence.

Suddenly, after the quiet of the afternoon, the solitude of his darkness, the sound of Noel's lone voice reading Keats, there is activity all around him. Mothers are trying to feed their children in the huts down by the river. Fortune is talking quickly at Thomas. Not to him, but at him, telling him what he must do for Baba Cripps in the hospital as she packs his few clothes into an old leather suitcase. And Leonard, in the rondavel behind him, sorting through his papers, chattering away to him, speaking loudly and clearly, telling him about his newborn son, who, as Baba Cripps recommended, he has named Horatio. His tone runs the full range of his voice, his low, serious conversation peeling off into high laughter as he describes how his son eats, walks, looks. And then, as he brings some piece of correspondence to Arthur's side, his voice is suddenly low and respectful again:

'There are two letters from Oxford University Press, Baba, shall I bring these, yes?'

Arthur answers but he feels this activity, the commotion, as if it were at a great distance. He is far away inside his blindness and his memories, thinking about leavings and how Ada is still alive, still in his world. He wants her to know that he has not left her either, never, however far away he has been. That, although they were never married, he has never stopped thinking of her as his wife. He calls Leonard to his side and tells him to open the trunk in his rondavel and find the blue folder.

'Which one, Baba? There are very many folders in the trunk.'

Arthur tells him it is not a folder of letters or poems but another folder, a folder of personal papers. He will know which one it is because it will hold a piece of paper with 'Last Will and Testament' written across the top.

Fortune and Thomas have moved Arthur inside so he can dictate to Leonard in peace. He is lying on his mattress again and Leonard is sitting on the old metal trunk, Arthur's old typewriter on his lap. Arthur listens as Leonard feeds his will into the roller: the crunching of the ratchets as he turns the handle, the metallic spring as he releases the lever to secure the sheet in place. As always he indicates he is ready by saying, 'Yes, Baba?'

Arthur speaks slowly and clearly. His own voice coming to him as if spoken through a sea shell, spoken through a sea.

'Centre page, capitals. Underlined. Codicil. C – O – D – I . .'

This, then, is what he will leave. Not a letter, too easily dismissed as the romantic despair of a dying man and too easily lost, but a statement. A statement of his memory, written in the one document that assures careful, considered thought. His Testament. Not legal, not financial, but emotional. She will know that he did not forget her. She will know that he did not leave her because of this, what he will leave her. Not the money, but the words.

'I the Reverend Arthur Shearly Cripps (comma) do hereby give and bequeath to (underline) Mrs Ada Neeves . . .'

And when she reads this statement, she will remember him, however briefly, perhaps as transiently as the baobab's flower, opening and closing overnight, but she will remember him and know that he remembered her. And for that moment, when she remembers, he will live again, resonating in her thoughts the way she has resonated in his for the fifty years since he last saw her: standing at the door of another man's house with their child by her side looking out at him from behind the folds of her mother's skirt.

Hampstead Heath, London, England

––––◇––––

Theresa is sitting on a bench on Parliament Hill waiting for her future. She is wearing her Sunday tweed jacket and skirt, her best ankle boots and a cloche hat given to her by her best friend, Dina. She sits with her bead handbag on her lap, and her hands on the bag, looking out over the grass, parched blond in patches by a late-flowering summer. Lifting her head slightly she looks out further, over the trees below, their pale and dark greens punctured by the fine yellow stone of two church spires.

The bench Theresa sits on is engraved along the back rest: '*For Albert, who loved this view*' carved into the dark wood. As she studies the land before her she tries to imagine who Albert was, and who engraved this bench in his memory. A wife? A daughter? There is no indication, just his name, living on in the place he made his. She remembers a line of Byron's, or rather part of a line: '*Live who you are.*' Perhaps that is why Albert's name is here, because this is where he lived who he was. And yes, she thinks, that should be celebrated, because living who you are is not as easy as it sounds, she knows that.

A kestrel is hovering above and in front of her. The bird has been tamed by the populated heath and it hangs in the air closer than she has ever seen one before. She can make out its grey hood and the black tipped markings on its wings and tail as it drops and rises, balancing on the currents of the breeze, poised with potential. Like a horse galloping or a fish swimming it is beautiful simply because it is doing what it has been born to do. Living what it is. She watches the delicate tight-rope act of its hovering, perfectly balanced between motion and stillness, and recognises how the bird's state describes so eloquently how she feels herself, sitting there on that bench: motionless, yet poised between two movements, ready to drop or to rise, depending on what the next half hour brings.

Theresa sits on the bench, waiting and watching the view with the same attention and expectancy as the hawk scanning the grass for its prey because she is waiting to discover how she will live: what kind of a life she will have, whether she will have children who will visit this bench in years to come and tell their children how their grandmother sat here, waiting. As she waits she feels the nervous energy of her anticipation swell inside her like a wave. With each minute that passes the surges get stronger and she tries to distract herself, first by looking at the view, then the hunting kestrel and then, with a force of effort, by thinking not of the years to come, but of the years that have been instead. The years that have brought her here, to this hill and this bench, risking her future because of her past, trying to live who she is.

It was when he was having his appendix removed on the kitchen table that her father (or rather Tom, the man she had known as her father) had finally apologised to Theresa. The white sheet over his legs and the wooden tabletop were both soaked in his blood. There was more of it on the flagstones, big dark splashes around where the doctor had been standing. He had lost a lot during the operation and she remembered how the kitchen had smelt not like a kitchen at all, but more like a slaughter-house.

Tom must have thought he was going to die and perhaps that is why he did what he did, hoping to make amends before he went, relieving himself of his sins before he met St Peter. She remembered him asking the doctor to leave the room, his voice weak and husky, and the doctor nodding solemnly as if he understood everything about this, pain and suffering and people. Picking up his black leather bag, he had walked out of the back door to his car, leaving just Tom, lying on the table, his head propped up on a cushion, Theresa and her mother. Lifting one arm Tom had taken Theresa's hand and drawn her closer to him. She remembered thinking how pale he was, pale and fragile, his naked chest collapsing with each breath, the tightly curled hairs dark against his skin. He was a farmer, and she had only ever known him with the colour of an outdoor life in his cheeks. With that colour drained she saw how old he was, really, behind his work and his clothes. It was ten years ago, she must have been twenty-two or twenty-three.

He didn't say much, but for him, she knew it was the most he would ever say on the matter. And she was not surprised when he didn't look at her as he spoke, but chose to stare at the ceiling instead, holding her hand limply in his.

'Theresa,' he'd said, 'I know I wasn't always fair. It was wrong, girl, I know that now.' A pause, during which he shuts his eyes and lets out a tired breath. Then he spoke again, 'Take care of your mother, won't you?'

But there had been no need for that passing request. A couple of months later he'd made a full recovery and was back to his old self. She was living in London by then, and though she came to visit them often he never mentioned it again, either his apology or what he had been apologising for. Theresa, however, knew only too well what he had been speaking about.

As a child she had never understood why her father always took against her. Why he punished her so harshly for reading in her room, or being late to the table, or for not doing a chore well enough. Her brothers, in comparison, always seemed to escape his anger whereas with her, he not only flew into a temper at the slightest provocation but even seemed to resent her any success. When she won a scholarship to Lewes Grammar School for Girls she had expected the news to cheer him, but it did the opposite. He remained in a black mood for days and found countless reasons to criticise her behaviour. As she got older she came to assume it was simply because she was a girl. That, unlike her brothers, she was not able to help her father on the farm with the heavy or manual work, that he had wanted a boy and that she, a girl, was no more than a burden to him. Over the years his treatment stopped seeming unfair or even unusual. It was just the way of things, and that is how she thought of it, until at the age of fourteen, she discovered the truth herself.

It was a package that did it. A package sent to the school in Lewes from her Aunt Lotty who had addressed the parcel (intentionally or accidentally, she will never know, her mother forbade her to speak to her aunt again) to 'Theresa Sargent'. It was then, and only then, after Theresa had written to her, that her mother came to Lewes and, no doubt fearing that someone else would tell her if she didn't, told Theresa the truth about her parentage. The truth about a young man called Arthur Cripps, a curate she had known in her youth, who, she admitted, looking red-faced and flustered at the floor, had been her lover. A young man called Arthur Cripps who was Theresa's father.

They were sitting in a tea house in Lewes. She remembers it all so clearly. Her mother's face, close enough to feel her hot breath on her cheek. Her hand over hers on the soft leather of the Bible she carried in her handbag, as she made her swear to never tell anyone about her parentage, ever. Then holding her tea cup, its handle hot against her fingers, its thin china trembling against her lip as her head swam and her eyes filmed over with tears. The feeling that sitting there, in that tea room, she was somehow drifting away from herself like a boat she had once seen, loosed from its mooring on Rye pier, slowly drifting out to sea, diminishing and fragile on the swell of the waves. Her mother carried on talking, but she could not hear her. Her mind was scattered, racing, unbelieving. Everything was altered, like when the optician had placed the testing spectacles over her eyes and slipped in lens after lens, turning the world strange.

Despite the shock and the shame, she did not cry. Not there in that crowded, smoky tea house. Nor did she cry outside, in the busy Saturday street. But later, when her mother had gone and she sat alone on her bed in her dormitory (the other girls had been at supper), retracing her life, testing her memories against what her mother had told her, then she had cried. Hard, bitter tears of frustration, confusion and anger, welling up from inside her, and drawing with them, like water drawn from a bore hole, a thousand unanswered questions. Who was Arthur Cripps? What type of a man was he? Where was he now? Why had he left? Why had her mother never told her before? Did her brothers know? Did the school know?

She was angry with everyone: her mother, the stranger who was her father, her aunt and even her brothers. But she was especially angry at Tom. She was sure this was why he had hated her. Knowing why, however, did not make his treatment of her any more forgivable. If anything, in Theresa's eyes, it made it worse. Because he had not hated her for how she was, but for who she was, and that was something she could never have done anything about, something she could never have changed. However much she had tried to win his favour, he would still have hated her, because she could not escape who she was to him: another man's child, reared as his own under his roof. An illegitimate. A bastard.

Theresa looks about the heath. The light is fading from the day, but the clouds are still bright on their flat undersides, and the heath is still moving with people. She takes a deep breath and looks at her wrist watch. Still five more minutes. She looks up again and is glad she chose a Sunday and not a weekday. On any other day she may have felt conspicuous, sitting here, waiting on her own, but on a Sunday the heath is full of people and no one was really alone. On her way up to the hill she had passed old men walking to swim in the ponds, their white hair blown in the wind, young, earnest men strolling along, their hands in their pockets, reaching decisions, mothers and nannies pushing their children in prams along the paths. On the bench just along from her there is another woman sitting alone, a lady older than Theresa, reading a novel and wearing a winter coat and a fur stole, despite the Indian summer sun. And along with the other individuals, there are groups of people to dilute her solitude too. Families laying out picnics (two boys squabbling remind her of her brothers), an outing of schoolchildren passing along in crocodile formation and gaggles of young women in hats, secretaries or office workers, followed by groups of young men, swaggering in their Sunday suits with cigarettes wagging at the corner of their mouths.

Theresa is waiting for her own young man, Stuart Hildred. Although, she supposes, neither of them is that young any more. She has left it late for this kind of thing, she knows that. Her mother can't understand why she has, but Theresa wouldn't have had it any other way. Unlike the other girls she'd spent her twenties travelling rather than looking for a husband, and she had needed those years. To find a bigger world, accessible, new and different. Just to know it was there, the possibility of escape, of undoing ties, pulling up roots. She and her best friend Dina would take off on their two-week holidays whenever they could: to Venice, the Italian Lakes, Biarritz, Switzerland. Back in her digs she had thick albums of photos and postcards from her travels, the plane tickets for each trip stuck on the pages in between. She had seen the Alps, the Dolomites, the waves of the Mediterranean. On one of their excursions, she had even met a man, an Italian called Mario. She has photos of him in her album too, his arm about her shoulder on the shore of Lake Como, a pipe in the corner of his mouth and his shirt sleeves rolled up to his elbows. When she returned to England he had written dramatic love letters to her, but she knew he would never follow the letters, that he was in love with love not her, and that he would never follow her to England.

There had, of course, been other men since: young clerks from the Barclay's Bank where she worked, an older man from the post office when she was in Portsmouth, but no one who she could seriously consider as a husband. Until Stuart. There had been something different about Stuart, a solidness and calmness that gave Theresa comfort, a balance that the other men seemed to have lacked. Perhaps it was because he was already married when she first met him.

Stuart worked in her office at the bank, and from the start she had known he was married. She had even met his wife, Nancy. Stuart introduced them at the manager's annual party. That was three years ago now, but even then she had noticed how frail Nancy was. How Stuart supported her at her elbow as if he was afraid the wind would blow her away or knock her down. 'Cancer,' he had explained the following day when she'd asked. 'The doctor says there's not much he can do.' He spoke with his head down, in a low voice as he sorted some papers on his desk. Theresa felt awful for asking but then Stuart had looked up at her and, sensing her awkwardness, he'd smiled at her, as if to tell her it was all right. 'But she's fine,' he'd said. 'Really. Fine.'

Theresa knew when Nancy had died. It was a Monday morning and when Stuart didn't arrive at his desk, everyone in the bank thought they knew why. It must have happened over the weekend. They'd been expecting it for some time, no one had seen Nancy for months and when they asked after her Stuart's replies had been getting briefer and briefer: 'Oh, she's well, well enough,' or 'Not bad. Very tired, though, very tired.' When he returned to work, two days later, he had the look of a man who was empty of something inside, like a blown bird's egg, complete but somehow lighter. His grief was not dramatic, black, but delicate, fragile and it was then, watching him move about the office in his usual way, a quiet vacuum at his centre, that Theresa knew for certain that she loved him.

They became good friends. They would go out for lunch together and Stuart would sometimes talk about his late wife to Theresa. She never felt jealous. In fact she had felt privileged to be so close to this fine, rarefied grief, this grief that was a gentle afterburn of love. She admired his ability to remember her, his ability to love and, strange though it was, that is why she had fallen in love with him herself: for his loving of another woman.

Stuart's hobby was music, composing for and playing the piano. Theresa had inherited both her mother's voice and an old carved piano she had kept under a blanket in the back room of the farm in Icklesham. That autumn Stuart started to visit her digs on the weekends, sitting at the piano and playing his songs when they had finished their tea, his long, pianist's hands running the length of its keyboard.

Encouraged by him, Theresa would sing the accompaniment. Then one day he had asked her if she would like to take a walk instead, and they had come here, to this hill and this bench, where, for the first time, he had kissed her. Just lightly and just once, but he had kissed her. And ever since this bench, Albert's bench, had become their regular place on the heath. It was the destination of their walks, their meeting place, where they brought their picnics last summer. It was also where, a week ago, almost exactly a year after that first kiss, Stuart had asked her to marry him. And that is why she hadn't needed to tell him where to meet her this evening. She had simply written, 'on the heath at 5 p.m.' He would know where to come, if he was coming at all. There was nowhere else she could have meant; for them, this was the heath. This bench and this view, consecrated as it was by their shared memories.

When Stuart proposed Theresa had wanted to say yes straight away, with all her heart. She could no longer imagine a future without him in her life. But she could not say yes, she knew that. Not without him knowing the truth about her. Not without her telling him what she had sworn on her mother's Bible in that tea room in Lewes never to tell anyone. So she had written to him that night, after he had walked her to her door and said goodbye, trying to keep the disappointment at bay in his voice. She had written to him and told him everything: about Tom not being her father, and about Arthur Cripps, who was. She even told him how Arthur had written to her once a few months after her mother had visited her at Lewes, a strange, polite, guarded letter: 'You must be, I think, that little girl of four I saw all those years ago . . .'

She finished the letter by telling Stuart that if he still wanted to marry her, then he should meet her 'Next Sunday, on the heath at 5 p.m.' She had said she would understand if he did not come, that she would understand if he never wanted to see her again. Then she signed the bottom of the paper, 'your Theresa', and blew on the ink to dry it. She did not read the letter over, but folded it, sealed the envelope, addressed it and walked out to post it straight away, before she had time to change her mind.

That was a week ago. Since then, she had heard nothing from Stuart, but that was what she had requested, a week of silence to consider what she had told him. But now, waiting for him on Albert's bench, she was beginning to wish she had never written that letter. What had she done? What would she do if he did not arrive, if he never came? How long would she wait for him?

Suddenly the kestrel drops from the sky, a brown streak, its talons drawn, landing in the grass with its wings outstretched. Theresa watches its dive, then its hunched position in the long grass and its grey hooded head, peering over its shoulder before turning away and stabbing with short, sharp jerks between its legs. A little boy points at it and tugs the sleeve of his father. Theresa thinks of the animal, the shrew or the mouse that is there, unseen and unheard but still there under the talons of the bird, struggling for its life.

She looks at her watch, two minutes past five, then back up at the heath with its wandering couples and individuals passing each other, each person involved in their own lives, their own futures; their thoughts unseen, unheard by her, but like the kestrel's prey, still there. She wonders what this evening means for them? What are they all remembering or considering as they stroll along, talking, or as they stand alone, pausing under a willow to look through its leaves at the sky? Were any of them, she wondered, feeling as she was: their life on a knife edge, everything they valued hanging by a thread that would either be rescued or cut loose in the next ten minutes? It was impossible to know. All she could be certain of is that like her, they would feel the low sun, flaring at the edges of their eyelids, the touch of the breeze on their faces. That some of them may have seen the kestrel dive, and that others would not. A million sensations were passing through them all as they shared this time and space on the heath. Passing through and passing on, a stream of thoughts and feelings, some which will snag and remain as memories, but most which will live and die in the passing of a breath.

And then, among the milling people on the path below, she sees him. Striding along, a bunch of red flowers bright against his brown suit, emerging from the anonymous crowd. And suddenly, he is there, in her world, breaking into her isolation. He is looking up at her and has been all the time she was watching the kestrel. She has been so alert, waiting, expecting him and now he has surprised her. Although he is far away below the hill he stops in the path, lifts the flowers and waves them at her. She can not make out the details of his face but she knows he is smiling. She feels a flood of relief rush through her and her eyes prick with tears. The scene she has been watching, which has been so clear, so sharp on her senses, swims back into an everyday focus. Because she is no longer waiting. He knows who she is, her story, and he has come to be with her, now and forever. He waves the flowers again, and as she lifts her hand to wave in reply, she feels her world fall back to her, as suddenly and violently as the kestrel, dropping to earth out of the sky.

1 AUGUST 1952

Enkeldoorn Hospital, Enkeldoorn,
Southern Rhodesia

◆

The corridors and the wards of Enkeldoorn hospital are quiet. This is the only time of the day and night when they are: in the twilight before dawn, sharp, bright stars in a sky which is draining from black, through purple, to blue. The groaning, the coughing, the sound of the nurses' shoes on the hard floors have all stopped, and the hospital is quiet. Even the trees outside the windows are still. There is no wind. The flies and the mosquitoes have not yet risen into the warmth of the day and the cicadas and grasshoppers have not yet begun their chorus.

Thomas Shonhe lies on the floor of a private ward in the European wing. He is the only African in this part of the building. The English Sister has made many complaints to the doctors about his presence, but the doctors are respecting Father Cripps' wishes. The old priest had said clearly when he was admitted almost a month ago that he wanted Thomas to stay with him. Since that day, 8 July, Thomas has not left Arthur's room. He has watched the nurses wash Baba Cripps, and give him medicine, then, when they are gone, he has cared for him himself, in the way that Fortune told him to and in the way that he knows Baba Cripps expects him to. He lies now, on the floor beside Baba Cripps' bed, drifting between sleep and wakefulness. When he wakes, he listens for the faint sound of Baba Cripps' breath, the passing of air in his throat and his lungs. It is a gentle breathing, a sighing, like the wind weaving through the reeds by the river.

Arthur is lying on his back, his forearms hanging off each side of the bed, his palms held upwards. It is nearly a month since he was brought here in a car from Maronda Mashanu. It is over ten years since Noel Brettell last visited him and read him Keats and Tennyson, over a month since Fortune washed him and over three months since he dictated the codicil of his will to Leonard. But tonight, here in the hospital, he has been living all these memories again. Tonight he has seen Bishop Gaul again, Frank Weston, the alleyways of Zanzibar. Tonight he has raced in the New Year games and watched soldiers and porters die on the shores of Lake Victoria. Tonight he has seen the building of his church and the burning of his mission stations. He has written his poems, read the letters of his life and walked across Mashonaland, sleeping under her stars with his red blanket about him. Tonight he has spoken with headmen about land, lain in his rondavel listening to the waking life of Maronda Mashanu, heard the whirr and tick of Leonard's bike's wheels. Tonight he has been cold in summer and hot in winter, heard when he is deaf, seen when he is blind. And tonight he has fallen in love with Ada again. He has lain beside her by the river, felt the heat in her hair, the sun on his face and remembered her voice in his ear.

The steel edges of the bed are digging into the backs of his arms, and as he lies there, between sleep and consciousness, between life and death, the blood flow to his hands is restricted. But he does not feel any pain. Instead, he feels, through the layers of his sleep, through the darkness of his blindness, that he is holding two glowing globes of light and warmth in each palm, two handfuls of sunlight, heating in his fingers.

The paper-thin skin of his cheek billows in and out with each shallow breath like a sail, catching the lightest of breezes. The breath tapers in the hollow of his mouth, plays in the canvas of his skin, softens, then dies. And with its dying, Arthur dies too, holding a globe of light in each palm and with a gold and red radiance firing behind his eyes, like the leaves of the musasa tree in spring, flicking on and off in the wind.

Lying on the floor, Thomas wakes and listens for Baba Cripps' breath, and hears nothing. Everything is still. He raises himself under his blanket and kneels by the bed. He looks up at Arthur's face in time to see the sinking of his one remaining eye, like a pebble easing itself into mud, until his eyelid is flat across the socket, calm as a windless lake.

Thomas looks at Baba Cripps' face and he knows it has happened. He stands, lifts Arthur's arms onto the bed and pulls the blanket up to his neck. Then he walks to the door and looks down the dim, bare corridor. There is nothing and no one. He looks back at Baba Cripps, at his face which is draining of life, of light, then softly closes the door as if he might still wake him. Rubbing the sleep from his eyes, he walks down the empty corridor to find the night nurse, the bare soles of his feet slapping on the hard concrete floor in the quiet twilight of Enkeldoorn hospital on the morning of 1 August 1952.

Dear Owen,

Sorry for delaying in writing to you. I was somehow busy but I did not give up.

My name is Thomas Shonhe, the one who was with your relative 'Arthur Shell Crips' for his last three years up to the day when he passed away.

When I was with him we walked together. On Mondays we would leave the mission Maronda Mashanu to Chivhu Town on foot to pray for the sick in Chivhu Hospital. People with their sick relatives would ask him to come and pray for the sick. We spent three days in Chivhu. On Wednesdays evening we left Chivhu back to Maronda Mashanu where he had a church service with sermon. This is how we were operating when I was with Shell Arthur Crips during my stay with him.

Shell Crips was old by the time I stayed with him. He suffered from diarreah for at least three months. I Thomas Shonhe, my duty was to direct him where to go since he was blind. I had to cook for him and wash him. Mr Mamvura was his clerk by that time.

Arthur Shell Crips died in Chivhu hospital when we were just two. We were in a private ward. After his death I went to call the nurses. The burial was arranged and he was buried at Maronda Mashanu.

After the burial they requested his clothes. I gave them.

Yours loving
Thomas Shonhe

A GREAT MULTITUDE
The Burial of Father Cripps

Father Cripps had many times expressed his wish that a lot of money should not be wasted on his funeral, and this wish was honoured in the very simple but moving burial services on the afternoon of Sunday, 3rd August. All the arrangements were made by Daramombe Mission, which incorporates the earlier Wreningham where he lived and worked for 25 years: the coffin was made in the Mission workshop. There was no hearse; the coffin was carried in a van lent and driven by Mudiwa Bill, the Enkeldoorn bus proprietor.

The body lay in the little church of St Cyril, where he used to minister in times past, from 11 on Sunday morning till half-past two, when the first part of the Burial Service began. It was read in English by the Rev. R. H. Clark, of Daramombe, and the Rev. Richard Nash, of Umvuma, played the organ. Two hymns were sung: 'Blest are the pure in heart' and 'Sun of my Soul'. The congregation of Europeans, Indians, Coloured and Africans was much too big for the church to hold.

From St Cyril's the procession of cars made its way to Father Cripps' home at Maronda Mashanu. A quarter of a mile from there the cars stopped and the coffin was taken up by the six bearers – Mr N.H. Brettell and Mr W. Stewart of St Cyril's; Inspector Dufton, B.S.A.P (representing the Civil Commissioner); Mr J. Mutasa and Mr G. Mandaza, old friends of Father Cripps, and Mr D. Taranyika, Headmaster of Daramombe School. A vast crowd of Africans was waiting there in silence. Suddenly three shots rang out, women began to wail, and a group of men broke into a war dance and a famous heathen song used only to honour a great chief, while old men who had known Father Cripps almost all their lives took the coffin from the pallbearers and bore it to the church of the Five Wounds, while the great company sang hymns, including one in Shona written by Father Cripps himself. The spontaneous tribute by heathen and Christian alike in the vast concourse was inexpressibly moving, showing how greatly the African people loved and admired him whose love for them was so sincere. As one of the Africans said, 'Father Cripps must have smiled in his coffin.'

A grave had been prepared in the chancel of the church of Maronda Mashanu – the church which had been largely built by Father Cripps himself after the style of Zimbabwe. It is now almost a ruin, but the people propose to build a new church round the grave. The service around the grave was conducted in Shona by the Rev. Langton Machiha, of Daramombe; the Lesson was read by the Rev. Edward Chipunza, who represented the Bishop, and Father Clark read the committal.

One other priest was present – the Rev. Cyprian Tambo, who as a young man worked for Father Cripps and was instructed and baptised by him.

All who loved Father Cripps will feel a deep gratitude to the Doctor and Staff of Enkeldoorn Hospital for their sympathy and care, and for their consideration for the many Africans who came to minister to him and to pay their respects. Foremost among these was Leonard Mamvura, Headmaster of Maronda Mashanu School and Secretary for Father Cripps, who cycled backwards and forwards each day after his work to spend as much time as possible with him, and Cecilia and Thomas, who attended him so faithfully.

Harare, Zimbabwe

---◇---

Last night I danced on your grave. There must have been more than two hundred of us crammed into the ruins of your church: old men and women, children, mothers with babies swaddled on their backs, young men in Nike and Puma tracksuits, young women wearing coloured headscarves. And all of us dancing, our bodies made large with layers of jumpers, coats, scarves and hats worn against the freezing edge of the night. Our breath steamed like incense in the beams of a powerful halogen lamp mounted on a truck outside the walls, a generator shaking and chuntering on its open back. Everyone was singing.

One man at the head of your grave blew long, low notes through an impala horn, another beat a tall *mutandarikwa* drum, his hands a blur above its tight skin. Above us the clear southern sky was full of stars, the Milky Way dusting a swathe across the blackness and the familiar constellations swung on their sides: Leo tipped, the Southern Cross between the legs of a rearing Centaur. And beyond the broken walls of the church the fires on the kopje were still burning in the deep black of the night, picking out the shape of the little hill in their pulsing spots of orange and yellow.

It is seven months since I was last here looking for you. Seven months since I camped in the Eastern Highlands, thinking over the story about you and Ada and Theresa. I have come back to Maronda Mashanu to attend the annual festival held in your honour. Leonard has been writing excited letters to me in London, telling me about the preparations and what to expect. Three days of services, singing, plays, dancing and feasting. 'Dear Owen,' he tells me, 'Our country is now very cold and please as you are coming for the Memorial Festival of Father Cripps, please try to wear some warm clothing. This is just to remind you.'

Although it has only been seven months, there are many changes since I was last in the country. There has been an election, marred by rigging, intimidation and ballot boxes found dumped in rivers as far away as Mozambique. The offices of the *Daily News*, the only voice of opposition in the press, were attacked with grenades. Journalists have been taken to detention centres and opposition leaders threatened. The land question that everyone was talking about when I was last here has become physical ('I do hope,' Leonard writes in one letter, 'that the dust of the land situation in this country will settle down on land invasion soon after the election'). But the farm invasions have continued, some of them turning violent. As you suspected, land has once again been the touch paper for unrest, but this time it is a black government, not a white, that is doing the taking and the giving, despite the economic disaster it will bring. Already there is almost no foreign currency in the country and there are often severe petrol shortages. Driving out of Harare to Chivhu I pass a large group of War Veterans protesting outside the Zanu PF building. There are much fewer white faces on the streets and the air is somehow tauter than it was when I was last here. On the edge of the town a packed commuter minibus slows in front of me, stutters forward, then stops. It rolls to the side of the road and joins the other vehicles abandoned there which have also run out of fuel.

Seven months, and there are changes with me too. I am no longer getting on the Blue Arrow bus, and I am no longer alone. I am driving a bright green hire car, its metallic shine incongruous against the dusty colours of the veld, and Jodi Bieber, a South African photographer who has come to photograph the festival for the *Saturday Times* is sitting beside me. As we drive south we pass through a temporary camp of War Veterans, a tattered Zimbabwe flag flying from a crooked wooden pole, then past a deserted petrol station with one lonely pump and a stack of empty blue Pepsi crates stranded on the forecourt. Every now and then a scattering of rondavels appear at the side of the road, bright washing hung on a line, but mostly it is the veld, all around us. Flat, rashed with green over its brown-red dust and dotted with granite.

Chivhu arrives suddenly out of this landscape. Just a brief warning of some breeze-block 'high density' housing, much of it half-built, and then the town itself is there. We approach the central square, with the cream and green of Vic's Tavern on one side, then turn left, past the post office, and up the main street of shops, before turning left again, past the old Dutch Reformed church, the hospital, then left again onto Cripps Road. Your road, long and yellow in the late afternoon sun.

I park the car outside the gate to Leonard's farm. Somehow it would seem wrong to drive it up to his house; even coated in a film of dust from the journey, it still feels out of place here. So I walk, as I did seven months earlier, up the track to his homestead, where not much has changed. The rondavels are still there, arranged around the patch of beaten earth, the chickens are still pecking in the grass and the dogs are still slouching around, some with puppies in tow. I do notice one change though – the wooden cattle kraal has been moved closer to the house, leaving just a square of churned earth where it once stood. I also notice that the new kraal is empty, its irregular fencing holding nothing but air and another patch of ground, less churned than the old one.

And then there is Leonard, who has not changed, beaming a smile, walking towards me with the awkward gait of his one stiff hip, his arms outstretched, and saying my name over and over. His wife, Actor, walks behind him, wearing a bright red woollen hat and a blue-and-white spotted dress. She is smiling too, laughing and wringing her hands, and shaking her head at her husband's extravagant welcome. Leonard embraces me, squeezing out our seven months apart with the pressure of his strong arms. Then, taking me by the hand, he leads me into his house for tea. Jodi follows us, the shutter of her camera clicking. As we enter the bungalow we pass a white goat tethered to a pole outside, bleating thinly, its narrow pink tongue vibrating in its mouth, shuffling its feet in the dust. Inside, its bleats are deadened by the walls, but the goat never stops calling, as if it knows something we don't, as if it is trying to warn us.

Actor busies herself over the sideboard in the dark little room of Leonard's bungalow, preparing some tea, then leaves to go and cook in the kitchen rondavel across the yard. Leonard and I sit at the shaky table in the middle of the room, just as we had done seven months before, and he brings me up to date as he pours out the tea and offers me sugar. He speaks about the election, the intimidation of the voters, the fuel shortages, the high price of Actor's medical treatment and of the land invasions. I think of your book, *An Africa for Africans* and of how you saw this coming, this problem of land, the sowing of the dragon's teeth: 'This unawakened race does not perceive yet the injury that has been done it. But one day it will arouse itself, become articulate . . . and then . . .?'

As Leonard talks, he shakes his head slowly, like a father disappointed with a promising child. I ask him why he has moved the cattle kraal nearer the house and he tells me. He had just two cattle left when one morning three months ago he found their heads and their skins lying in the mud of the kraal. They had been slaughtered and butchered while Leonard and his wife slept. 'We are suspecting they came from Chivhu town with cars to carry the meat,' he explains of the thieves. 'There is no law here anymore.' He shakes his head again, his eyes down, and he seems older than when I met him outside. Older and tired. For a moment he is quiet, and just the bleating of the goat fills the silence, but as I watch him I see a smile grow on his face, rising through his features to his bald forehead. Looking up, he begins to tell me about the preparations for your festival, and suddenly, he is no longer eighty years old but eighty years young, excited and energetic, his hands making the shapes of his words in the air.

When I walk out of Leonard's house onto the small porch the sun is already low in the sky and an African evening light has taken hold of the world, casting long shadows from everything it touches. A chicken struts past, pulling a grotesque jabberwocky shadow behind it. Patches of midges vibrate in the air and the cicadas and crickets trill and tune themselves in from the long grass around the homestead. Leonard is still inside the house, packing vestments and pewter candlesticks into a big canvas bag and preparing to leave for the festival site. I notice that the goat tethered outside which has been bleating has stopped. I turn around and it is no longer there. Then I hear its cracked, pathetic call again, further away, behind the house. I walk to the corner of the bungalow and see Sabethiel, who helps Leonard on the farm, and a couple of bare-footed young boys in torn shorts and T-shirts leading the goat away. The rope around its neck is taut as they pull it behind them up towards a large flat stone surrounded by thorn trees and one leaning jacaranda. Sabethiel sees me watching and waves, then beckons, so I follow them up towards the stone.

When I get there I find the seclusion of the place emphasises the peacefulness of the evening. The sun is now a bloated orange disc, setting the branches of the trees into razor sharp silhouettes. A swallow dips in the air above us and, higher, an eagle circles in the sky. I watch as Sabethiel leads the goat up onto the stone and the other boys follow. It is only then I see Sabethiel is holding a long-bladed knife, and I know what is about to happen.

With a practised movement he catches the goat by its legs, one hand around the hindquarters, the other around the forelegs, and swings it onto its back. The animal lets out a short, shocked bleat, more of a sudden groan. One of the other boys crouches and quickly ties the animal's legs with string while Sabethiel holds it still. The goat carries on bleating, faster, more urgent than before, its broken voice the only sound in the still evening above the constant static of the cicadas. Sabethiel puts his hand under its chin and presses, forcing its head back and exposing the taut white throat where its windpipe thrums beneath the skin. He shifts his hand up from its chin to around its mouth, trapping the tip of its tongue between its teeth, and its bleats become muffled, strangled, its nostrils flaring with the effort of its breathing. Then, with his other hand, Sabethiel brings the blade of the knife to its throat, and starts sawing with a rapid motion.

For a second nothing happens and for some reason I think nothing will. It seems impossible that this animal, so vibrantly alive, will ever stop being so. But then its muffled bleats fill with liquid, turn to a gurgle, and the blood rises, shockingly red against its white hair, spilling onto the stone beneath. Goats, however, are stubborn and this one does not die easily, its tied legs jerking against the flow of blood from the vivid wound in its neck, and Sabethiel has to use the point of his knife, twisting it through the throat to find the spinal cord. Leaning on the handle with all his weight, he tries to snap the vertebrae, which eventually give, cracking with the sound of a branch breaking. And it is only then that the goat empties of life, the splash of its blood spreading from its neck like an extravagant bright red ruff.

Leonard comes out of the house as the boys hoist the animal from the jacaranda tree by its tied hind legs. Some of the tree's seed pods are shaken loose as it is jerked higher, falling around it like confetti. A few land on its rump, catch in its fine white hair. A dog slouches up behind me and nervously licks at the pool of blood on the stone, already congealing in the last light of the evening. I hear Leonard call out for me, 'Owen, where are you?' I walk down towards him; he is smiling one of his big smiles again.

'Ah yes, the goat, you have seen the goat? Now we will have meat with the sadza for the festival, yes, yes.' He puts an arm around me, pulling me close and I feel his strength again. He tells me to get my bags – 'Otherwise we will be late, Owen, yes, yes, and we mustn't be late.' Maybe it is the white of the goat still playing in my mind, but for a second, Leonard's haste and concern makes me think of the white rabbit in *Alice in Wonderland*, hurrying, hurrying.

We walk down towards the car, where Jodi is waiting, her cameras slung around her neck and her khaki photographer's gilet bulging with film. I take a look back at the flat stone and see Sabethial cutting into the goat's groin, sliding his knife down its belly and chest. The skin folds away, as if undone by a zip, opening to the red of the flesh beneath.

When I was last in Zimbabwe I noticed how the dark does not fall in Africa but grows, thick and black and quick, and this night seven months later is no exception. Within two hours of Leonard and me walking away from the goat strung up in the jacaranda tree, night has claimed the ground again and I cannot see my hand in front of my face without the aid of a match or a torch. In those two hours we have driven down to your church, unloaded our bags into your rondavel and walked throughout the site of the festival. On the way down we pass a boy by the side of the road, hammering a sign into the ground with a red arrow on it pointing down the track through the bush to your church. 'Shearly Cripps Festival' is written above the arrow, also in bright red paint. At the clearing the silence of your ruins has been overtaken by the activity and noise of preparation. A group of men are erecting a tall circular thatch wall on which another sign is nailed, 'VIP Toilet', and another group are building a temporary kitchen while women file up from the pump by the river, plastic containers filled with water on their heads. Leonard introduces me to old men who knew you, most of whom are wearing dark suits and old trilbies, the ribbon loose above the brim, and blue deacons' sashes across their chests. I also meet Horatio again, wearing a thick woolly hat against the cold evening. He tells me he is the Festival Vice Chairman, and as we shake hands there is a friendly conspiratorial air about him, as if he, too, is remembering our walk to Wreningham and the stop at the beer hall. Moses Maranyika is also there, scanning the preparations with the eyes of a man who is in charge. I notice a pair of handcuffs glinting at his belt and he tells me that he is the Special Officer for the area, as well as being the headmaster and the Festival Secretary. 'In case of trouble,' he says, indicating the handcuffs and giving them a little rattle at his hip. I think of a Rixi taxi driver in Harare who warned me that the festival could become the target of Zanu PF intimidation. He said the Anglican Church was not popular with the government right now, and that one priest had even urged his congregation to pray for Mugabe's death.

The darkness is complete by the time I unpack my bag in your rondavel and roll out my sleeping bag next to Leonard's. For two years now I have been trying to inhabit your life, trying to get under your skin, and as I make a rough pillow out of my rucksack, I wonder if this is as close as I will get: sleeping the night in your hut, listening to the song of the veld that you listened to outside its round stone walls. As I have moved through your life, from your letters, to Zimbabwe, to here, I have always encountered the problem of imagination, a struggle between what happened and what may have happened, a colonisation of fact by fiction. But this, the hard polished dung of your rondavel's floor, the single slit window where you kept the portrait of your mother, the rustle of mice moving in the thatch, this, I feel, must be real. I lie down and I know I am lying in the shadow of you. I can sense the penumbra of your body on this floor, the touch of your skin on these walls. I think I understand, but I cannot be sure.

Leonard has taken the torch to go to the toilet and I can't find my matches, so, deprived of my sight, I strain my ears to try and get a picture of what is happening outside. I can hear people, but it is hard to say how many. There is excited chatter, the rustle and thump of bags and packages being let to the ground, greetings and shouts. A drum has been beating a rhythm for the last ten minutes, and every now and then a man's voice joins in, singing. The metal racket of one engine sputters into the clearing then stops with a sudden clank, leaving just voices in its wake, men and women's, speaking quick Shona.

I have no idea how many people are coming to your festival. Leonard was hoping for around three hundred, but it has been a hard seven months – the petrol shortages, inflation, farm workers losing their homes in the land invasions – and I can't help thinking that Leonard is being optimistic in his expectations. But then, through the open doorway of your rondavel I see the fires. Where the night air above the clearing had been filled with pitch black there are now constellations of pulsing orange spots. I watch as more come out over the kopje like stars emerging in the night, each one a little higher than the next. After half an hour there are so many that the shape of the hill is clearly marked out by the rough triangle of orange and yellow flickering lights.

I get up from the floor of the rondavel and walk out of the doorway towards the fires, and it is by their light that I see the clearing and the trees at the base of the kopje are teeming with people. Many are still arriving, baskets and bags carried on women's heads, toddlers dozing in the arms of the men and babies tied to backs, their sleeping faces squashed against their mother's spines. I walk on into the trees and into an ethereal atmosphere of firelight through wood smoke, the smell of roasting peanuts sweet and rich in the air. I see Jodi in there, darting between the fires, a big grin on her face, the small black camera always either at her eye or poised just below her chin. She sees me and shouts across, 'I'm trying to find the light. It's tough, hey?' Her South African English sounds surprising on my ear after the sea of Shona I have been walking through.

I walk on, and I am stared at. I am the only white man here, but I don't want to miss a thing. I am stunned by the volume of people, out here, in the veld, at night, all here for your festival. Most of them are surprised to see me, but after the surprise there is interest. The older people are interested in me because of you, the younger because of my watch, my shoes or for whether I know David Beckham. Everyone wants an address, a point of contact. Letters are still alive here, as a way of hope, just as they were for you. One boy in an Adidas tracksuit and a bobble hat pulled low over his eyes asks me quite simply why he can't come back to Britain with me, 'to help with your work, I can work with you'.

A woman surrounded by children asks me to sit by her fire. She introduces herself as Happiness and offers me some of the peanuts twitching on a flat pan above the flames. The children crowd at her shoulder, then, as she tries to teach me to count in Shona, at mine. *Poshi, piri, tatu, ina, shanu, tanhatu*, the children chant along with me, screaming with laughter when I make a mistake. Happiness introduces me to her daughter Sandra, who is doing her O-levels this year and who wants to be a teacher. Her younger brother wants to be an airline pilot. In fact, all the boys want to be airline pilots. And then we talk about you. Because everyone knows your story here, which is told to me again and again, the same phrases reoccurring in different mouths, your life as a fable: 'he loved the Africans', 'Arthur Shearly

Cripp, he lived just as an African', 'Baba Cripps, he would walk *one hundred miles* into Salisbury.'

Two powerful beams of light sweep through the trees from behind me, passing across the dark tree trunks and the groups huddled around the fires like two searchlights. Walking out into the clearing with Happiness and Sandra I find that the lights belong to an open-backed truck which is pulling up beside your church carrying what looks like a load of blankets. The driver cuts the engine and it rattles out, sending a shiver down the truck's chassis. Almost immediately the blankets begin to move, and as the driver gets out of his cabin to flip down the tail, children emerge from under them. They drop to the floor, young boys and girls rubbing sleep from their eyes, some of them carrying even younger children. They wear strange combinations of ill-fitting clothes and many are bare-footed. They stand around the back of the truck, disorientated by sleep, shivering and their teeth chattering audibly as a woman in a nun's habit and large glasses ushers them into some kind of order. Watching them, I realise how cold it has become. There is no wind but the air now has a frozen edge to it, and the heat of the recent afternoon feels like a distant memory. I remember Leonard's letter: 'Our country is now very cold.' Then, as if I had thought him there, Leonard's hand is on my shoulder. He gestures towards the nun and the children, who are still slipping off the tail of the truck onto the ground. 'This is Sister Dorothy from the Shearly Cripps Children's Home. They have come from Juru, that is *five hours* away,' he adds, his voice rising to his now familiar pitch of astonishment. 'I will go and help them, but you must talk to this man,' he says, indicating a huge man at his side. 'His name is Patrick and he also knew Baba Cripps.'

'My name is Patrick Bwanya who comes from All Saints Wreningham in Manyeni Reserve, near Chivhu town where Cripps came in 1901 to work among the Vaheri people. He was welcomed by my three grandfathers, these being Wade*sango* (the one who loves the bush), Gava*jena* (white fox) and Mu*pem*hi (Beggar).'

Patrick and I are sitting inside the walls of your church, a few feet from your grave. We have come in here because Patrick wants to tell me all he knows about you, and the singing in the clearing has got so loud that it is hard to hear each other talk. I have brought a mini-disc with me this time and Patrick talks slowly in his deep growl of a voice in deference to the clumsy microphone I am holding out to him. As he tells me the story of your life again, I glance up at the sky above us. Your church is roofed with stars now, not grass, the constellations of Virgo and Hercules looking over you. Beyond the walls the singing lifts and falls above a steady rhythm of maracas and drums, the women's voices flowing on like an endless stream, answered every now and then by the deeper voices of the men. Patrick tells me how he moved to Maronda Mashanu with his father, and a story about seeing bees stop a car. Then he describes your funeral, how the congregation of whites, blacks and coloureds was so big it did not fit inside the church, and how the people of Maronda Mashanu sang as they are singing now, songs only ever sung for the burial of a Mashona chief. He finishes with a big laugh and a nod towards you in your grave as he says what I have heard so many people say today, 'Yes, because Baba Cripps, he was like an African.'

The singing and witnessing does not stop all night, drawing me up through layers of sleep again and again in time with the rising and falling of its cadences. Leonard is sleeping beside me, and when I wake I listen to his heavy breathing and to the lighter breaths of Jodi who sleeps beyond Leonard, her head on her camera bag. The music becomes part of my dreams, and I find it hard to tell when I am awake or asleep. For most of the night I think I am neither, but somewhere in between.

It is the singing that finally draws me to full wakefulness in the morning, a small group of men around a fire near the rondavel, passing a song between them like a round. I get out of my sleeping bag, step over Leonard and walk through the open doorway to go and wash in the river. Outside, the sun has not yet taken the edge off the night and the air is still cold. Those sleeping in the open are stirring from where they lay under blankets beside the embers, children stumbling around, sleep still heavy in their eyes and their breath steaming in the cold as if they are exhaling the smoke of last night's fires. There are now around 700 people here, all going about the morning chores of washing and eating and passing on the singing from group to group.

After a breakfast of boiled eggs and toast the festival proper begins. The festival committee all carry schedules that Leonard has typed out on his old typewriter and the day proceeds with a strange mix of strict efficiency on the part of the committee and casual nonchalance on the part of the crowds. By mid-morning the Bishop of Harare has arrived in his wine-red cassock and an altar is prepared outside the walls of the church. The priests and the deacons gather for the memorial service, all wearing their white vestments as they proceed towards the altar, the choirs accompanying them, and a tall wooden cross held before them. I can't help thinking of the photo of you I found in Rhodes House Library, that odd juxtaposition of the veld and your ecclesiastical dress. The scent of incense mixes with the smell of fires.

The congregation sit on the ground around the altar, the women of the Mothers' Union in their bright blue headscarves and shawls and the choirs from other churches each in their own bright uniforms of yellows, reds and purples. I join a group of boys from the Children's Home, crouching at the back. The service is long and the sun is hot and after a while they start to yawn and play, shooting pieces of straw from the clam-like dried seed pods of the jacaranda tree and drawing biro tattoos on each other's arms: a Nike swoosh, an Adidas logo, 'Power Rangers' written below.

After the service I chat with Sister Dorothy about your Children's Home. She tells me the children help in all areas of the home, in the garden, the kitchen and even with teaching the younger children. She asks me if I can send the boys football magazines and then tells me very proudly that many of their pupils go on to university. Two boys have even become airline pilots with Air Zimbabwe.

Over a lunch of sadza and beef after the memorial service the talk turns to politics. Some of the men admit that Zanu PF only won this area in the recent election because of their intimidation tactics. Chivhu is a long way from Harare, and it is easier for things to go unseen here. All the men I speak to are worried about the situation, and more than once I am told by someone shaking his head that Zimbabwe is at the lowest point of its twenty-year life. They know the land situation must be reformed, that some of the land should be redistributed, but none of them support the violent farm invasions. They are also all too aware of Mugabe's political shorthand of black and white, and they know it isn't as simple as that. That the 'race card' is a smoke screen for inter-African political struggles, between Zanu PF and the MDC. As one man says, for himself, he is more concerned about their boys coming back in body bags from the war in the Congo than the land problem. You are mentioned again by a local farmer, who gives thanks that you left your land to the Africans. 'Otherwise,' he says, a serious frown on his face, 'I would not have my farm now, and my children would not be in school. That is why I am here.'

That evening I help Leonard up to the evensong which is being held on the summit of the kopje and the irony does not escape him. As he leans on my arm he tells me how you used to lean on him on the road into Chivhu, your fingers digging into his shoulder when you were in pain. He says he hopes his grandchildren are there to help me walk when I am old.

On the kopje I meet more people who knew you including an old woman with pencilled eyebrows like sweeps of italic ink. As we sit on a flat stone, still warm from the touch of the sun, she tells me she always called you her father. The congregation gather around us, the choirs fanning out in their bright vestments like the wings of different species of butterfly. The old woman tells me her christened name is Cecilia, but that everyone calls her Fortune.

A younger woman approaches with a tiny old man on her arm. She says she wants to introduce me to her grandfather, Thomas, who was with you when you died. I shake hands with the old man, who is wearing a brown suit and a shirt and a tie. His lower lip hangs loose from his mouth and he has soulful, sad eyes. His voice is very weak as he asks for my address so he can write to me. All he says about your death is that you died quietly.

I watch the evensong from a rock behind the priest's head. The congregation fans out beneath, a mix of the choirs, Mothers' Union, suited older men and children in shorts and T-shirts. Once again I listen to the singing, rich, full and flowing, Christian hymns tinged with veld life, the sound of a single impala horn running beneath. Throughout the service Tendai, a ten-year-old boy from the Children's Home, translates for me, solemnly whispering into my ear, his soft, serious voice a second delayed after the preacher's. The evensong ends with two women and one of the priests dancing in the dust, kicking up the dry earth with their bare feet.

A few hours later and everyone is kicking up the dust with their feet, dancing in the clearing around your church. Night has taken hold again, with its deep, absolute blackness and its shocking stars that send a plumb line to the centre of the soul. The clearing is packed with people and the drummers have whipped the crowd into a frenzy, women, men and children dancing in the African way: leant over at the waist, elbows out, knees bent, shaking their pushed-out bottoms in time to the drums, like bees performing a directional dance. The smaller kids are on older children's shoulders, one woman yells out a line of song, and everyone answers: a lowing, liturgical swell of voices. The drums get faster, and the dancing more frantic. The lightning flash of Jodi's camera illuminates everything for a second, then passes, plunging us back into night and torches and sound and feet, shuffling and kicking up dust.

I think of the goat, its slaughter like a sacrifice, then the High Church vestments, candlesticks and incense, the services, the heavy black Bibles, then this singing and this dancing, the canopy over your grave, an appeasement to you as a rain spirit, the Christian memorial service and what the porter at the archives told me about Shona ancestor worship. And I realise I was wrong. Lying in your hut, listening to the sounds of the people arriving was not the closest I would get to you. Nor was it reading your letters, or tracing the work of age on your face in the photographs I found. Nor was it even in the memories of the people who knew you, who told me your stories. It is here, now, as I am carried along by the push and tide of the crowd, as we move as one towards your grave, as the singing swells and falls like waves, like a voltage passed through the hundreds of bodies. This is when I am closest to you.

I don't think I have ever really known why I have been following you. Maybe to fill a hole in me with another man's life, maybe natural curiosity, or perhaps just to feel the proximity of history, touching the same paper, stones, hands that you touched. Sitting in the Red Cave in the Eastern Highlands I thought I would never know the true stories, because true stories pass away with the moment. But here, I think I have finally got close to the true story and whatever the reason I came looking, I think I have found you.

The next morning, I am woken by singing once more. Many of the people have not slept for three nights and as I walk out to wash again they have a slightly crazed, disorientated look in their eyes. There is another service after breakfast, a smaller one, and then the festival begins to ebb away. Families begin packing up their belongings and pans in blankets, a pick-up arrives and takes a load of young men, sitting in facing rows in its back, down to the town. An hour later it returns and I realise it is a shuttle service, getting people down to the bus station in Chivhu. By midday the VIP toilet has been dismantled and there is a steady stream of people walking away down the track through the trees towards your road. The seven-tonne truck starts up its engine, working up to speed like a grumpy titan woken from a long sleep. The children from the Children's Home pile into its back and disappear under blankets as Leonard and Jodi roll up their sleeping bags and get into the hire car which I have driven round to the front of your rondavel. We follow the truck up to Leonard's homestead, where Leonard and Actor present the Home with their annual contribution of grain. I have seen how little grain he has to spare in the back room, but Leonard gives the sack to Sister Dorothy with one of his huge smiles, and then as the children sing a song of thanks he dances a shuffling, twisting dance in reply.

Half an hour later Leonard is still smiling, one arm around Actor, the other waving high above their heads as they both diminish in the shaky frame of the hire car's rear view mirror. We bump away from them, down Leonard's track towards your long straight road, turning yellow in the evening sun. I indicate left, but I don't know why. No one is watching.

◇

My second visit to Zimbabwe ends strangely, but perhaps appropriately. After a flat tyre (picked up on your road – you never did like cars) and dropping off a couple of boys from the festival in one of the high-density housing estates on the edge of the city, Jodi and I are back in Harare. We are staying at the Cresta Oasis hotel on Nelson Mandela Street, and tomorrow morning we will fly out of Zimbabwe, Jodi to Johannesburg and me to London. The modern country is all around us. The long carpeted corridors lead to bedrooms with power showers and a business suite with an internet connection. Businessmen with shiny leather briefcases and Disney ties stroll through the lobby or shake each other's hands and pat each other's backs, a deal well done.

Jodi and I are sitting in the hotel bar which has a long window that looks out onto the deserted pool, its umbrella shades furled until summer. The sound of the city filters through to us: car horns, newspaper vendors, people on the pavement, a commuter minibus blaring out *jit* dance music that rises then falls as it passes. It is hard to

297

believe this is the same country as the one I woke up in this morning.

The mobile phone of the man sitting next to me rings and a few tinny bars of 'The Ride of the Valkyries' cut through the murmur and chatter of the bar. He looks at the number on the screen and frowns. He is Zimbabwean, in his early fifties, wearing a smart dark green suit, and he is partly bald, so when he frowns I watch the wrinkles pass like ripples right to the top of his head. He looks up at me and smiles a massive smile. 'You are British, aren't you?' he says. Yes, I say, I am. He holds out the ringing phone to me. 'Then you answer this, tell them I am drinking with a British man, they will like that.'

I take the phone, uneasy at his request and aware he seems to find it a little too funny. He laughs with the men around him as I press the green telephone button and answer the call. The woman on the other end of the line is from South African Broadcasting, and she wants to know if Dr Hunzvi is available for interview. I put my hand over the phone and ask him if he knows Dr Hunzvi.

He laughs again. 'Tell them Dr Hunzvi will call them back.'

And that is how I discover I am drinking with Dr 'Hitler' Hunzvi. I have heard the name before. When the men at the festival were talking about the intimidation during the election. And I have seen it before too – in the papers, where it was always preceded by his self-invented moniker: Dr 'Hitler' Hunzvi, Zanu PF MP, leader of the War Veterans and organiser of the farm invasions. The leader of Mugabe's unofficial private army and responsible, according to the whispers I have heard, for recent torture and intimidation. I remember reading a letter in *The Herald* asking Dr Hunzvi to declare exactly which regiment he fought with in the War of Independence. Many veterans have no memory of fighting with him, and some doubt he fought at all.

Dr Hunzvi takes back his phone. 'They have been calling me a terrorist,' he says, 'the most dangerous man in Africa! Hah! Well, would I be drinking here with you if I was a terrorist?'

I admit he probably wouldn't, but somehow I don't think he would mind if I disagreed with him on this point. He pronounces the word 'terrorist' with a hint of disgust but with more than a dash of pride as well. Jodi tugs at my arm and tells me to keep him talking while she goes and gets her camera, so I turn back to Hunzvi and try to flatter him into conversation.

As we talk he reminds me of a child. He is obviously clever but seems to have a slight grasp on lots of subjects and no firm hold on any one, as if he is repeating dictums and ideas he has heard else-where. He is keen to let me know of his power in the country.

'I can get anything done and anything changed in this country. I have the power to do what I want.'

Judging from the nervous laughter from around the bar, I believe him. I ask him about the popular support for the Movement for Democratic Change, the main opposition party, and for its leader Morgan Tsvangirai.

He laughs again and, taking out a piece of paper and a red pen, says, 'Shall I tell you what MDC stands for?' He writes the three letters down the page, then adds a word to each, turning it into a mnemonic. He hands me the paper but I do not understand the Shona, so he tells the barman to translate for me. The barman leans over from where he is cleaning glasses and reads the three words. He smiles weakly and says quietly, 'Morgan Tsvangirai eats shit.' Hunzvi laughs hysterically at his own joke.

When Dr Hunzvi asks me what I am doing in Zimbabwe I tell him about you and your festival. At the mention of your name he nods slowly, and his smiling face clouds over. He says he knows you, and then, turning to his drink, he dismisses you with a wave of his hand. Another 'colonist', one of the whites who took the land in the first place. I tell him I think he is wrong, and that, however different his means, he actually shares some of the same aims as you. You wanted land for the Africans and, at least publicly, so does he. He turns back to me and tells me that no, I am the one who is wrong. 'Your uncle came here and stole from us, like everyone else.'

I feel my anger rise and I realise that your name undermines his oversimplified view. Your rare talent a hundred years ago was for see-ing in colours other than just black and white, while Hunzvi's vision is solidly monochrome.

Trying to keep as calm as I can I ask him if he has read your book *An Africa for Africans*, which inspired early African leaders like Charles Mzingeli and Chief Mangwende. I know I am opening myself up by asking him this. The conclusion you reach in the book, as a des-perate measure, is a plea for segregation, separate areas of the country for black and white. You clearly say this would only work on a basis of absolute racial equality, but Hunzvi could still claim this an early model of apartheid. But he does not. He has not read the book and he even tells me that the book no longer exists, that there are no copies to be found in Zimbabwe. I tell him I read one in his own government's National Archives.

He stares at me and I am continuing with my argument when I feel a squeeze on my thigh. Stopping mid-sentence, I notice the bar is very quiet. I think it must be Jodi, but turning around I see it is one of the men with Dr Hunzvi, a man who he introduced to me earlier as his 'driver'. Like Hunzvi he wears a smart suit with a floral tie over a purple shirt. Keeping his hand on my leg he tells me to take it easy, and then, when Hunzvi has turned away to talk to a Zambian businesswoman on his other side, that it is best if I stop talking to Dr Hunzvi now. Looking down at me he makes it clear that if I do not, he may be asked to 'make you quiet, my friend'.

I go back to my drink with Jodi and we watch Hunzvi flirt with the businesswoman. She is here to sell and buy handbags, she explains to him in a soft, patient voice. She is very beautiful, delicate, her long fingers covered in gold rings and her eyelids heavily painted with bright blue eye-shadow. She responds to Hunzvi's jokes and touches, but she is obviously uncomfortable. Maybe Hunzvi senses this, or maybe he has somewhere else to go, but after ten minutes or so, he leaves, dropping the businesswoman his card and walking out of the bar followed by his entourage of silent men in suits. The air in the room loosens. The businesswoman turns to us and smiles, then orders another drink from the barman, who also looks more relaxed, leaning against the till as if he is exhausted.

But then, over Jodi's shoulder I see Hunzvi's driver re-enter the bar. He strides towards us and I feel the adrenalin run through my veins. Jodi sees him too and we exchange a glance, not sure if we should stay or get up and go. He comes up to me and holds out his hand for mine to shake. I am hesitant, but he is smiling, so I do.

'I am from Chivhu,' he says proudly as we shake hands, talking quietly and quickly as if he hasn't much time, 'and I know of your uncle. I know Father Cripps and I love what he has done. I am very pleased to meet you.' Relieved, I say I am pleased to meet him too. Then I thank him for warning me earlier. He just says, still smiling, 'It was best.' And then he leaves, jogging back out the door to Hunzvi, who is waiting for him in the passenger seat of his black government car, its engine ticking over among the pick-ups and Mazdas in the back lot of the Cresta Oasis hotel, Harare.

So, I thought you would like to know this. That your name still carries a powerful charge in Zimbabwe, that it still disturbs the power people who want to keep things black and white, rich and poor. But more importantly, that it still resonates in the memory of the people. That farmers still thank you for leaving your land to the Africans, that your Children's Home is still taking in orphans, that two of its pupils have become airline pilots. That your church is still there. That your daughter married a man who loved her, that he didn't care about her past, and that together they played the piano you gave Ada. That the people of Marondą Mashanu still remember you as someone who tried to help. As someone who loved their parents and grandparents. As someone who 'lived as an African'. That history can be closer than you think and that a life can carry on living after the person who lived it does not. I thought you'd like to know.

> Dust in the air suspended
> Marks the place where a story ended
> T. S. Eliot, 'Little Gidding'

Leonard and Actor with the author, July 2000

Epilogue

◇

Except, of course, stories don't always end; sometimes they are just brought to one. Behind the dropped curtain Hamlet's Denmark continues. The bodies are cleared from the stage and Fortinbras takes his place at its centre. The last page of a novel is not where the characters dissolve into the white of the paper, just where the writer and the reader let go of them, where they part company. The storyteller concludes, but the story continues.

The stories of many of the people I have written about didn't end where I left them: they continued, past the last date, the last page number, moving on under their own momentum, some of them to their own individual ends.

Cullen Gouldsbury did publish a novel in which the protagonist, Father John, was based upon Arthur. He called it *God's Outpost* and I read it in the Rare Books reading room of the British Library, recognising Arthur in its pages. In the book Father John is a Catholic not Anglican priest, but Arthur is definitely there in his running and walking, in his physical appearance, in his Franciscan philanthropy. *God's Outpost* was published in 1907. Nine years later Cullen was killed in the war and Arthur returned the literary favour, writing an elegy for his friend which he published in his book of war poems, *Lake and War*:

Cullen Gouldsbury
Poet of 'The Pace of the Ox,' and 'The Shadow-Girl'
[Late of Lake Staff and 1st King's African Rifles,
died at Tanga on August 27th, 1916]

So as a war's forc'd loan we've lent thee now,
Our land finds few interpreters, and thou
Wast one. Methought not wisely but too well
Thou would'st chameleon parts aforetime play –
Wearing our hues alike of Heaven and Hell.
Yet who, that reads between thy lines, would say

Thy fellow-feeling for our petty views
(More narrow than our dorp's gum-avenues,)
Was all benevolent complacency,
Ah! For those earthly beasts our land may know –
Our veld, its daylight calm, its twilight glow –
Bests money buys not, bests that priceless be –
How broad they love, how big thy reverence!
Much hast thou given us ere thy going hence,
Now take what we may give, and leave the rest, –
Take earth of ours thy world-wide Church hath blest,
Sleep, body, by our sea, beneath our stars!
Go, soul, to peace in honour from our wars,
Interpret there a land than ours more kind –
A land for all its colours – colour-blind!

Pastor Liebenberg, the Dutch Reformed minister in Enkeldoorn, also died before Arthur, on 6 October 1933. Considering himself unworthy to travel in the carriage behind his friend's coffin Arthur ran ahead to the cemetery instead, and was waiting at the grave when the funeral cortège arrived. During the funeral he performed the graveside service, just as he had done twice before for two of Liebenberg's children.

Noel Brettell survived Arthur and went on to become a respected Rhodesian poet himself. He often wrote about the old man, in his prose memoirs and in his poetry. This is part of a poem he wrote called 'Maronda Mashanu', the first poem in his book *Bronze Frieze: Poems mostly Rhodesian*:

Maronda Mashanu
To Arthur Shearly Cripps, in his blindness

It stood alone, that grim euphorbia:
Goat boy in dangling monkey skins,
Whistling his surly beasts after sparse nibbling,
Could scramble up through clefts where no path was,
And yodel a summer's day under its shade –
But I could not.

. . . Alone, asleep, that strange sequestered church;
Blue starlings flirted round its broken altars,
And climbed and hung, and climbed and hovered,

> Thin spire of smoke not teased by any wind
> Against the gentle evening dim with rose
> > And apricot.

The final two stanzas of the poem are addressed to Arthur himself:

> Rest so, never in doubt,
> Never in doubt that beauty and truth are one,
> That truth will rise, resolute, unconfined,
> Like water drawn unerringly from deep wells
> To carry in drought to drooping loveliness
> > The smell of rain.

> Rest so, ever in peace,
> Your knuckles steady on your homely stick;
> And may the sunset that so often for us
> Underlines cheeks with harsh violet shadows,
> Be like a benison on your patient eyes,
> > Soft, with no pain.

During the War of Independence Noel and his wife Eva somehow survived a vicious mortar attack on their house. The building itself, however, was demolished and they moved to Harare to be closer to their son, John. Some years later Eva died as a result of a car accident. Noel followed his wife in December 1991, aged eighty-three, the same age as Arthur when he died.

Captain Meinertzhagen served in the British Army for another ten years, rising to the rank of Colonel. After East Africa he served in Palestine on the Gaza front, where he conceived and engineered the dropping of a GHQ officer's notebook close to enemy lines. The notebook contained detailed false information about the impending British attack along with a letter from an imaginary wife about the birth of a son for added credibility. The Turkish were suspicious of such a lucky find, but the Germans fell for Meinertzhagen's trick, which proved successful and significant enough for T. E. Lawrence to mention it in his *Seven Pillars of Wisdom*. Years later, on a visit to Constantinople in 1933, some Turkish officers tracked Meinertzhagen down to celebrate with the man behind the famous 'dropped notebook'. They took him on a tour of the city's nightlife of cabarets and dancing girls. Meinertzhagen records the event in his *Army Diary 1899–1926*, which he eventually published in 1960 at the age of eighty-two. 'I got to bed,' he writes, 'at 4 a.m. after quite an amusing evening.'

Theresa and Stuart Hildred got married in a church in St James's, London. Theresa's Italian lover Mario got wind of the marriage and did actually come to London to try and win Theresa back. On the morning of the wedding day he burst into a church in St James's hoping to interrupt the ceremony, and, had he got the right church, would have been successful.

On 5 February 2001 I received a letter from Leonard's daughter, Florence, a nurse in Masvingo:

> Dear Mr Owen,
>
> I am writing to let you know that my father Leonard Mamvura died of cancer on 12th January 2001. He was laid to rest on his farm on 14/01/01. He was very unfortunate that his diagnosis had been missed until a day before his death. The doctors said the cancer had spread from the prostate gland to the kidneys and intestines but he had been admitted to Harare hospital as a case of acute renal failure.
>
> I would be very pleased if you could spare a few cards of him which you took during the Cripps Festival.
>
> Best wishes
> Florence Shindi

I don't think I have ever met anyone possessed of such an ability for joy and love as Leonard. I had seen him just six months before I received this letter. He must have already been very ill, but still everything about him spelt life, energy and laughter. As Ray Brown wrote to me later, he was the best part of Arthur's legacy.

Ray Brown himself is still in Zimbabwe, still in the same house on The Chase, although it is currently up for sale. The disruption in the country is driving him out, as it has already done to so many of the others I met while looking for Arthur.

Pelline and Laci returned from church one day to find their house and farm occupied by 'War Veterans' and Zanu PF Youth. They were given five hours to pack and leave. They are now living in a flat in Budapest, Hungary, which, Pelline writes, is 'alright, but snowy'.

Contrary to what I expected, their son, Miki, also left his farm and has taken his family to Mkushi, three hours from Lusaka in Zambia, where he is establishing a new farm from scratch. And Alice and Stassi

Callinicos have left too. They are both teaching in the North of England, Stassi at Stonyhurst and Alice at a sixth-form college in Blackburn. Canon Holderness, though, is still in Zimbabwe, in a nursing home in Harare. His daughter's farm was invaded and he lost most of his papers and books, which were stored there. I haven't heard from Betty Finn, and no one seems to know what's happened to Jeremy.

Since I met him I have discovered that Dr Hunzvi was the man at the root of much of this disruption that has sent so many people out of Zimbabwe, and that threatens those who have remained with economic breakdown and famine. It was Hunzvi's petition for pensions and large 'gratuities' for the 40,000 war veterans and his own embezzlement of these funds that triggered the country's economic crisis. Then, once Mugabe had bought them off, Hunzvi and his organisation became the President's private army, leading the violent land invasions and torturing, raping and beating any opposition to Zanu PF. The Zimbabwe Human Rights NGO Forum has since singled Hunzvi out as being personally implicated in acts of torture during the 2000 General Election at Chikomba, Bikita West and in his own doctor's surgery at Budiriro.

Hunzvi died on 4 June 2001, officially from malaria, but his long battle with AIDS was well known. Drivers in Harare celebrated his death by honking their horns in the streets while his supporters stood vigil outside his hospital ward, swearing revenge on the celebrants.

The Arthur Shearly Cripps Children's Home has also suffered from the disruption and unrest in Zimbabwe. An increasing number of children are arriving at the home with AIDS, but the local clinic has closed down. The sisters have no transport to take sick children to the clinic in Harare and have to depend on the local headmaster's car, when he can find petrol. The Home finished the last of its fruit jam (a crucial source of nutrition) last July. Now they are almost down to their last groundnuts and have recently had to kill all their chickens for meat, depriving the children of eggs. Meanwhile, the government-controlled grain supply is either sold off for profit or handed out to card-carrying Zanu PF members only. Donations to the Home can be sent to: The Shearly Cripps Children's Home, P.O. Box UA378, Union Avenue, Harare, Zimbabwe.

And then of course, there is Mazzy Shine, Theresa's daughter, who I finally found in a mansion flat in Belsize Park, London. Mazzy, who has travelled much of Africa as a nurse, gave me coffee over her large wooden kitchen table and once again I heard Arthur's story, but this time from the lips of his granddaughter. Her mother only told Mazzy about Arthur on the night of Stuart's death; until then his existence and her lineage had been a secret. But Mazzy had indeed been to Zimbabwe before me; she had stood up in Ray Brown's seminar, she had been to the festival and introduced herself to my great aunt and she had been to her grandfather's grave in Maronda Mashanu.

Mazzy found some old photo albums her parents had left her, and together we flicked through their stiff black pages. I saw Theresa's postcards and photographs of Europe, Mario, the British European Airways tickets and a black-and-white picture of the silver aircraft that flew her and Stuart to Paris for their honeymoon (Mazzy remembers her mother telling her how the plane's roof had leaked on the way, dripping water onto her new dress).

There was just one photo of Ada, as an old woman, sitting in a deckchair at the coast. She smiles comfortably into the camera, her grey hair tucked under a hat and a shawl about her shoulders. Mazzy says she remembers the day well, the whole family at the seaside. Ada, however, was fast subsiding under the weight of senile dementia and the young Mazzy couldn't work out why she kept offering her cake, over and over again. Ada died a few years later, in 1957, five years after Arthur.

Before I left Mazzy she told me she once had a collection of letters from Arthur written to Ada and Theresa. She'd taken them over to Zimbabwe and had left them with Canon Holderness. We have since both tried to locate these letters, but at the time of writing they are still lost, perhaps along with the papers and books Holderness had stored at his daughter's farm, perhaps elsewhere in Zimbabwe. But then maybe that is how it should be, and maybe that is where Arthur would want them: in the country he cared for, lost in its turmoil, lost to history, their words and the love they spoke of written somewhere in its dust.

Afterword

◇

When I wrote this book about Arthur and the legacy of his life I never expected or wanted to write a biography. I was more interested in letting my imagination move between the 'stepping stones' of the stories, photographs and texts I could still find fifty years after his death. This movement was always fed and guided by my research and by what I felt to be the true essence of Arthur and his story: by the arc of his life and the principles and passions that drove him. Since publication more driftwood from Arthur's life has found its way to the shore of my desk. Letters, handwritten manuscripts, the memories of those still alive (including the man who built his coffin) and a scattering of new photographs. Many of these materials have simply confirmed or added texture to the story I've written. Others though, have shed new light on him and his relationships and I feel it's only right to share some of these fresh illuminations here. I began with Arthur's letters, so maybe it's appropriate I end with them too.

The way I received the first batch of new letters eloquently illustrates how time can play with what we leave in the world, with the footprints we make. The article I'd written with Jodi found its way, in a copy of *The Saturday Times Magazine*, to a dentist's waiting room in Harare. Here it sat on the table in the middle of the room for two years before it was picked up and flicked through by Keith Martin. Keith had just spent the morning clearing out his late aunt's house. In the attic he'd found a bag full of letters. They were all postmarked 1940 or 1941, and were all written to or by Arthur S. Cripps. Arthur had apparently left the letters with Keith's aunt when he stayed at her house after one of his hundred-mile treks up to the capital from Maronda Mashanu. Keith recognised his name in the article and kindly sent the letters to me.

Most of the letters I'd seen previously had been written by Arthur, whereas most of these were addressed to him. As such, like a soil sample taken through years of sediment, they gave a fascinating glimpse into the other side of his fifty-year epistolary dialogue with the world.

Their content describes the peculiar pattern of his concerns and pre-occupations around this time: the Southern Rhodesian Minister of Justice writing like a scolded schoolboy, explaining himself in response to Arthur's outrage at the racist language he'd used in a speech on native wages. Fond letters from Bishop Paget, recently back from visiting the African troops in the Western Desert; 'I was greatly impressed with the attitude of European troops toward the Africans in the Division' he assures Arthur, who is obviously worried the inequality he witnessed in the First World War will be echoed in the Second. Rejections of his poems from publishers as diverse as Black-wells in Oxford and the *Cape Times* in South Africa. Returned poems themselves in which Essex and rural England are remembered and praised in Arthur's strangely archaic verse. A plea for help from the *New Times and Ethiopia News* on behalf of their Djibouti correspondent, expelled from the country by the French. An entreaty from an old friend to 'write your poems in Shona only'. A letter of sincere thanks from the African leader Charles Mzingeli, and even one from Arthur's brother William, in which he talks of 'bad air raids' and of relishing 'the chance to use my rifle on a German parachutist'.

Two letters from this batch make a particular impact. The first is another from Bishop Paget and is obviously from a long series of letters between the two men. In it, he confirms his support for Arthur's protest against the government's 'iniquitous' Maize Control Regulations. It's a discussion that rings a note of disturbing familiarity. At the time of writing the current Zimbabwean government are employing similar policies. The country is facing the prospect of real famine and yet ZANU PF, the ruling party, are strictly regulating the grain supply. Anyone found carrying more than three sacks of grain faces a fine and having all their sacks confiscated. Once again food is being used as an electioneering tool, as a lever of influence. Despite so much of what Arthur fought for fifty years ago having been achieved, it seems that for the ordinary people of Zimbabwe government injustice is still a fact of life. It's a situation that would deeply sadden Arthur were he to return now to the country he loved so much.

The second letter is folded inside an off-white envelope with 'ON ACTIVE SERVICE' written in red crayon across the top left hand corner. When I open it I find it's written by my grandmother from Alexandria, where she was serving as a nurse during the war. In it she describes how Rommel is closing in on the city and how she has been instructed to leave for England along with all the other servicemen's wives. I show this letter to my grandfather. He reads it, his hands shaking slightly, and his eyes brighten with tears. He explains to me that my grandmother had only recently become a wife. They had just got married in Alexandria and already they were facing separation, perhaps for ever. This was the last letter she must have written before she boarded a boat up the Suez canal. That boat was torpedoed and sunk, and it was then my grandmother received the long scar running down her shin that she would show me so many years later. This letter, which had lain for so long in the attic of Keith Martin's aunt, brought all this back to my grandfather. This letter which had been sent from Alexandria to a hut in Maronda Mashanu, then carried on foot up to Salisbury, where it stayed undiscovered for sixty years as the city about it became Harare. My grandmother's handwriting, the date, her use of my grandfather's name, all of it opened again, as such letters do, a brief fissure in time, through which emotion and memory seeped once more.

Seven months after publication I thought I'd seen the last of new letters and memories stirred up by this book, but I was soon proved wrong. One night last September I got a phone call from Mazzy Shine. We've kept in touch since we first met and in another of those strange coincidences have even discovered that Mazzy is the godmother to one of my childhood friends. She told me she'd found some more letters in a suitcase under the bed in her Belsize Park flat. She said she thought I'd find them interesting. They were all written by Arthur and all addressed to Mrs Teresa Hildred.

I met Mazzy a couple of weeks later in London. It was a wet autumn night with a blustery wind funnelling between the tall buildings of Villiers Street. I saw Mazzy walking towards me, a silhouette against the orange street lights of the Strand, the wind catching under her umbrella which she was trying to keep tilted against the slanting rain. We hugged there in the street than ducked into a café and ordered some coffees. Mazzy was not long back from a three-month trip to Zimbabwe, where she'd been working as a nurse for an NGO. She was still buzzing with Africa, slipping into the cadences and accents of the people she'd met as she told me about her travels in the country. When we'd caught up she pulled a small brown envelope out of her bag and handed it to me. Once again I found myself pulling out those thin sheets of browning paper on which Arthur wrote. They felt so fragile under the café's strip lights it seemed as if it was only the fabric of his looping black handwriting that held them together and stopped them disintegrating. There were some photographs with the letters and it was these we looked at first. Among the sepia snapshots of trees and groups of people there were three that especially caught my eye, each another punctuation point in Arthur's eighty-three-year-long life. The first was taken from the kopje overlooking Maronda Mashanu, looking down into the clearing. At its centre stands Arthur's church at the height of its glory, two massive thatched conical roofs suspended above the bleached grass on slender wooden poles. Beside the church I can see Arthur's hut where Leonard and I slept during the festival, while on the other side a group of people are dwarfed by this African cathedral. Beyond them the veld opens up, dotted with trees and bushes, flat and massive.

The second photograph is of Arthur and a younger man standing outside the entrance to the church. Arthur, as ever, looks away from the camera while his friend stares straight into its lens. Arthur looks old but strong, the skin of his face and bald head nut brown above the gleaming white of his dog collar, his large hands resting on his walking stick. This same stick appears in the third photo, but this time Arthur is sitting and it rests against his knee, its curved handle passing over his right shoulder. The photograph is dated 1949 so I guess this is Arthur's eightieth birthday. He looks like a modern-day Tiresias with his stick, his collapsed mouth and his destroyed eyes that have seen too much. As always he is wearing his dog collar, looser now, but as white as ever, a gleaming neck-manacle against his weathered skin.

I decide to save the letters until I get home, so Mazzy and I leave the café and make our way up onto the Strand. We've met here because we've both heard about a bar under the Zimbabwean embassy. We've been told it opens every Friday night for embassy staff and any other Zimbabweans living in London. Mazzy wants to visit this bar because she's missing the flavour of the country, while I'm curious to take the temperature there as some kind of a benchmark for the state of things in Zimbabwe. I've long been hearing now, on the news and from individual sources, how the situation is worsening in the country, how political thought is becoming increasingly indoctrinated with ZANU PF rhetoric. I hope I might be able to get some idea of the extent to which this is true by talking to some of the people in the bar tonight.

Mazzy and I walk out of the rain through a side door in the embassy building. The sound of rush-hour cars and buses on the Strand diminishes as we approach a glassed-in reception. The man at the desk is preoccupied on the phone, apparently trying to sort out his son's student fees. 'No, no,' he says, 'it is not me who is going to university. I am fifty years old, my friend. Today, today I am fifty.' He finishes with a chuckle, and signals for us to sign in. We write our names, addresses, occupations. I say I'm a teacher, as I've been warned it wouldn't be wise to admit to being a writer. The same person who told me this, once a close colleague of Robert Mugabe, also told me to watch out in the bar. 'That place is a hotbed of CIO operatives and spies,' he said. 'Listen – don't talk. Don't get drunk and just say you love the country. Don't say anything they can use against you.'

Mazzy wishes the doorman happy birthday in Shona. He smiles in response and indicates towards a door on his right through which a large Zimbabwean man in a suit has just walked. This man holds the door open for us with one hand, his mobile phone in the other, and smiles as we pass, then calls down the stairs after us, 'Enjoy yourselves!'

Downstairs we find a low-ceilinged room with groups of chairs and sofas arranged over a brightly swirling carpet. In front of us is a long hatch bar through which we can see the bright lights of a working kitchen. Zimbabwean music plays tinnily through speakers hung on the walls. Two men, one wearing a black suit, the other a grey, are sitting at the bar talking with the barmaid, a young Zimbabwean woman with her hair in braids. Behind her I can see the familiar cans of Zambezi and Castle beer stacked into mini-pyramids on the otherwise bare white shelves. Mazzy and I order a beer each. As the barmaid gets the cans the two men welcome us and ask what we do. I say I'm an English teacher. The grey-suited man frowns, takes a sip of his beer then laughs, looking over at his friend. 'Teacher, eh?' he says, shaking his head. 'Not good. Teacher cheater, teacher cheater, eh?' Black suit laughs while the barmaid simply smiles and shakes her head too, as if she's heard this all before. At first I'm confused but then I remember something else I've been told about the situation in Zimbabwe. Teachers in the country are often supporters of the opposition party, the MDC, and because of this the occupation as a whole is viewed with suspicion by ZANU PF. Trying to change the subject, I ask grey suit what he does. He tells me he works for Corydon council before turning his attentions to Mazzy. As he does black suit introduces himself to me. 'Hello, I am Peckham,' he says handing me a white business card. 'This is for you,' he tells me 'it may be useful.' I look down at the card: *Peckham Chibonga: Free Professional Will-Writing*. I thank him, although I'm less than convinced about the generosity of his gesture.

The conversation turns to memories of Zimbabwe and eases as it does so. The kitchen serves up dishes of piled sadza and meat and the music is turned up a couple of notches. Grey suit asks me what Zimbabwean musicians I like. 'Thomas Mapfumo,' I tell him and for the second time that night his face clouds over. 'Aah,' he says, dismissing the name with a downward wave of his arm, 'he is an old man now. He has lost it, someone should put him out of his misery.' Thomas Mapfumo was one of the most important musicians of the second *chimurenga,* the Zimbabwean war of independence. His songs inspired the guerrilla fighters and gave a popular voice to the revolution. More recently he's given a popular voice to protests against Mugabe's dictatorship and this is why, I suspect, grey suit dismissed him so. Once again I find myself wondering what Arthur would make of Zimbabwe now, a country where the government persecutes teachers, shuts down independent voices in the press and threatens musicians with imprisonment. I know he'd still recognise the resilience, generosity and humour of the people, but something tells me he'd also still be writing his letters from a hut in the bush, sending out a tide of words against the government of the day just as he did against the colonial administration fifty years ago.

When I return home I'm able to study the letters Mazzy gave me. Carefully unfolding them from their envelopes, they make first confusing, then fascinating reading. The earliest is dated 19 October 1936 and the latest 24 August 1952. Once again I watch the ebb and flow of Arthur's handwriting, his decent into blindness, his stubborn unwillingness to yield up his pen until, as in the other letters, there is the gradual surfacing of another's hand, giving his voice words on paper again. There is also, once again, the unique punctuation he used. 'Dear Mrs Hildred' the first letter begins, 'Thank you so much for your kind letter!!!' Those three exclamation marks, so boyish in the handwriting of a sixty-seven-year-old man.

From what I can tell Teresa started writing to Arthur as an interested patron and their correspondence grew from there. Over the years she begins to send him photographs of the area where she grew up, of Rye and Icklesham, as if asking him to recognise her. Then, around the beginning of 1938, she must have signed with her first name, 'Teresa Hildred.' It's a PS in Arthur's reply that leads me to this conclusion.

> P.S. Is it not possible that your mother was a real friend of mine in ancient days at Icklesham? Is it not possible that I saw you as a small child the last time when I came to that countryside in 1898 or thereabouts? If it be so, I do want to send the very heartiest of greetings to your mother, whom I have so

blamefully lost sight of for so many years now of my time in Africa.

I had such cheering news on Easter Monday – that the Oxford University Press had made an offer to publish a considerable selection of my 'An African Shepherd's Song-Books', at the poet's expense. I would so much like to send a copy both to you, and to your mother, if she be my old friend of Icklesham days. It is your name 'Teresa' that has made me think that she is. It seems so strange indeed if an old friendship should be renewed in the way [*here the writing goes up the side of the page*] that I hope this soon maybe, if God please. 'There's a divinity that shapes our ends, rough hew them how we will.' A.S.C.

This, then, is the moment when Arthur realises he has been corresponding with his estranged daughter. The language is careful and battened down, but when I read it I can sense, welling beneath this surface, the strange admixture of joy and worn regret that carries him towards his conclusion.

From this date on Arthur's letters are fuller, more intimate, and nearly always written on Teresa's birthday. They are still formal in tone, however, and he never addresses her as anything other than 'Mrs Teresa Hildred'. There is also an oddly formulaic quality to many of his openings. A comment on the lateness of the rains, birthday wishes, imaginings of what the Sussex or Essex countryside must look like at this time of year, best wishes sent to her mother and to her mother's husband. After a brief period of indecipherable letters his handwriting is gone altogether, apart from a wispy A.S.C. at the close. On 28 February 1952 he writes, now in another's hand, 'About April last, diarrhoea attacked me and from time to time seemed to be with me. I seemed to have lost my old power of walking. But, God be thanked, the power seems to be coming back to me.' Then, a few months later, it is not Arthur writing at all, but Leonard. In a strange pre-echo of the letter his own daughter, Florence, will send me informing me of his death, so Leonard writes to Teresa, telling her of her father's. Arthur's voice is woven so intimately with Leonard's own that they seem to be writing as one man. With this in mind I'd like to leave the last words to Leonard, so often the voice of Arthur in his blindness , and always in the long years after his death.

My Dear Mrs. T. E. Hildred

Many thanks indeed for your very kind letter! Our noble father and beloved friend went into the hospital on July 8th, Tuesday 1952 seeking for a cure of diarrhoea and peaceful passed away on Monday 1st August in the Hospital. May our hero rest in peace and rise in joy!!

He has outsoared the shadow of our night, he stood for Liberty, Equality and Fraternity, did he not? Des Gratias!!!

I have written a few lines about him, should I get them printed I will send you a copy.

Our veldt noted poet missionary and who was calling himself a Christian Missionary in Mashonaland who believed in the inter-denominationalism was buried in his beloved church of Maronda Mashanu 'Five Wounds' mission on Sunday 3rd August and we had a huge gathering of about more than a thousand and some hundred of Europeans Indians and Africans who attended the service.

I shall try to write you about books later but at present I need a financial support from any kind hearted people to keep me going with correspondences of our noble father and beloved friend. Oh! Madam I do miss him so much.

Here I would like to thank you for your tributes, sympathy and kindness extended to me and others in our recent sad bereavement. He was a misunderstood Christian who taught and lived – 'Be ye followers of me ever as I am of Christ.'

Yours with Best wishes for you all!!!

Leonard M. T. Mamvura

Acknowledgements and Glossary

◇

In this book I have written an imaginative story based upon certain events and characteristics of Arthur Cripps' life. This task would have been impossible, however, without the more factual and comprehensive touchstones of two existing books, and I am hugely indebted to them and their authors. *God's Irregular* (SPCK, 1973) by Douglas V. Steere is an invaluable account of Arthur's life and philosophy, while *Arthur Shearly Cripps* (G. K. Hall & Co., 1975) by John R. Doyle Jr. is a perceptive study of Cripps the writer. Countless other books have informed my research, but I am particularly indebted to the following:

Arthur Shearly Cripps: A Selection of His Prose and Verse, compiled and introduced by G. R. Brown, A. J. Chennells and L. B. Rix (Mambo Press, 1976)
Side-Gate and Stile, by Noel Brettell (Books of Zimbabwe, 1981)
God's Outpost, by Cullen Gouldsbury (Eveleigh Nash, 1907)
Old Rhodesian Days, by Hugh Marshall Hole (Books of Rhodesia, 1976)
The Arab and the African, by S. Tristam Pruen, MD (Seeley & Co., 1891)
Army Diary, 1899–1926, by Colonel Richard Meinertzhagen (Oliver and Boyd, 1960)
The Great War in Africa, by Byron Farwell (Viking, 1987)
Battle for the Bundu, by Charles Miller (Macdonald and Jane's, 1974)
The Spiritual Beliefs of the Shona, by Michael Gelfand (Mambo Press, 1977)
Keats, by Andrew Motion (Faber and Faber, 1997)

Thanks are also due to the staff and administrators of Rhodes House Library, the British Library, the University of Zimbabwe Library, the National Archives of Zimbabwe and the Imperial War Museum. Also to, the Arts Council of Wales for a Writer's Bursary, Robert Minhinnick at *Poetry Wales* for asking me to write about Zimbabwe in the first place and Gill Morgan at the *Saturday Times Magazine* for making it possible for me to return there for the Cripps festival.

Over the last four years I have benefited from the advice, hospitality and support of many individuals, but I am especially grateful to the following people:

Zimbabwe: Alice and Stassi Callinicos, Ray and Barbara Brown, Betty Finn, Canon Richard Holderness, Pelline, Laci and Miki Marffy, Jeremy, Richard, Justin, Sabethiel, Jodi, all of the Mamvura family and everyone at Maronda Mashanu.

Britain: Mazzy Shine, Alan Wilkinson, Donald Allchin, Lee Brackstone, Angus Cargill, Annette Green, Tania Kindersly, my grandfather, Elizabeth Roberts for her generosity of spirit and memory, Richard Sidwell for sourcing so many titles so quickly, Louis and Cathy and Liz and Mike for housing both me and the book, Tom for the running and talking, Martin for being the other side of the tracks and my parents for everything.

And of course my deepest thanks to Cat, for having the best ideas first and sharing everything with me from Salome's Garden to the final draft. Without you, neither this book or its author would exist in the way they do today.

◇

chimurenga poetic Shona for war of liberation
D.V. Deo Volente (God willing)
kopje a small hill, often no more than a pile of boulders on an otherwise flat plain
kraal either an enclosure for livestock or a fortified village of huts
n'anga a shaman or medicine man
mufundisi a priest
mbira thumb piano, comprising 24 narrow iron keys mounted in rows on a wooden sound board
rondavel a round, often thatched hut
ruga-ruga German irregular native troops of the First World War
sadza Shona for maize meal porridge